Teaching Modern Arabic Literature in Translation

Teaching Modern Arabic Literature in Translation

Edited by
Michelle Hartman

The Modern Language Association of America
New York   2018

MLA and the MODERN LANGUAGE ASSOCIATION are trademarks owned
by the Modern Language Association of America. For information about
obtaining permission to reprint material from MLA book publications, send
your request by mail (see address below) or e-mail (permissions@mla.org).

Library of Congress Cataloging-in-Publication Data

Names: Hartman, Michelle editor.
Title: Teaching modern Arabic literature in translation / edited by Michelle
    Hartman.
Description: New York : The Modern Language Association of America, 2017. |
    Series: Options to teaching series ; 42 | Includes bibliographic
    references and index.
Identifiers: LCCN 2017031958 (print) | LCCN 2017034124 (ebook) | ISBN
    9781603293167 (EPub) | ISBN 9781603293174 (Kindle) | ISBN
    9781603293143 (cloth : alk. paper) | ISBN 9781603293150 (pbk. : alk.
    paper)
Subjects: LCSH: Arabic literature—Study and teaching (Higher)—United
    States. | Arabic literature—Translations.
Classification: LCC PJ7505 (ebook) | LCC PJ7505 .T43 2017 (print) | DDC
    892.7/071—dc23
LC record available at https://lccn.loc.gov/2017031958

Options for Teaching 42
ISSN 1079–2562

"The War Works Hard," by Dunya Mikhail, translated by Elizabeth Winslow,
from *The War Works Hard,* copyright © 2005 by Dunya Mikhail. Reprinted
by permission of New Directions Publishing Corp. Original Arabic text:
الحرب تعمل بجد. Reprinted by permission of the author.

"Travel Ticket," by Samih al-Qasim, translated by Abdullah al-Udhari, from
Victims of a Map: A Bilingual Anthology of Arabic Poetry (London: Saqi Books,
1984). Reprinted by permission.

Cover illustration of the paperback and electronic editions:
Untitled, 2013, by Etel Adnan, oil on canvas, 35 x 45 cm, Unique. Courtesy
of the artist and Sfeir-Semler Gallery Hamburg / Beirut.

Published by The Modern Language Association of America
85 Broad Street, suite 500, New York, New York 10004-2434
www.mla.org

Contents

Part III: Comparative Contexts, Youth Culture, New Media

Acknowledgments

This volume is a result of a collective effort, and I would like to thank all of the contributors for their hard work, perseverance, and help in shaping it from beginning to end. A series of anonymous readers contributed to this process and offered many useful and important comments, as did the Publications Committee of the MLA. Thank you to them. Thanks are owed as well to the two acquisitions editors at the MLA who worked on this project: Margit Longbrake and James C. Hatch.

Specific thanks are owed to Dunya Mikhail for enthusiastically allowing us to reprint her poem. Both Philip Metres and I would like to thank Adam Rovner for generously offering to transcribe Hebrew quotations in the text.

Several people read, commented on, and edited drafts of different parts of this work for me. I would like to acknowledge Dana Olwan and also Aziz Choudry, who was part of the inspiration for the project. Katy Kalemkerian worked extremely hard with me, in several bursts of activity especially at the end, and deserves more thanks than can be expressed in a short line here.

Having taught Arabic literature in translation for many years, I am constantly inspired by my students, and it is for them that I put this book together. It is in that spirit of mentorship and collaboration that this volume is dedicated to my students, past, present, and future. They are, or will soon become, the teachers. It is thus dedicated to Shirin Radjavi, Katy Kalemkerian, and, most especially, Dima Ayoub.

Michelle Hartman

Introduction: Why Theory, Politics, and Ethics Matter

Rationale for the Volume

In 2010, the contemporary Arabic novel found a place in no less a mainstream American literary magazine than *The New Yorker*. In "Found in Translation: The Contemporary Arabic Novel," Claudia Roth Pierpont asks, "What do you know about how people live in Cairo or Beirut or Riyadh? What bearing does such information have upon your life?" She suggests that modern Arabic novels can "offer a marvelous array of answers to questions we did not know we wanted to ask." Her surprise at the breadth and depth of this literary tradition is not only common but also indicative of how modern Arabic literature in English translation is received and circulates both inside and outside the academy, particularly in North America. As it moves into English, its reception is fraught with clichés: it is about "us" understanding "them," about what we here need to know about mysterious people who live and events that happen somewhere called over there. The discourse invoked by Pierpont holds Arabic literature as something to be found or discovered—it will unlock the secrets of a hidden world and provide that elusive glimpse behind the veil. This approach remains dominant in the North American academy, where

1

Arabic literary works are more often taught as exemplary documents and sources in political science and history courses than integrated into mainstream literary curricula.

This volume is being published at a time when Arabic literature is being translated more and more, when the Arab world is constantly in the news, but when understanding of the complexities of Arab politics, history, and culture—let alone literature—is still sorely missing in North America. There has been very little written on how to teach this literary tradition in a society that constructs it as other—controversial, dangerous, difficult, esoteric, and exotic. This is why we have produced a volume with a deeper, contextual approach to teaching modern Arabic literature in translation.

We focus here on teaching modern Arabic literature in English translation, not on all facets of the vast and diverse Arabic literary traditions. We look only briefly into some of the many texts, authors, genres, approaches, and themes of the much larger category of modern Arabic literature. For example, there could be an entire book of essays devoted to teaching modern Arabic poetry in English translation. Our volume offers more essays on teaching fiction than on teaching poetry and drama. We draw more examples from texts by writers from Egypt, Syria, Lebanon, and Palestine than from North Africa and the Gulf countries. Although our subject is broad and expansive in many ways, it does not provide coverage in either a geographic or generic sense. Rather, we seek to offer suggestions on how to teach these materials in different ways.

Modern Arabic literature of course is a problematic and contested term. In this volume we limit its definition to creative works of all genres written in Arabic from the late nineteenth century until today. Our focus on teaching these works in English translation means that we do not take up the vibrant and exciting literature penned by Arab authors working in English, French, or Spanish, for example. Works written in English by Arab authors, Arab Americans included, are increasingly diverse and in dialogue with texts written originally in Arabic (Fadda-Conrey; Hassan; Hout; Salaita, *Arab American Literary Fictions* and *Modern Arab American Fiction*). But only Arabic texts translated into English are discussed in this volume. Its contributors hone in on the crucial and complex question of what it means to teach works in English translation.

Defining literature as modern suggests a break from the literary traditions of the past, but it is not entirely clear how relevant such a break is in Arabic literature or if it is indeed the best way to conceptualize or teach the subject. Indeed the question of what *modern* means and is preoccupies much of the study of the Arab world today. Choosing texts that most consider modern does allow us to take on political questions that affect us today directly. Moreover, the issues that so many of us grapple with in our teaching are best reflected in modern Arabic literature. The essays collected here deal with texts ranging from the late nineteenth century, a period of literary revival often referred to as the *nahda* (نهضة) and commonly translated as the "Arab Renaissance," to 2013.

There is now a fairly well established literature on the study of modern Arabic literature in English (Allen, *Introduction*; Badawi; Starkey). Of the standard reference works, Roger Allen's *An Introduction to Arabic Literature* is particularly useful in setting up parameters that help problematize the field and the terms that define it. This collection contributes to the field in a different way, by offering insights and suggestions to anyone interested in thinking through how to read and teach literary works written in Arabic and translated into English. The essays in this volume challenge and work beyond the discourses that overdetermine both our own and our students' approaches to these texts. The focus on how the theory, politics, and ethics of translation inform their production and reception in English addresses the concerns that teachers have about bringing texts into their classrooms and teaching them in new and relevant ways in the twenty-first century.

With the increased interest in and attention paid to the Arab world in twenty-first-century North America, not only are more Arabic literary works being translated into English but there are also more spaces for working with them. It is no longer only specialists and experts in the field who wish to include them in their classrooms. This volume invites those working in other fields to participate in the conversation. The more the participants, the more we will learn from one another.

Structure of the Volume

This volume is divided into three sections that respond to three of the main challenges faced by people who teach modern Arabic literature in the university and elsewhere. In the first section, "Situated Literatures: History, Current Events, and the Politics of Teaching Arabic Literature," essays engage the politics of teaching Arabic literature in English translation, dealing in particular with some of the events and issues that students are likely to be familiar with before they come to class. The second section, "Engaging the Canon in Modern Arabic Literature," deals with canonical authors and works and also challenges traditional notions of canonicity. These essays offer exciting new possibilities for teaching texts like Salih's *Season of Migration to the North* (موسم الهجرة إلى الشمال ; Mawsim al-hijra ila al-shamal), Shidyaq's *Leg over Leg* (الساق على الساق فيما هو الفارياق ; Al-Saq 'ala al-saq fima huwwa al-fariyaq), and Habiby's *The Secret Life of Saeed* (الوقائع الغريبة في اختفاء سعيد أبي النحس المتشائل) ; Al-Waqai'i al-ghariba fi ikhtifa' Sa'id Abi al-Nahas al-mutasha'il). In the third section, "Comparative Contexts, Youth Culture, New Media," the essays consider texts written by young authors or for young readers; discuss how authors invoke and reshape new media, social media in particular; and offer resources for teachers.

Contexts for Essays and Sequence of Reading

The essays of this volume do not need to be read in order. For example, the teacher new to Arabic literature might begin with Allen Hibbard's "Teaching Modern Arabic Literature in Translation in Middle Tennessee," which suggests approaches and gives resources for teaching translated Arabic poetic and dramatic texts. Anne-Marie McManus offers a guide to accessible resources for the teaching of Syrian literature in "Syrian Literature after 2000: Publics, Mobilities, Revolt." In "Arabic Poetics through a Canonical Translation: Teaching Tayeb Salih's *Season of Migration to the North*," Rula Jurdi tells how she used her experience of reading the original text in Arabic to work through the translation with students at the University of Akron.

Many readers will be interested in national traditions, either to work with texts from one nation or to compare nations. "Syrian Literature after 2000," by McManus, and "Teaching New Egyptian Writing: Experimental Style in Arabic and the Undergraduate Reader," by Mara Naaman, take up questions related to their specific national contexts and to teaching a local literature in a larger pan-Arab context. A number of typically underrepresented national traditions are touched on, including those of Yemen (see Seymour-Jorn's essay) and Sudan (see Jurdi's essay).

Many paths to teaching about Palestine are suggested. "Teaching (beyond) the Conflict: A Contrapuntal Reading," by Philip Metres, which considers both Palestinian and Israeli literature about the conflict, can be read usefully with Stephen Sheehi's reflections on teaching Mahmoud

Darwish's poetry. Both essays explore pedagogical techniques that challenge how students have been accustomed to approach the study of Palestine. Palestine looks different in Maya Kesrouany's approach to teaching Habiby's complex satire *The Secret Life of Saeed the Pessoptimist*. The moments of impossibility of translation in her essay, "The Joke's on Me," parallel the supposed impossibility of return for Palestinians. In "Untranslatability, Discomfort, Ideology: Should We Teach Arabic Literature?," Sheehi connects the dispossession of Palestinians to that of the indigenous peoples of North America.

Kesrouany's essay on Habiby can be usefully read with Rebecca Johnson's "In Translation: Cosmopolitan Reading in the *Nahda*." The three essays, by Kesrouany, Sheehi, and Johnson, all offer ways to bring texts from the *nahda*, a fecund period of Arabic literary production, into the classroom. Kesrouany pairs *nahda* texts with a reading of Habiby; Sheehi pairs modernist European poetry with anticolonial poetry in Arabic; Johnson works with two of the most canonical texts of the *nahda*—Tahtawi's *An Imam in Paris* and Shidyaq's *Leg over Leg*—through the concept of cosmopolitanism.

Another way to organize the reading of the essays is to focus on literary matters, in a particular style. In "Teaching New Egyptian Writing: Experimental Style in Arabic and the Undergraduate Reader," Naaman probes different methods of teaching difficult stylistic features to students who do not know Arabic. She uses techniques to connect students to texts that they feel distant from because of style. McManus moves between genres in her discussion of contemporary Syrian literature. Hibbard offers the perspective of a teacher working with poetry and drama in Tennessee whose students are unfamiliar with the language and rhetoric of Arabic literary traditions.

Although the novel is the predominant genre discussed in this volume, the essays that deal directly or indirectly with poetry provide insights into a range of approaches and texts. Hibbard's essay shows ways to bring poetry alive in the classroom. McManus brings several genres together in teaching Syrian literature, including works by the Syrian Kurdish poet Golan Haji. Sheehi juxtaposes European modernist and Arab anticolonial poetry, echoing M. Lynx Qualey's explanation of irony in "The War Works Hard," by Dunya Mikhail, an Iraqi. Lynx Qualey and Sheehi both reflect on how to teach texts in classrooms located at the center of empire, which is waging imperial wars in the Middle East.

Lynx Qualey's "Teaching Arabic Literature in Open Spaces" can be paired with Sheehi's essay in another way as well. Both seek to answer the question, What elements of the complex North American context of translating Arabic literature into English do we need to think about in order to develop an ethical teaching practice? Both authors argue for an emphasis on deep context and comparison. Lynx Qualey discusses how she administers an educational blog about Arabic literature in translation—an "open space"—and details some of the changes and differences in teaching that this space entails in comparison with classroom teaching. Sheehi suggests that in the ways that we conceive of the texts and issues that we teach we challenge American privilege to develop a radical pedagogical practice. Hartman and Jurdi describe how explanations of translational techniques and strategies lead their students to develop empathetic readings of texts. Seymour-Jorn broaches the question of ethical teaching and translation by discussing how Marilyn Booth's translation of *Girls of Riyadh* was changed and how Booth responded to that change.

How can we bring politics and poetics together in the classroom? How can we highlight the language of texts while working with their content? Several essays address this question. McManus compares literary works that challenged Assad's regime through the more traditional form of the novel with newer post–Damascus Spring writing that experiments with form. Both groups of texts are deeply political, but both are also artistically developed and challenging. Focus on form is taken up in Naaman's discussion of experimental writing in Egypt. Naaman shows how young authors experience and articulate politics in ways different from those of their predecessors. These two essays work well with Kesrouany's linking of Habiby's exploration of the impossible return to Palestine with difficult translational moments, particularly the translation of the names of female characters. In Habiby's work, formal elements are linked to an Arabic literary heritage, elements that are extraordinarily difficult to express in translation but are crucial to understanding the politics of the text.

Purpose of the Volume

To create a toolbox of ideas for approaches to teaching modern Arabic literature in English translation, this volume pays close attention to the dynamics of that translation. A great challenge facing all teachers of modern

Arabic literary works in English is that many of the translations available to us are problematic and flawed. Therefore they must be critiqued: which can be used in the classroom and which cannot?

Though it is only recently that a handful of scholars have started working with the insights of translation theory specifically in relation to Arabic-English translation, these insights are crucial to developing our reading and teaching practices as more and more works become available to us in English. Lawrence Venuti's seminal study *The Translator's Invisibility: A History of Translation* emphasizes the importance of recognizing translated works as translated. Historically, transparency and fluency were valued, but Venuti advocates a different approach, foregrounding the role of translator as creator. He suggests that, if we see translation as interpretation and intervention, we will understand how translational ideologies affect the resulting texts.

Issues and debates in the field of translation studies provide points of entry to classroom discussion of Arabic literature in translation. The change from conceptualizing translation as conveying words or phrases to conveying an entire culture is important not just in the development of the field but also in thinking through what translation actually means (Bassnett and Trivedi). Is it partly or primarily a metaphor for explaining culture (Bhabha)?

The idea of lexical equivalence, that a word-to-word correspondence exists that will enable us to understand a given text, has been thoroughly debunked, and the notion of translation as a more expansive practice is being applied to postcolonial translation studies in particular (Bassnett and Trivedi; Bhabha). But equivalence in general has been shown by many theorists to be a complex and multifaceted area of inquiry. Mona Baker's exploration of different levels and layers of what equivalence means, for example, compels us to think about how we use this notion when evaluating Arabic translations. Are we talking about words, phrases, texts, implied meanings, or something else when we critique a given translation? Maria Tymoczko and Venuti use this approach in very different ways to develop larger theories about how to produce more ethical translations.

What should we do to produce an ethical theory and practice of translation? Tymoczko's collection of essays *Translation, Resistance, Activism* questions which texts we translate and why and advocates for a deep contextualization of works not only linguistically and culturally but also temporally and politically. In her concluding essay in the volume, Tymoczko argues against some of Venuti's prescriptions for foreignizing translation; she gives in detail a number of cases where such foreignizing would not be possible ("Space").

Acknowledging the differences in literary traditions makes clearer the power of differences among languages and their associated literary traditions in the world. Though Arabic is the fifth most spoken language in the world, Arabic literature is only in the top twenty languages from which literary works are translated, and Egypt is the only Arab country in UNESCO's list of top fifty countries whose works are most translated (www .unesco.org/xtrans/bsstatexp.aspx?crit1L=1&nTyp=min&topN=50). This disparity affects the circulation of Arabic literary works and also the dynamics in our classrooms, wherever we are located in the world.

Drawing attention to translation choices allows teachers to open different kinds of discussions of Arabic literary works and to demonstrate some of the dynamics of interpretation and power relations in action. Roger Allen discusses the choice to render the titles of the volumes of Naguib Mahfouz's famous *Cairo Trilogy* (ثلاثية القاهرة ; Thulathiyat al-Qahira) by translating the Old Cairo street names—as "Palace Walk," "Palace of Desire," and "Sugar Street"—instead of transliterating them ("Happy Traitor"). The simultaneous domestication and exoticism inherent in these book titles is indicative of the issues faced in translating modern Arabic literature. The English titles do not immediately conjure up street names, and, because they are familiar words, they do not necessarily evoke Cairo. Translation has tamed the streets, making them less challenging to the reader and more easily consumed. This is a common problem in Arabic translation, unlike translation from most European languages. Allen points out with irony that no one refers to the most famous street in Paris as the Elysian Fields; in English we simply call it the Champs Elysees (479). Another example is the changed title, inclusion of photographs, and addition of a prologue and epilogue to Hanan al-Shaykh's memoir of her mother. There is a significant ideological shift in titling a text, originally called حكايتي شرح يطول (Hikayati sharhun yatul), which literally translated is "My Tale Is Too Long to Tell," as the *The Locust and the Bird*. The Arabic title of the daughter's written rendition of her illiterate mother's life story is patently ironic. It also privileges the mother's voice: she asserts something about her story before it begins. But the English title, invoking a fable, gives the work an almost mythical cast, as do the additions made to the translation (Hartman, "My Tale"). Observing these changes leads to discussion in the classroom of genre in relation to readers' expectations. Why might English readers expect the story of an Arab, Muslim peasant woman to be told not in her own powerful voice but rather as a fable? Why were the prologue and epilogue in the author's voice requested by the English-language publisher but refused by the Arabic publisher?

Making the translation "visible," to borrow Venuti's terminology (13), allows us to think about literature in broader ways. We can address loss in translation, talking about the violence done to a work by moving it from one language, context, and tradition into another. We can also consider what might be the gains of translation. A work can acquire a new or different life in another language. According to David Damrosch, works of world literature are those texts that "gain on balance in translation" (289). *Season of Migration to the North* enjoyed a wide following in English that it did not have in Arabic; it took on the role of being an exemplary text of postcolonial fiction representing Africa, a role very different from its place in the Arabic literary scene as a novel in conversation with a long history of Arabic writing and with other contemporary literary works written in the region. In both the original and the translation, the romantic relationships between the African (Sudanese) protagonist and his Western (British) women are the center of attention, but those relationships are read in different ways by the different audiences.

The first substantial review of *Other Lives* (حيوات أخرى ; Hayawat ukhra), by Iman Humaydan, underlined not only the strong characterization of the protagonist but also the intimacy of a text written about a woman by a woman and translated by a woman (see Lynx Qualey's essay). In Arabic, this work is arguably also a woman's novel, in all the positive senses of that term. The review made me realize, however, that the author and I (I was the translator) had discussed gendering the text when we were working closely to produce the English translation, that on several occasions we ended up choosing feminized versions of expressions where the Arabic grammar called for masculine pronouns. English, in this case, was more flexible. The way our choice changed the text could perhaps be considered a gain. Such examples connect the theory and practice of teaching translated works to both ethics and politics.

Conceptual Framing of the Volume's Topic

The construction of Arabs and Muslims as the twenty-first century's other has its roots in a much longer history of orientalism and colonialism.

Edward Said's now-classic 1978 study *Orientalism* emphasized the role of arts and literatures in creating and perpetuating the myth of an Orient defined against the West. Western scholarly studies of the Orient, later relabeled the Middle East, used literary and linguistic evidence to bolster their claim to the superiority of the West. Said traced the effect of these discourses on colonial ambitions and on people's material, everyday existence. The various and contested namings of the region in which Arabic-speaking people live—the Orient, Near East, Middle East, North Africa, MENA (Middle East and North Africa), Maghreb—point to the different and overlapping legacies tied to the interests of Europe and later North America.

Colonial intervention in the region is often talked about as something that started and ended in the past, in other words bounded by dates. We know that Napoleon landed on the shores of Alexandria in Egypt in 1798. We date British colonial power in Egypt to 1882. When we talk about the fall of the Ottoman Empire after World War One and the carving up of its former domain by the European powers, we list the dates of independence of new nation-states—for example, Lebanon's in 1943 and Syria's in 1946. The date 1948 is of course crucially important as the Nakba (النكبة ; "catastrophe"), the establishment of the State of Israel in historic Palestine and the loss of the Palestinian homeland. But this attention to dates does not convey how lives were affected. Conversations about the War of Independence in Algeria are still current in France, partly because of the impact that the brutal colonial period still has on Algerians. The refugee crises created by colonialism and its afterlives, for Palestinians, Iraqis, and Syrians, are tragically familiar in mainstream North America, but the histories in which they are rooted often are not. Lasting colonial legacies pervade every aspect of daily life in the Arab world, whether directly or indirectly, and they live on today in North America and Europe too—consider the United States imperial ambitions throughout the region.

The so-called global war on terror has had a deep resonance in the United States, not only in the prevalence of misinformation, hostility, and stereotyping but also in the ways in which Arabic literature can and cannot circulate within and outside literary venues, the academy, and the classroom. The English-language reception environment for Arabic literary works today, particularly in North America, is fraught with complicated and conflicting views about a subject virtually unknown to most readers. Iraq is not home to some of the most important poets of a vast and rich literary tradition but a scary place full of improvised explosive devices. Beirut is not a city of many bookshops and a multilingual reading public but an unstable location for an overflowing Syrian refugee population. Egypt, having lost its temporary luster in the United States popular imagination with hopeful visions for a democratic society, is now portrayed as irrational and violent. In this context, the choice of Arabic literary works to teach is politicized, and many of us assign the same supposedly less difficult or less controversial works to teach again and again. Moreover, relatively few works are translated from Arabic to English. Most appear with small presses; works often go out of print; many translations are problematic, because they are so transformed from their original versions or have glaring errors; and some are unusable in classrooms. Most translations from Arabic into English are done not by writers or professional translators but by university professors who want to teach certain texts in their classes. The literary quality of these translations is uneven—and it is notoriously difficult to convey the aesthetics of Arabic literary techniques in English. In addition, some of the better known and more widely distributed translations clearly speak more to market interests and current events than to literary value.

Literary works are published throughout the Arab world by both small and large presses, but Cairo and Beirut have traditionally been the centers of this publishing. Censorship in different places and times is an issue for texts written in Arabic and not always for the reasons that people assume: texts are scrutinized for involvement in local politics much more than for sex and sexuality or for heresy, though these instances tend to be what make the news. Texts published in one Arab country circulate in others, increasingly so with the advent of the Internet and as many publishers and bookshops have online services, the largest of these being Neel wa Furat, which has almost half a million titles in its catalog. Online publishing and reading are new realities that will no doubt influence people's reading practices—McManus and Lynx Qualey's essays in this volume show this—but have not existed for long. In some locations, access to the Internet is expensive and not as accessible as in others; where Arabic literature is published, works in other languages are often available; and in all Arab countries, translations of literary works from other languages into Arabic are common. In the Arab world, there is great diversity in how people write and read.

Yet the English-language representation of Arabic literature is narrow, partly because of the lack of translators, the history of translating Arabic literature for political reasons rather than literary ones, and the relatively low interest among English-language publishers in translations in general. So how are we to teach the politics and poetics of Arabic literature in translation? What strategies can we use to highlight the language and poetry of texts while also working with their content, particularly if we don't know Arabic?

Bringing Politics and Poetics Together in the Classroom

Teachers of literature always struggle to balance poetics and politics, aesthetics and issues, form and content in their courses. Even before Fredric Jameson's famous article claiming that all Third World literary works were national allegories, the idea that some literary traditions are more inherently political than others—and less important aesthetically—infused the study of modern Arabic literary works. Texts that were complex or difficult to understand were derided for being irrelevant, extravagant, or without purpose or sense. The approach of using Arabic literature to unlock the secrets of an ancient past or esoteric otherness dates back to well before there was such a thing as modern Arabic literature. The use of pre-Islamic poetry to teach about the life of Bedouin Arabs is an example. I have demonstrated how the English-language critical construction of the poetic figure of the first Arabic female poet, the fabled al-Khansaʾ, tells us much more about the needs of orientalist scholars and Western feminists than about this poet, her works, or the life of people in the pre-Islamic Arabian Peninsula ("Arab Woman"). This construction also highlights the role that gender plays in our assumptions about the Arab world, stereotypes influenced by orientalist discourses: Arab women must be exotic and passive, Arab men aggressive and warlike.

This legacy deeply informs how we study and teach modern Arabic literature today. The argument that all Third World literature is an allegory for the nation was made in the 1980s, yet its resonance is remarkably vibrant today. Jameson's claim is still upheld, in various ways by many, despite the strong response by Aijaz Ahmad and others to it. Scholarly articles in the field of Arabic literary studies still use the Jameson-Ahmad debate as a framing device. I have found that it is effective in teaching Arabic literature to undergraduates. In 2013, I assigned students at McGill University both Jameson's article and Ahmad's, together with Adania Shibli's *Touch* (مساس; Masas) and Alexandra Chreiteh's *Always Coca-Cola* (دايما كوكا كولا ; Daʾiman coca-cola). These novels helped them work through issues of nation, narration, politics, and poetics in relation to gender dynamics. Both texts, written by young women, question the gender roles to which men and women are meant to conform. I then assigned the students roles— Jameson, Ahmad, Shibli, and Chreiteh—and they prepared their argu- ments in groups. This debating exercise dramatized for them not only the issues at stake in this criticism but also how authors and their texts hold up to such scrutiny.

Whereas it is the politics that draws most students to our classes, it is often the aesthetic and formal aspects of Arabic literary texts that make them stay. Even when working with flawed and stilted translations, stu- dents appreciate the poetic values of the originals—Salih's *Season of Migra- tion to the North* is exemplary in this regard. Students like Mahfouz's *Cairo Trilogy* for its attention to detail and compelling portrait of a family against the backdrop of modern Egyptian history. They develop a love-hate rela- tion to Habiby's brilliantly constructed *The Secret Life of Saeed* because of its formal challenges and because it draws on Classical Arabic literary devices and traditions (see Kesrouany's essay in this volume). The narra- tive styles of Shibli's and Chreiteh's books could not be more different. Chreiteh's rendition of everyday life in a simplified version of formal Ara- bic makes a dramatic contrast to Shibli's stylized elliptical narration, which leaves out more than it includes and tells its story by evoking sensations.

The students' interest in politics, history, and current events should not be discouraged, even when it makes it difficult to teach poetics, but should be contextualized An example is to remind students that, although we teach much more fiction (particularly the novel) than poetry in our classrooms, the opposite is true in the Arab world, whose literary tradition has always prided itself on its poetry. Another example of how classroom practice reflects the biases of our own society is provided by the essay "Pal- estinian Women and the Politics of Reception" (Saliba and Kattan), which shows that in Palestine students read and are taught texts by Palestinian women writers that differ from texts used to teach Palestinian women's writing in the United States.

Is Arabic Still Controversial? Translation and Conformity

In his article "Embargoed Literature," published in *The Nation* in 1990, Said relates that, when he suggested names of Third World writers to be translated and published in response to a request from a major commercial New York publisher, he was told that Mahfouz—who would go on to win the Nobel Prize—could not be included because "Arabic is a controversial language" (278). Today there is still resistance to having Arabic literary works translated into English. Hosam Aboul-Ela details the poor state of Arabic-English literary translation and publishing in 2000: it was difficult to access texts, works quickly went out of print, most translators were not professional, and sales figures of works translated from Arabic were dismal.

With the recent increase of interest in Arabic literature, more works are being translated and therefore more texts are available for teaching. Better funding—for example, new literary prizes like the Arabic Booker (the informal name for the International Prize for Arabic Fiction), which is sponsored by the Emirates Foundation in Abu Dhabi and others—has promoted the publication of Arabic works in English translation. Book fairs in Arab countries have long been a meeting place for authors, publishers, teachers, and readers and are increasing in size, scope, and visibility. Fairs in the United Arab Emirates are particularly prominent now—in Abu Dhabi, Dubai, and Sharjah. Yet Arabic literature in English translation is still a small, underfunded, and marginal area of publishing.

Literary works that do not conform to predetermined notions of what will sell to a mainstream audience are still often passed over as uninteresting or unrepresentative. Pierpont's article unleashed a small wave of critical pieces that pointed out these dynamics. Ibrahim Farghali, for example, offers a scathing indictment of the state of translation from Arabic into English (as well as into French and German), suggesting that despite all the prizes and attention given to translation today, little has changed. His blog post is titled with his main question: "Is it really necessary to translate Arabic literature?" Hilary Plum, an editor and writer, criticizes Pierpont's unspoken assumption that literature should satisfy what a white, American, mainstream readership desires. She suggests that we change this attitude, not for ethical but for literary reasons:

> Literature in translation is a crossing of borders, but shouldn't be thought of just as one of the easier border crossings—tourism, reportage, whatever sort of casual interest or genealogical research—but remembering the violent invasions and migrations that make up our real world and thus the theoretical field of translation. It's *useful* to think of reading literature in translation not as a means of gathering "insight and information," but as a means of experiencing acts of resistance that occur between languages, between cultures, "simply" between reader and writer.

The Texts We Teach: Availability, Circulation, and Problematic Translations

Plum is engaged in the project of bringing more texts to the public that break with conventional ideas of what Arabic literature in translation should be, in helping establish the imprint Clockroot Books at Interlink, one of the small independent presses dedicated to publishing Arabic literature in translation. It is joined by Archipelago Books and City Lights Books in the United States, Ithaca Press and Saqi Books in the United Kingdom, as well as by the now defunct Bloomsbury Qatar Foundation Publishing. University presses in the United States, like Syracuse University Press, University of Arkansas Press, and Indiana University Press, also frequently publish modern Arabic literary works in English translation. The American University in Cairo Press has long been an important source of translated Arabic fiction into English—particularly of Egyptian titles—and these circulate around the world. Many colleagues—specialists and nonspecialists alike—prefer to use works for teaching produced in English and easily available in North America.

Availability of texts is a major factor in the creation of a reading list and teaching syllabus. This volume offers an exciting range that its contributors draw on to discuss their choices of texts and teaching methods. There are both classic, canonical works of the Arabic tradition and works by newer and less-well-known authors. Habiby's *The Secret Life of Saeed* is entertaining but a challenge to teach. Salih's *Season of Migration to the North* is used in many classrooms as an exploration of the ravages of colonialism, and here new approaches to it are explored. Syrian novels like Khaled Khalifa's *In Praise of Hatred* (مديح الكراهية ; Madih al-karahiya) is becoming better known but still not widely used in classrooms. Works by younger authors include Ahmed Alaidy's *Being Abbas el Abd* (أن تكون عباس العبد ; An takun ʿAbbas al-ʿAbd); Hamdi Abu Golayyel's *Thieves in Retirement* (لصوص متقاعدون ; Lusus mutaqaʿidun); Haji's poetry; and Zaher Omareen's short stories.

Works both recent and well established are plagued by poor translations. We must address this problem frankly. A sticky issue is how the concepts of domestication and foreignization work politically in connection with Arabic literature. Because Arabic is seen as so exotic in English-language reception environments, foreignizing techniques, as advocated by scholars like Venuti, can serve to exoticize a translation further. In translation theory, quite new in the conversation about Arabic works into

English, discussion about errors of word equivalence and about vague notions of accuracy is slowly giving way to more holistic evaluations of a translation.

People who regularly work between original Arabic texts and translated English ones have called attention to the flawed nature of many of the translations they must deal with—even some of the most famous ones. The ethical imperative to draw attention to the question of translation in our classrooms is more pressing for us than for colleagues who teach other literary traditions: we face not only the problems of word-to-word translation but also the more dramatic changes to a translation that can happen—particularly cutting and censorship. Mohja Kahf's argument for how cutting reshapes the autobiography of Huda Sha'rawi, an early Egyptian feminist, shows the connection between ideology and the so-called need for a shorter text. Amal Amireh's essay on Nawal El Saadawi examines the changes that this feminist icon undergoes in translation from Arabic to English. I have shown how the image of the Arab woman is flattened in a comparison between an ancient poet and al-Shaykh, a contemporary Lebanese novelist ("Gender"). Al-Shaykh's *Women of Sand and Myrrh* bears only passing resemblance to the Arabic text from which it was translated, given the changed title, reordered chapters, and significantly different ending. Booth reflects on the dramatic changes that took place between the translation she submitted to Penguin, the publisher of *Girls of Riyadh*, and the version that was eventually published ("'Muslim Woman'" and "Translator").

Studying texts and their translations side by side mirrors the larger issues in the English-language reception of Arab authors. Gender and gender stereotyping is perhaps the most important of these issues and deeply connected to others. It is not only in translated women's texts that problematic gender dynamics are revealed. In "Packaging 'Huda,'" for example, Kahf shows how male characters are written out of the text and female characters given more prominent roles in the name of making the work shorter in translation. The positive treatment that Huda Sha'rawi gives her father and brother therefore fades, and these stereotype-defying Arab men are removed from a book that is renamed *Harem Years*, a title that points to the oppression of women by domineering men. It is not a vague presence of prejudice but rather concrete translation and editing choices that support ideologies and gender stereotypes in translated texts.

How can we work with the politics of the writing we are studying and its contexts while acknowledging our own context? We must find ways in the classroom to talk about translation and bring together the challenges of the theory and practice of translation with translation politics. The ethical issue facing all teachers of modern Arabic literature in English translation, wherever they are situated, is that of working with both the constraints of our own location and the discourses and material conditions of the region from which the literature came.

Works Cited

Aboul-Ela, Hosam. "Challenging the Embargo: Arabic Literature in the US Market." *Middle East Report*, vol. 219, 2001, pp. 42–44.

Ahmad, Aijaz. "Jameson's Rhetoric of Otherness and the 'National Allegory.'" *Social Text*, vol. 17, 1987, pp. 3–25.

Allen, Roger. "The Happy Traitor: Tales of Translation." *Comparative Literature Studies*, vol. 47, no. 4, 2010, pp. 472–86.

———. *An Introduction to Arabic Literature*. Cambridge UP, 2000.

Amireh, Amal. "Framing Nawal El Saadawi: Arab Feminism in a Transnational World." *Signs*, vol. 26, no.1, 2000, pp. 215–49.

Amireh, Amal, and Lisa Suhair Majaj, editors. *Going Global: The Transnational Reception of Third World Women Writers*. Garland Publishing, 2000.

Badawi, M. M., editor. *Modern Arabic Literature*. Cambridge UP, 2006.

Baker, Mona. *In Other Words: A Coursebook on Translation*. Routledge, 1992.

Bassnett, Susan, and Harish Trivedi, editors. *Post-colonial Translation: Theory and Practice*. Routledge, 1999.

Bhabha, Homi. *The Location of Culture*. Routledge, 1994.

Booth, Marilyn. "'The Muslim Woman' as Celebrity Author and the Politics of Translating Arabic: Girls of Riyadh Go on the Road." *Journal of Middle East Women's Studies*, vol. 6, no. 3, 2010, pp. 149–82.

———. "Translator v. Author (2007): Girls of Riyadh go to New York." *Translation Studies*, vol. 1, no. 2, 2008, pp. 197–211.

Chreiteh, Alexandra. *Always Coca-Cola*. Translated by Michelle Hartman, Interlink Publishing, 2012.

———. دايما كوكا كولا [Da'iman coca-cola]. Arab Scientific, 2009. Translated as *Always Coca-Cola*.

Damrosch, David. *What Is World Literature?* Princeton UP, 2003.

Fadda-Conrey, Carol. *Arab American Fiction: Transnational Reconfigurations of Citizenship and Belonging*. New York UP, 2014.

Farghali, Ibrahim. "هل هناك أهمية لترجمة الأدب العربي إلى لغات أجنبية حقا؟" [Hal hunak ahamiyya li-tarjamat al-adab al-'arabi ila lughat ajnabiya haqqan?]. *Ibrahim Farghali*, 21 Aug. 2012, ifarghali.blogspot.ca/2012/08/blogpost.html. Translated as "Is It Really Necessary to Translate Arabic Literature?"

———. "Is It Really Necessary to Translate Arabic Literature?" *Qisasukhra*, qisasukhra.wordpress.com/2012/09/14/is-it-really-necessary-to-translate -arabic-literature/.

Hartman, Michelle. "An Arab Woman Poet as a Crossover Artist? Reconsidering the Ambivalent Legacy of Al-Khansa'." *Tulsa Studies in Women's Literature*, vol. 30 no. 1, 2011, pp. 15–36.

———. "Gender, Genre, and the (Missing) Gazelle: Arab Women Writers and the Politics of Translation." *Feminist Studies*, vol. 38, no. 1, 2012, pp. 17–49.

———. "My Tale Is Too Long to Tell: *The Locust and the Bird* between South Lebanon and New York City." *Journal of Arabic Literature*, vol. 46, 2015, pp. 1–25.

Hassan, Waïl S. *Immigrant Narratives: Orientalism and Cultural Translation in Arab American and Arab British Literature*. Oxford UP, 2011.

Hout, Syrine Chafic. *Post-war Anglophone Lebanese Fiction: Home Matters in the Diaspora*. Edinburgh UP, 2012.

Humaydan, Iman. حيوات أخرى [Hayawat ukhra]. Arrawi, 2010. Translated as *Other Lives*.

———. *Other Lives*. Translated by Michelle Hartman, Interlink Publishing, 2014.

Jameson, Fredric. "Third-World Literature in the Era of Multinational Capitalism." *Social Text*, vol. 15, 1986, pp. 65–88.

Kahf, Mohja. "Packaging 'Huda': Shaʿrawi's Memoirs in the United States Reception Environment." Amireh and Majaj, pp. 148–72.

Lynx Qualey, M. "The Illusions of Intimacy and Reading *Other Lives*." *Arabic Literature (in English)*, 8 May 2014, arabllt.org/2014/05/08/the-illusions-of-intimacy-and-reading-other-lives/.

Pierpont, Claudia Roth. "Found in Translation: The Contemporary Arabic Novel." *The New Yorker*, 18 Jan. 2010, pp. 74–80, www.newyorker.com/magazine/2010/01/18/found-in-translation-2.

Plum, Hilary. "Field Guides to Elsewhere: How We Read Languages We Don't Read." *The Quarterly Conversation*, 16 Feb. 2010, quarterlyconversation.com/field-guides-to-elsewhere-how-we-read-languages-we-dont-read.

Said, Edward W. "Embargoed Literature." *The Nation*, 17 Sept. 1990, pp. 278–80.

———. *Orientalism*. Vintage, 1978.

Salaita, Steven. *Arab American Literary Fictions, Cultures, and Politics*. Palgrave Macmillan, 2007.

———. *Modern Arab American Fiction: A Reader's Guide*. Syracuse UP, 2011.

Saliba, Therese, and Jeanne Kattan. "Palestinian Women and the Politics of Reception." Amireh and Majaj, pp. 84–112.

Shibli, Adania. مساس [Masas]. al-Adab, 2001. Translated as *Touch*.

———. *Touch*. Translated by Paula Haydar, Interlink Publishing, 2010.

Starkey, Paul. *Modern Arabic Literature*. Georgetown UP, 2006.

Tymosczko, Maria. "The Space and Time of Activist Translation." Tymoczko, *Translation*, pp. 227–54.

———, editor. *Translation, Resistance, Activism*. U of Massachusetts P, 2010.

Venuti, Lawrence. *The Translator's Invisibility: A History of Translation*. Routledge, 2008.

Part I

Situated Literatures:
History, Current Events,
and the Politics of
Teaching Arabic Literature

Ken Seigneurie

Arabic Literature and World Literature

A short essay on the role of Arabic literature in world literature cannot defuse all the theoretical charges buried along the way: What is the *world* of world literature? Is it the same in Arabic? How does *world literature* differ semantically and functionally from the corresponding Arabic term, الأدب العالمي (al-adab al-'alami)? These questions will have to keep. Instead, if *world literature* may be defined as texts of exemplary artistic value that have appealed to a wide number of readers from a range of cultures, then it would be a useful service to literary studies to explore these texts and their contexts of transmission and reception. This essay highlights but a sliver from the bulk of Arabic literature that has contributed, and continues to contribute, to a cross-cultural literature of the world. The aim is to raise awareness of a part of world literary heritage by helping instructors build Arabic literature into undergraduate courses on world literature in an English-language environment.

The prominence of the *One Thousand and One Nights* in anthologies and world literature syllabi may lead one to assume that Arabic literature is a one-hit wonder of world literature. The six-volume third edition of the *Norton Anthology of World Literature* contains fewer than a dozen examples of Arabic literature, most relating to Islam and, of course, the

One Thousand and One Nights, along with a few token modern representatives (Puchner et al.). Of course, anthologizing is a thankless task and always open to quibble. Yet even in the highbrow press, contemporary authors writing in Arabic command little attention in the burgeoning upper-middle-class market for world literature. The New York–based magazine *n + 1*, sometimes likened to the authoritative *Partisan Review* of yore, recently devoted an eight-thousand-word article to world literature, citing several dozen names and titles but only one Arabic text, again the *One Thousand and One Nights* ("World Lite"). So when one hears, as in the now famous and oft-cited 2002 United Nations Arab Human Development Report, about how few books are translated from and into Arabic, one might assume that what little literature the Arabs possess—the *One Thousand and One Nights*, Islamic texts, and a few modern also-rans—is adequately represented in anthologies of world literature (Gearing).

Yet the notion that Arabic has little to contribute to world literature is nothing short of embarrassing. The problem is not the dearth of material but rather its massive quantity. How can we do justice to a literature that before the end of the first millennium was doubtless among the most widespread literatures on the planet and one that is still commonly in use on every continent? How to explain the role of the House of Wisdom (بيت الحكمة ; Bayt al-hikma) from the ninth to the thirteenth century: Was it simply the largest library in the world drawing from European, African, and Asian language cultures? Or shall we complicate matters by saying it was also a center for translation and research in the humanities and an institute for science? In the tenth century, Abu al-Faraj al-Isfahani attempted to get a handle on the literary wealth of Arabic, producing an encyclopedic twenty-five-volume collection of poems, songs, and commentary known as the *Book of Songs* (كتاب الأغاني ; Kitab al-aghani), which remains today a staple of public and even personal libraries throughout the Arab world (Kilpatrick). By the twelfth century, numerous Arabic texts were already exemplars of world literature, having traveled by ship, caravan, and word of mouth to northern Europe, sub-Saharan Africa, Gibraltar, and Indonesia. And like the cargo that traveled with them, texts were often supplemented or pared down along the way, bearing the intertextual and translational traces of cultures encountered en route.

Indeed, if we are going to talk about Arabic literature from the standpoint of world literature, many features stand out. First is its astonishing spread across spatial, cultural, and temporal borders since the emergence of the written language in the fifth century CE. The Qur'an is, of course, the most important text and Muslim culture the most important vector (Blatherwick and Toorawa). The *One Thousand and One Nights* is almost as well-known, yet many other texts have traveled widely as well. Ronit Ricci has shown how a tenth-century text known in English as the *Book of One Thousand Questions* contributed to the spread of Islam into South and Southeast Asia. A product of "several centuries of prior texts circulating in the form of hadith tradition and Qur'anic commentaries," the *Book of One Thousand Questions* depicts a Q-and-A between the Prophet Muhammad and a Jewish leader who is eventually persuaded to convert to Islam (34). The text was adapted in content and language to its many target cultures, among them Latin, Portuguese, Dutch, English, Persian, Urdu, Tamil, Javanese, and Malay. So protean was the text that it existed in numerous tellings rather than versions, since *version* assumes an identifiable original.

The complex identity and itinerary of the *Book of One Thousand Questions* illustrate a second feature of Arabic literature in the context of world literature: it has been a crucial mediator among different text cultures and value systems. The contribution of Arabic literature to intercultural dialogue was not only, or even principally, related to Islam, even in earlier periods. Everybody has heard of the dizzyingly complex itinerary of the *One Thousand and One Nights* from India to Persia, the Arabian Peninsula, central Asia, and points west (Irwin 42–62; Rastegar 35–74). Expressed graphically, the movement of *Nights* around the globe would look like a bird's nest with points of origin and destinations difficult to distinguish. Such complex text networks were not uncommon in the ancient and medieval literature of the Near East (Selden). Among the many other famous examples is the *Panchatantra*, a collection of talking animal fables, first recorded in Sanskrit early in the first millennium. By the seventh century, Middle Persian and Syriac versions of the text appeared, and around 750 a Persian scholar, Ibn al-Muqaffa', translated the text into Arabic along with three other tales from the *Mahabharata* and one from a Buddhist legend (Marroum). The resulting Arabic text, *Kalila wa Dimna* (كليلة ودمنة), became the source for most European versions from Greek to Swedish, including the renowned fables of La Fontaine (Marroum 537; Dandrey 26). So Arabic literature, like other literatures in different times and places, has played a key role in the dialogue among cultures in which texts pass from one language group to another and then back again.

A third contribution of Arabic to world literature goes to the heart of European culture. Scholars have long recognized the role of Arabic-language culture in preserving and developing ancient Greek philosophical and scientific ideas. Yet the contribution of Arabic to the humanistic practices of early modern Europe is less well recognized. The Arabic term most often cited as equivalent to "literature" in English, *adab* (أدب), includes a constellation of features such as a formal prose style used in a didactic spirit, a tendency toward realism, use of the personal voice, and attention to particular incidents in the world—all crucial elements in the transition from an otherworldly to a humanistic world. Several scholars have explored the role of the ninth- and tenth-century Arabic literary *adab* tradition in developing and conveying principles and practices that would eventually find their way into fifteenth-century European humanism (see Allan; Bonebakker).

Several indicators suggest that their work is finally being recognized by mainstream scholars. For one thing, the ninth-century Mu'tazilite scholar al-Jahiz, who embodies the gold standard of classical *adab*, merits a twelve-page excerpt of his works in the *Longman Anthology of World Literature*, probably the best of the general anthologies when it comes to Arabic literature (Damrosch and Pike). Of deeper significance is New York University's Library of Arabic Literature series, devoted to translating worthy Arabic texts in parallel-text format: the original Arabic and English translation on facing pages. This series, along with the Cambridge History of Arabic Literature series and the Edinburgh Studies in Classical Arabic Literature series, provides non-Arabist English-language students and scholars the opportunity to see Arabic as an integral part of the world literary patrimony.

A fourth and perhaps even greater role for Classical Arabic in world literature may well turn out to be its serving as a major constituent of the worldwide language of love. The earliest and most prestigious pre-Islamic Arabic poetry, the ode (قصيدة ; qasida), most often includes an amatory prelude (نسيب ; nasib) to the absent beloved. Deeply imbued with longing, the poem pictures the poet standing by traces or ruins, consisting of overgrown paths, campfire ash, old tent pegs, et cetera, that remind him (the poet is usually a he) of a former love, whereupon he delivers himself of the melancholic pain of desire (Stetkevych 50–102). From this powerful beginning of the ode, Arabic literature developed a genre of love poetry, the *ghazal* (غزل), which remains a rich part of Arab culture to this day. Other literatures appropriated the *ghazal*, including Persian, which soon developed the form to high levels, but also Hebrew, Turkish, Pashto, Urdu, Nepali, Hindi, Punjabi, Gujarati, Malay, German (via Goethe), and recently English (Bauer and Neuwirth). The *ghazal* often recounts the separation of famous lovers who pine for each other to the point of exhaustion yet whose intense emotion is at the same time paradoxically revivifying.

Of the many legendary loves in Arabic literature, the most famous is the story *Majnun Layla* (مجنون ليلى ; "Fool for Layla"), whose ninth-century rendering by Ibn Qutayba should probably be called a retelling of older texts. The story takes place in seventh-century Arabia, where Qays and Layla experience a childhood paradise while herding their parents' flocks (Khairallah). As they grow up, Qays declares his love for Layla in passionate poems, and Layla's parents forbid him to see her. Qays's father takes Qays away to cure him, and Layla is forced to marry another. Qays goes mad, roaming about half-naked and taking refuge in the wilderness, his only link to society being poetry. From this narrative kernel, the Persian poet Nizami created a world-renowned version that continues to resonate throughout many language cultures and modes (most notably mysticism) until today. From dozens of examples of modern versions and adaptations, suffice it to note the first opera in Azerbaijan was *Leyli and Mejnun* in 1908, and, on the other side of Asia, the first Malay film was *Laila Majnun* in 1933 (Khairallah 238). In France, Louis Aragon's 1963 *Le fou d'Elsa* was immensely popular, and the story of Majnun Layla was eventually adapted in a song by Eric Clapton. Yet it is inaccurate to depict the travels of *Majnun Layla* unidirectionally. Its various versions and adaptations have in turn reentered Arabic culture to reinvigorate new versions over the centuries. Instead of talking about the influence of one work on another, we could talk about a dialogue among cultures around this story.

The role of Arabic literature in forming a cross-cultural, worldwide language of love is not exhausted with the *ghazal* and the stories of its legendary lovers. Arabic has also arguably played a role in what has traditionally been considered the quintessentially European culture of love. Long before the famous medieval Provençal troubadours first set finger to fret, tenth-century Iberian Arabic love poetry developed the *muwashshah* (موشّح). A good number of Iberian Arabic *muwashshahat* were formally distinguished by a final verse in Mozarabic, the Romance vernacular of the Iberian Peninsula that was related to Provençal. According to Maria Rosa Menocal, the presence of the Mozarabic verse known as the *kharja* (خرجة) as part of the Arabic poem strongly suggests a link between this Arabic-Romance hybrid form and the later poetry of the Provençal troubadours. Comparing the poetry of the early troubadour William IX of Aquitaine (1071–126) and the Andalusian poetry of the *muwashshahat*, Menocal affirms:

It is . . . difficult to escape the conclusion that there are strong affinities between the original, and in some ways revolutionary, poetry of William and his progeny and the hardly less revolutionary Andalusian poetry of the *muwashshah*, or that a study of these two groups of poems side by side can give us a more complete and convincing picture of the nature of the innovations that were taking place in lyric poetry throughout Europe in the eleventh and twelfth centuries. An examination of the poems of both schools aimed at seeking out the distinguishing features of courtly love from such a perspective would lead us to conclude that the "rules" of courtly poetry written in Romance are quite similar to those that must be assumed in order to read the *muwashshahat* with their *kharjas* as integral and meaningful poems in their own right. (108)

To juxtapose a hybrid Arabic form and the origin of love poetry in Europe was once controversial; today, it is precisely such attentiveness to cross-cultural literary relations that distinguishes the best scholarship in world literature.

Modern Arabic Literature

The past few decades have seen excellent studies that have gone a long way toward revising the once undisputed notion that Arabic literary history followed a model that may be summarized as Rise, Fall, and Redemption (thanks to Europe). This model had Arabic literature beginning with a creative flourish in the pre-Islamic period and developing in sensibility and sophistication throughout the period of Muhammad and the first four "rightly guided" caliphs (622–60) through the Umayyad (660–750) and Abbasid dynasties (750–1258), before entering a long "period of decadence" (عصر الانحطاط ; ʿasr al-inhitat) until 1798, when Napoleon invaded Egypt and sparked a "renaissance" (نهضة ; nahda) in Arabic letters. Most scholars today take issue with this periodization of literature based on nonliterary factors (Allen, *Essays* 1). Indeed, from the standpoint of world literature, it may be precisely the period of decadence that is most interesting, inasmuch as it was during this period that much popular literature developed and spread. The Lebanese comparatist Asʿad E. Khairallah writes:

Compared to the traditional works within the Arabic canon, it has been easier for popular works to cross cultures. They probably benefit from being closer to the collective unconscious and its archetypal patterns, while being less burdened by the strong thematic and stylistic conventions of classical Arabic literature. (241)

While it is surely overly schematic to draw a clear line that separates elite and popular genres, it is illuminating to consider that the fine flowers of Arabic literature may not be as influential in world culture as the hodgepodge tales of the *One Thousand and One Nights*, the hybridized *muwashshah*, the protean *Book of One Thousand Questions*, the breathless multiversioned love story of *Majnun Layla*, or any of the texts that space prohibits from discussing in this essay, such as numerous polyreligious saints' lives; the philosophical allegory and proto–*Robinson Crusoe Hayy ibn Yaqzan* (حي ابن يقظان), by Ibn Tufayl; or the Arabic popular epic (Heath). So here might be another way in which Arabic literature sheds light on world literature: if, as some would say, world literature has donned the mantle of Arnoldian culture as "the best which has been thought and said" (Arnold 5), then that best can be popular, unauthored, and of dubious cultural parentage.

From the early-nineteenth-century European colonial intervention in the Arab world, Arabic literature underwent great changes. Just as earlier Arabic literature enriched itself by direct and indirect contacts with Sanskrit, Syriac, and Persian cultures, among others, modern Arabic developed a literature that is in dialogue with foreign as well as classical literatures. Among the principal figures of Arab cultural modernity is the nineteenth-century Lebanese intellectual Ahmad Faris al-Shidyaq (1804–87), whose travels through Egypt, Malta, Tunis, England, and France are recounted in his 1855 book الساق على الساق فيما هو الفارياق (al-Saq 'ala al-saq fi ma huwa al-Faryaq), recently translated as *Leg over Leg* by Humphrey Davies. This book, part travelogue, part autobiography, is remarkable for both its cultural insights and literary quality. Al-Shidyaq was a crucial figure in the modernization of the Arabic language, playing an important role in the Arabic press and offering biting critiques of sectarianism, feudal society, and sexism. This work, along with his collaboration in producing a modern translation of the Bible, makes al-Shidyaq a key force in establishing the register of much subsequent modern Arabic literature and linking Arabic to world literary currents (Rastegar 101–25).

In the early twentieth century, a group of Syro-Lebanese emigrant poets, among them Jibran Khalil Jibran, Amin al-Rihani, and Mikha'il Na'ima, brought the Romantic sensibility in Arabic to full maturity (Allen,

Essays 14). Jibran, best known in the West as Kahlil Gibran (1883–1931), is the author of the English-language *The Prophet*, whose mega-best-selling popularity obscures his contributions to Arabic and world literature (Bushrui and Jenkins; Hallaq). Beyond their Romanticism and mysticism, these poets, collectively known as the Pen League of Arab Poets, mediated the transition from fixed neoclassical meters and forms to a poetry more in tune with the subtle movements of feeling. Although its Romantic idealism is out of style, Jibran's 1912 short lyrical novel الأجنحة المتكسرة (Al-ajniha al-mutakassira; *Broken Wings*) is interesting today precisely for its alienating sensibility. It is a testament to an earlier phase of the historic struggle between traditional and modern values in the eastern Mediterranean, which has since evolved into wholly new forms (Imangulieva). It also reveals that Arabic literature's contribution to the worldwide language of love did not end in the medieval period.

This essay cannot do justice to the depth and breadth of Arabic twentieth- and twenty-first-century poetry, whose range and influence go from formalist experimentation to an engaged poetry of commitment (Jayyusi and Tingley 574–83, 599–604). Among the more innovative mid-twentieth-century poets was Nazik al-Mala'ika (1923–2007), whose experiments in free verse along with those of her fellow Iraqis, Badr Shakir al-Sayyab and 'Abd al-Wahhab al-Bayyati, opened new avenues of expression in Arabic. Among her most famous poems, "Revolt against the Sun" (ثورة على الشمس ; Thawra 'ala al-shams) whipsaws between aesthetic and thematic extremes. While the title declares stark opposition to the sun, the first line of the poem thrusts the speaker's heart and the sun together like quarreling lovers:

وَقَفَتْ أمام الشمـس صارخـةً بها   يا شمسُ، مثلُكِ قلبيَ المتمــرِّدُ

"O sun! Like you is my rebellious heart!"
She stood before the sun screaming.

The title and first line (بيت ; bayt), consisting of two hemistichs (عجز ; 'ajaz and صدر ; sadr) also politicize the pain of love. "Revolt" (ثورة ; thawra), especially in the Arabic of al-Mala'ika's time, applies to a more limited semantic range than the English equivalent, referring most often to concrete opposition to authority or state of affairs. Her figurative use therefore is more striking and more clearly resonant with politics than in the English. "My rebellious heart" (قلبيَ المتمــرِّدُ) reinforces the oppositional sense established in the title, and the word "screaming" introduces a sense of psychological extremity in stark contrast to the pining lover one might otherwise conjure.

In tension with these modern features are the traditional split-line verse structure, line-ending rhyme (قافية ; qafiyya), and the topic of the poem: the pain of love. My English rendering below of the first verse of the poem obviously fails to preserve the traditional structure and rhyme of the Arabic, but the diction of the translated first stanza does convey something of the modern emotional register of the Arabic:

يا شمسُ، مثلُكِ قلبيَ المتمـــرِّدُ   وقَفَتْ أمام الشمـس صارخـةً بها

وَسقَى النجــومَ ضياؤه المتجدّد   قلبي الذي جَرَفَ الحياةَ شبابُـهُ

في مقلتيَّ ، ودمعـــةٌ تتنهَّدُ   مهلاً ، ولا يخـدعُكِ حـزنٌ جائرٌ

تحت الليالي ؛ والألوهةُ تَشهـــدُ   فالحزنُ صورةُ ثورتـي وتمـرُّدي

"O sun! Like you is my rebellious heart!"
She stood before the sun screaming,
"Whose youth swept life away,
And whose renewed light watered the stars.
Hold on, don't be misled by a cruel
Sadness and sighing tear in my eyes,
God be my witness, beneath the night,
Sadness is but the image of my revolt and rebellion."

The image of renewed light watering the stars (وَسقَى النجــومَ ضياؤه المتجدّدُ) in line 4 demonstrates the poet's ability to create beautiful imagery and suggests an idyllic past. Yet this imagery of light relating to the sun/heart in the first, second, and fourth lines (شمسُ, الشمـس, ضياؤه) contrasts with night (الليالي) in the seventh line and in the rest of the poem. The night, moreover, does not simply negate the light of the sun/heart in "sadness" (الحزنُ) but also conceals a very modern psychological well of "revolt and rebellion" (ثورتـي وتمـرُّدي).

Al-Mala'ika's mastery of traditional structure and her subtle grasp of the theme of wasted youthful passion alone would make this a great poem. But her blending of psychological complexity in the imagery of light and darkness as well as her use of the vocabulary of political struggle make "Revolt against the Sun" strikingly modern. Al-Mala'ika thus manages a natural transfer of the Arabic poetic sensibility into a thoroughly modern register.

If al-Mala'ika uses politicized imagery to express subtle states of mind, other poets often reverse the polarity, employing the imagery of love and everyday life to convey social or political injustice. Mahmoud Darwish (1941–2008), still probably the best-known Arab poet in the world, composed his famous "To My Mother" (إلى أمي ; Ila ummi) to allegorize the Arabs' loss of Palestine. Like al-Mala'ika's poem, Darwish's occupies the traditional emotional register of the contrast between childhood innocence and adult alienation. The longing expressed in the poem for mother and home is most often read as the longing for pre-Zionist Palestine, yet the association is complex. Thinking of the lost nation as lost childhood innocence, while emotionally powerful, might be politically debilitating, because once childhood is gone, it is gone forever. At the same time, however, the mother-nation association also inspires the will to renewal:

لأني فقدت الوقوف
بدون صلاة نهارك
هرمت، فرُدّي نجوم الطفولة
حتى أشارك

Without your daylong prayer,
I've lost the will to stand.
I have aged!
Return to me the stars of childhood
To guide me. (my trans.)

Coming toward the end of the poem, not only does this passage stress the primary sense of the child's longing for the mother but also its invocation of the "stars of childhood" (نجوم الطفولة) transforms the political struggle into the realm of visionary inspiration. In both this poem and in "Revolt against the Sun," students may well note the religious diction: the "day-long prayer" (صلاة نهارك) and "God be my witness" (الألوهةُ تَشْهـدُ), respectively. While it would certainly be erroneous to exaggerate the role of religion in either poem and in Arab culture as a whole, it is equally unhelpful to pretend that such invocations can be reduced to "your good wishes" and "I hope," respectively. Such invocations should be taken as formulaic performatives that recognize, and gesture beyond, the limits of human will in the way that "Lord willing" can in English.

Darwish's poem has been translated many times. My version of the lines above is slightly more literal than other, readily available online versions, which makes it a bit rougher on the anglophone ear but also gives more of a sense of the original Arabic. In the context of world literature, the choice to present a smooth idiomatic translation must, of course, be balanced against the risk of giving the impression that the Arabic original is merely alternative code for an otherwise transparent message. Another advantage of studying a famous text like "To My Mother" is the availability of other media versions of it. Using Marcel Khalife's renowned performance of the poem can be a meaningful classroom experience for students. Reading a famous poem in the classroom and letting students hear an equally famous musical rendition of it—another example might be Nizar Qabbani's كلمات (Kalimat; "Words") or قارئة الفنجان (Qari'at al-finjan; "The Fortune Teller")—can convey the literary value of both Arabic poetry and song. As Allen Hibbard points out in this volume, this kind of comparison happily relativizes the students' culture, showing how powerful feeling can be expressed in other languages and other cultures.

Perhaps the most exciting recent development in Arabic drama, at least from the standpoint of world literature, is the translation into English of several of Saʿdallah Wannous's plays. One of the most insightful playwrights in any language in recent decades, Wannous (1941–97) unleashes an acerbic critique of the regime in Syria and, by extension, other Arab regimes while exposing through the audience participation both the complicities and resistances of citizens. Wannous's "theater of politicization," designed to supplant traditional political theater, provides a vision of the potential efficacy of art today (Swairjo). His work, moreover, embodies one of the major concerns of modern Arabic literature: its relation to the past and to literary tradition. One play, *The Adventures of the Mamluk Jabir's Head* (مغامرات رأس المملوك جابر; Mughamarat ra's al-mamluk jabir), calls for the creation of a traditional Arab café atmosphere of interaction between a *hakawati* (حكواتي; "storyteller") and the audience. Another, *The King Is the King* (الملك هو الملك; Al-Malak huwa al-malak), deploys a subtle intertextual fabric from the *One Thousand and One Nights* and the work of one of the Arab world's first modern playwrights, Marun al-Naqqash (Dorigo). Wannous, the UNESCO World Theatre Day Message Author of 1996, stated his hope for the role of the theater in society, which could also stand for the role of world literature among societies:

> Culture now stands in the forefront of the forces that seek to confront the egocentric inhuman process of globalization. . . . For in such a context, the theatre, through example and participation, can teach us how to rebuild and recreate and how to engage in the dialogue for which

we all thirst—the serious and comprehensive dialogue that should be
the first step toward confronting the frustration that besets the world
at the turn of this century. ("'Our Lot'")

Wannous's soaring reputation has led to a MacArthur Foundation grant
in support of the work of Robert Myers and Nada Saab to translate what
some say is his masterwork, *Rituals of Signs and Transformations* (*Four
Plays* 267–394).

Although the novel in Arabic did not begin with Naguib Mahfouz
(1911–2006), its entry into world literature did begin with the Egyptian master, whose world renown is not unmerited (Hartman). His novels
span historical, realist, and postmodern genres and forms, demonstrating command of character, plot, and tone to a high degree. Before translation of Mahfouz's novels, almost all accounts available in English of
everyday life in Egypt passed through the eyes of Western travelers. Mahfouz himself gave an indication of how different these perspectives could
be when he was asked what he thought about Lawrence Durrell's wildly
popular *Alexandria Quartet*: "It is very beautiful, but it is about foreign-
ers" (Dickey 102).

In addition to the most famous work by Mahfouz, a family saga, the
Cairo Trilogy (ثلاثية القاهرة ; Thulthiyat al-Qahirah; 1956–57), deservedly
on many syllabi of Arabic literature already, *Midaq Alley* (زقاق المدق ;
Zuqaq al-Midaq; 1947) and *Miramar* (ميرامار ; 1967) are among his
most trenchant novels. Like much of his work, they depict the effects of
illegitimate power and corruption on the lives of characters from all classes
and milieus. *Midaq Alley* is a compendious realist account of the mid-
twentieth-century encounter between tradition and modernity in a lower-
middle-class Cairene neighborhood. It follows the intertwining lives of
several characters as World War II conditions their desires and separate
fates. *Miramar* focuses on the 1960s well after the euphoria of the 1952
Revolution, the Bandung Conference, and the nationalization of the Suez
Canal in 1956 (Colla; Halim, "*Miramar*"). Its narrative centers on the sordid events in an Alexandrian hotel told from multiple points of view, each
representing one sociopolitical perspective on Egyptian life, and therefore
this novel, like others of Mahfouz, has been read allegorically (Halim, *Alexandrian Cosmopolitanism* 182). In retrospect, its depiction of postrevo-
lutionary decay, like that of his 1966 *Adrift on the Nile* (ثرثرة فوق النيل ;
Tharthara fawqa al-Nīl), seems prescient in the light of the 1967 military
defeat at the hands of Israel.

If Mahfouz has earned deserved acclaim, a host of other writers who have much to offer a world readership have suffered neglect. Abdelrahman Munif's absence from discussion of world literature is a great loss, especially given the dearth of novels in any language on the effects of the oil industry on societies. Munif was born Saudi but stripped of his citizenship for speaking out against Saudi corruption; he led a cosmopolitan life in Amman, Baghdad, and Damascus and traveled throughout Europe, the Soviet Union, North America, and Japan. His magisterial quintet of novels published in the 1980s on the depredations of big oil on Arabian society begins with a small community's encounter with American oilmen in the 1930s, an event recounted in the first volume of the quintet—the only one that has been translated to date, *Cities of Salt* (مدن الملح ; Mudun al-milh). Not only does the novel thematize the rise of oil in the Gulf Arab states but also its narrative style is innovative, shunning the European realist novel's reliance on focalization through individual consciousness and seeking a broader social subjectivity.

Cities of Salt is a good example of some of the tensions the Arab novel faces in being received as world literature. Some critics, such as the American author John Updike, find Munif's narrative strategy unappealing (618). Others disagree; Karim Mattar, for example, argues, "Munif 'registers' through his use of decentered narrative form the social logic of the modernity specific to Saudi Arabia and the Gulf region." The cultural payoff, Mattar claims, is that "Munif creates, in short, Arabic peripheral modernism as form." Munif's literary practice thus broadens the parameters of world literature beyond a New York, London, Paris, and Frankfurt axis to include social-literary spheres that relativize Western norms.

Arabic literature also introduces new intertextual networks into world literature. While one could cite dozens of texts that allow the reader entry into the vast intercultural world of Arabic literature, Emile Habiby, a Palestinian novelist and Communist Knesset member, offers among the richest and most provocative syntheses in his 1974 novel, translated into English as *The Secret Life of Saeed: The Ill-Fated Pessoptimist* (الوقائع الغريبة في اختفاء سعيد أبي النحس المتشائل) ; Al-Waqa'i' al-ghariba fi ikhtifa' Sa'id Abi al-Nahas al-Mutasha'il). Habiby's tapestry novel stitches together Arabic and Western literary histories and monotheistic religious discourses into a trenchant critique of the twentieth-century political history of Palestine/Israel. Much of his irony and humor emerges in the seam between what Angelika Neuwirth calls "two life-worlds ideologically based respectively on a Jewish messianic 'saga,' and an Arab heroic ideal" (197).

By identifying a dual legacy in *The Secret Life of Saeed* that includes the Western picaresque tradition and the Arabic *maqama* (مقامة), Neuwirth shows how this novel is "an audacious attempt from the Middle East to create a counternarrative, to 'foundational texts' setting and sustaining cultural identity" (197). The novel's wealth of Classical Arabic, Qur'anic, and contemporary political references in the form of allusions, puns, and incongruous juxtapositions serves to expose the "grotesqueness" of Zionist certitudes such as "the bringing home of the dispersed members of the Jewish nation, *qibbuts ha-galuyot* ('ingathering of the exiles')" (208). Most important, in recent years, according to Neuwirth, Habiby's work has "found its fitting sequel" in the work of post-Zionist Israeli thinkers (207). There is no reason to think that other examples of Arabic literature cannot have a similar salutary influence if allowed into the mainstream of world literary discourse.

Few see the role of world literature as that of preserving vanishing cultures, likewise few recognize Arabic literature as a lingua franca for non-Arabic societies. Yet consider the nomadic Tuareg of the western central Sahara, a people numbering fewer than a million and a half across Niger, Mali, and Algeria into southwestern Libya. Their language is a branch of Berber, and Arabic is a second language for many. From their number, Ibrahim al-Koni worked his way onto the stage of Arabic literature by dint of relentlessly depicting a little-known desert society. With some sixty volumes in Arabic to his credit and translations into thirty-five languages, he is among the most prolific contemporary writers in Arabic. He has lived in Russia, Poland, and Switzerland, where he currently resides, but most of his writing harks back to the desert. His novels and short stories often trope various aspects of the desert through animal imagery, Sufi mysticism, and Tuareg mythology. He uses these elements to develop his abiding themes: the conflict between the present and the past, the conflict between nomadic and sedentary ways of life. Although al-Koni shuns the mantle of political writer, his *The Puppet* (الدمية ; al-Dumya) does deal with corruption. His other novels currently available in English, such as *Gold Dust* (التبر ; al-Tibr), tend to be more visionary and allegorical. For both its literary prowess and its cultural value as a testament to a waning way of life, al-Koni's work is an invaluable contribution to world literature.

Arabic literature also contributes to world literature for the different perspectives it brings to contemporary social issues, such as those of gender and sexuality. It is increasingly common for Arab writers and artists to bring into question, in the context of Arab culture, antiquated laws and customs relating to sex and gender. Vigorous feminist work on issues of gender equality, for example, form the basis of a strong current in literary scholarship (Makdisi et al.; Ashour et al.). Many scholars have also contributed to ongoing debates and conversations that have pushed LGBT and queer studies in new directions, again demonstrating that such conversations are not unidirectional (Hadeed; Massad).

Yet Arab writers also refuse to see Arab society on a chain of being leading to Western progressivism. Thus while deeply critical of unjust legal and social practices in their countries, they also question the pieties of Western society, often by introducing a breath of human complexity that leavens debate. In an ambitious 1990 novel, *The Stone of Laughter* (حجر الضحك ; Hajar al-dahik), Hoda Barakat explores the shifting nexus of gender, violence, and sexuality during wartime. Her protagonist, Khalil, is an androgynous young man who enjoys housework, shuns violence, and exults in male beauty. The characterization tempts readers to categorize him as gay, which many Arab and foreign critics have done, framing the novel as a pioneering work in defense of gay rights in the Arab world. But nothing in the text denies or confirms that categorization. Indeed, by the end of this antibildungsroman, Khalil's performance of two coercive sex acts, one homosexual and the other heterosexual, effectively demonstrates how the debasement of his humanity through violence renders the question of sexual orientation irrelevant, even priggish (202, 208).

Rachid al-Daif has devoted a good number of his novels to gender and sexuality issues. His most recent text to appear in English is a novelized biography of a gay German writer, Joachim Helfer, which appears along with Helfer's response in a book translated into English as *What Makes a Man? Sex Talk in Beirut and Berlin* (عودة الألماني إلى رشده ; 'Awdat al-almani ila rushdih). As a frank dialogue on sexuality, al-Daif's text is at pains to represent a common, by no means elite, Arab point of view on homosexuality. Helfer's response, offered with equal sincerity, is equally enlightening. In this way, modern Arabic literature takes part in a social debate of worldwide relevance.

Let us consider what a world literature would look like that integrated the non-Western component that is Arabic. This world literature would:

> recognize the worldwide reach of Arabic-language culture beyond Islam and the *One Thousand and One Nights* to reveal a highly porous East-West divide

acknowledge the infusion of Arabic literature and literary practices
into European culture to deflate the notion of European cultural
exceptionalism

complicate cultural identities by casting into relief translational and
indigenizing practices

offer accounts of life in foreign lands translated from indigenous texts

surpass the mirror effect that privileged, so-called native informants
often provide by valorizing ideologically diverse texts

give access to non-Western text networks that relativize European
networks

enrich intertextual resonances beyond the sphere of European cultures

challenge culture-bound truths and thereby interrogate tradition and
modernity

Side by side with foreign and comparative literature programs, the inclusion of Arabic and other non-Western literatures into an English-language
world literature curriculum is a responsible way for the humanities to deal
with an increasingly globalized world. By underscoring the fact that we are
all both more related and more different than we habitually think, world
literature can be a means of promoting human solidarity and thereby reduce the anxieties and resentments that arise from essentialized differences. This world literature would offer the breadth of vision that alone
can earn for the humanities a leading role in the university.

Works Cited

Al-Daif, Rachid, and Joachim Helfer. عودة الألماني إلى رشده [ʿAwdat al-almani
ila rushdih; "How the German Came to His Senses"]. Riad el Rayyes, 2005.
Translated in *What Makes a Man?*

———. *What Makes a Man? Sex Talk in Beirut and Berlin.* Translated by Ken
Seigneurie and Gary Schmidt, Center for Middle Eastern Studies at the U of
Texas, 2015.

Al-Isfahani, Abu al-Faraj. كتاب الأغاني [Kitab al-aghani; "Book of Songs"]. World
Digital Library, Library of Congress, www.wdl.org/en/item/7442/.

Al-Koni, Ibrahim. الدمية [al-Dumya]. Al-muʾassasa al-ʿarabiya li-dirasat wal-nashr,
1998. Translated as *The Puppet.*

———. التبر [al-Tibr]. Dar al-tanwir, 1992. Translated as *Gold Dust.*

———. *Gold Dust.* Translated by Elliott Colla, Arabia Books, 2008.

———. *The Puppet.* Translated by William M. Hutchins, Center for Middle Eastern Studies, U of Texas, 2010.

Allan, Michael. "How *Adab* Became Literary: Formalism, Orientalism, and the
Institutions of World Literature." *Journal of Arabic Literature*, vol. 43, 2012,
pp. 172–96.

Allen, Roger. *The Arabic Literary Heritage: The Development of Its Genres and Criticism.* Cambridge UP, 1998.

———. *Essays in Arabic Literary Biography, 1850–1950.* Harrassowitz Verlag, 2010.

Al-Mala'ika, Nazik. "Revolt against the Sun." Translated by Emily Drumsta, 28 Feb. 2013. *Jadaliyya,* www.jadaliyya.com/pages/index/10391/revolt-against -the-sun-by-nazik-al-malaika.

———. الشمس على ثورة [Thawra 'ala al-shams]. *Adab.com,* www.adab.com/modules .php?name=Sh3er&doWhat=shqas&qid=458&r=&rc=19. Translated as "Revolt against the Sun."

Al-Shidyaq, Aḥmad Faris. *Leg over Leg; or, The Turtle in the Tree: Concerning the Fāriyāq, What Manner of Creature Might He Be* [هو ما في الساق على الساق والأعجام. العرب عجم في وأعوام وشهور أيام أو : الفارياق ; al-Saq 'ala al-saq fi ma huwa al-Faryaq]. Edited and translated by Humphrey Davies, New York UP, 2013.

Arab Human Development Report, 2002. United Nations Development Programme, www.arab-hdr.org/publications/other/ahdr/ahdr2002e.pdf.

Arnold, Matthew. *Culture and Anarchy: An Essay in Political and Social Criticism.* Edited by Jane Garnett, Oxford UP, 2006. Oxford World's Classics.

Ashour, Radwa, et al. *Arab Women Writers: A Critical Reference Guide, 1873–1999.* American U in Cairo P, 2008.

Barakat, Hoda. الضحك حجر [Hajar al-dahik]. Riad al-Rayyes, 1990. Translated as *The Stone of Laughter.*

———. *The Stone of Laughter.* Translated by Sophie Bennet, Interlink Publishing, 2006.

Bauer, Thomas, and Angelika Neuwirth. Introduction. *Ghazal as World Literature: Transformations of a Literary Genre,* edited by Bauer and Neuwirth, Orient Institute, 2005, pp. 9–11.

Blatherwick, Helen, and Shawkat M. Toorawa, editors. "The Qur'an in Modern World Literature." Spec. issue of *Journal of Qur'anic Studies,* vol. 16, no. 3, Oct. 2014, pp. 1–215.

Bonebakker, S. A. "*Adab* and the Concept of *Belles-Lettres.*" '*Abbasid Belles-Lettres,* edited by Julia Ashtiany et al., Cambridge UP, 1990, pp. 16–30.

Bushrui, Suheil, and Joe Jenkins. *Kahlil Gibran: Man and Poet.* Oneworld Publications, 2007.

Colla, Elliott. "*Miramar* and Postcolonial Melancholia." Hassan and Muaddi Darraj 171–83.

Damrosch, David, and David L. Pike. *The Longman Anthology of World Literature.* Vol. 1, Pearson Longman, 2008.

Dandrey, Patrick. *La fabrique des fables: Essai sur la poétique de La Fontaine.* Klincksieck, Paris, 1991.

Darwish, Mahmoud. "To My Mother." Poemhunter.com, www.poemhunter. com/poem/to-my-mother-45/. Translation of أمي إلى [Ila ummi].

Dickey, Christopher. *Expats: Travels in Arabia, from Tripoli to Teheran.* Atlantic Monthly Press, 1994.

Dorigo, Rosella. "Intertextual and Intratextual Processes in *al-Malik huwa al-malik* by Sa'd Allah Wannus." *Intertextuality in Modern Arabic Literature since 1967,* edited by Luc Deheuvels et al. Manchester UP, 2009, pp. 117–32.

El-Ariss, Tarek. *Trials of Arab Modernity: Literary Affects and the New Political.* Fordham UP, 2013.

Gearing, Jes. "A Note on Arabic Literacy and Translation." *Beyond Words—Language Blog*, 10 Aug. 2009, www.altalang.com/beyond-words/2009/08/10/a-note-on-arabic-literacy-and-translation/.

Gibran, Khalil. *The Broken Wings.* Translated by Juan R. I. Cole, White Cloud Press, 1998.

Habiby, Emile. الوقائع الغريبة في اختفاء سعيد أبي النحس المتشائل [Al-Waqa'i' al-ghariba fi ikhtifa' Sa'id Abi al-Nahas al-Mutasha'il; "literal translation"]. Hilal, 1974. Translated as *The Secret Life of Saeed.*

———. *The Secret Life of Saeed: The Ill-Fated Pessoptimist.* 1985. Translated by Salma Khadra Jayyusi and Trevor LeGassick, Interlink Publishing, 2001.

Hadeed, Khalid. "Homosexuality and Epistemic Closure in Modern Arabic Literature." *International Journal of Middle East Studies*, vol. 45, no.2, May 2013, pp. 271–91.

Halim, Hala. *Alexandrian Cosmopolitanism: An Archive.* Fordham UP, 2013.

———. "*Miramar*: A Pension at the Intersection of Competing Discourses." Hassan and Muaddi Darraj 184–202.

Hallaq, Boutros. *La refondation littéraire arabe: Gibrân et Manfalûtî.* Atelier National de Reproduction des Thèses, 2007.

Hartman, Michelle. "Teaching Mahfouz as World Literature." Hassan and Muaddi Darraj 41–52.

Hassan, Waïl S., and Susan Muaddi Darraj, editors. *Approaches to Teaching the Works of Naguib Mahfouz.* MLA, 2012.

Heath, Peter. *The Thirsty Sword: Sirat 'Antar and the Arabic Popular Epic.* U of Utah P, 1996.

Helfer, Joachim. *Die Verschwulung der Welt: Rede gegen Rede.* Suhrkamp Verlag, 2006.Ibn al-Muqaffa'. كليلة و دمنة [Kalila wa Dimna]. JiaHu Book, 2014.

———. *Kalila wa Dimna: Fables of Friendship and Betrayal.* Translated by Ramsay Wood, Saqi, 2008.

Ibn Tufayl. حي ابن يقظان [Hayy ibn Yaqzan]. Ar.wikisource.org.

———. *Hayy Ibn Yaqzan: A Philosophical Tale.* Translated by Lenn Evan Goodman, U of Chicago P, 2009.

Imangulieva, Aida. *Gibran, Rihani and Naimy: East-West Interactions in Early Twentieth-Century Arab Literature.* Translated from the Russian by Robin Thomson, Anqa Publishing, 2010.

Irwin, Robert. *The Arabian Nights: A Companion.* Tauris, 2004.

Jayyusi, Salma Khadra, and Christopher Tingley. *Trends and Movements in Modern Arabic Poetry.* Brill, 1977.

Khairallah, As'ad E. "The Story of Majnūn Laylā in Transcultural Perspectives." *Studying Transcultural Literary History*, edited by Gunilla Lindberg-Wada, Walter de Gruyter, 2006, pp. 232–43.

Khalife, Marcel. "I Long for My Mother's Bread." *YouTube*, www.youtube.com/watch?v=JB_YKodKoJ4.

Kilpatrick, Hilary. *Making the Great Book of Songs: Compilation and the Author's Craft in Abû l-Faraj al-Isbahânî's Kitâb al-aghânî.* Routledge, 2003.

Mahfouz, Nagib. *Midaq Alley*. Translated by Trevor LeGassick, Doubleday, 1991.

———. *Miramar*. Translated by Fatma Moussa Mahmoud, edited by Maged el Kommos and John Rodenbeck, Doubleday, 1993.

———. *Palace of Desire*. Translated by William Maynard Hutchins, Lorne M. Kenny, and Olive E. Kenny, U of Cairo P, 1991.

———. *Palace Walk*. Translated by William M. Hutchins and Olive E. Kenny, Doubleday, 1990.

———. *Sugar Street*. Translated by William Maynard Hutchins and Angele Botros Samaan, U of Cairo P, 1992.

Makdisi, Jean, et al., editors. *Arab Feminisms: Gender and Equality in the Middle East*. I. B. Tauris, 2014.

Marroum, Marianne. "*Kalila wa Dimna*: Inception, Appropriation, and Transmimesis." *Comparative Literature Studies*, vol. 48, no. 4, 2011, pp. 512–40.

Massad, Joseph. "Re-orienting Desire: The Gay International and the Arab World." *Public Culture*, vol. 14, no. 2, 2002, pp. 361–85.

Mattar, Karim. "The Shabaḥ of World Literature: Bedouin Cartographies in Abdulrahman Munif's *Cities of Salt*." *ELN: English Language Notes*, vol. 52, no. 2, 35–52. *Editorial Manager*, www.editorialmanager.com/eln/Default .aspx?pg=login.asp&username=.

Menocal, Maria Rosa. *The Arabic Role in Medieval Literary History: A Forgotten Heritage*. U of Pennsylvania P, 1990.

Munif, Abdelrahman. *Cities of Salt*. Translated by Peter Theroux, Vintage, 1089.

Neuwirth, Angelika. "Traditions and Counter-traditions in the Land of the Bible: Emile Habibi's De-mythologizing of History." *Arabic Literature: Postmodern Perspectives*, edited by Neuwirth et al., Saqi, 2010, pp. 197–219.

Puchner, Martin, et al., editors. *Norton Anthology of World Literature*, 3 ed., W. W. Norton and Company, 2012.

Rastegar, Kamran. *Literary Modernity between the Middle East and Europe: Textual Transactions in Nineteenth-Century Arabic, English, and Persian Literatures*. Routledge, 2007.

Ricci, Ronit. *Islam Translated: Literature, Conversion, and the Arabic Cosmopolis of South and Southeast Asia*. U of Chicago P, 2011.

Selden, Daniel. "Text Networks." *Ancient Narrative*, vol. 8, pp. 1–23.

Sheehi, Stephen. *Foundations of Modern Arab Identity*. UP of Florida, 2009.

Stetkevych, Jaroslav. *The Zephyrs of Najd: The Poetics of Nostalgia in the Classical Arabic Nasib*. U of Chicago P, 1993.

Swairjo, Manal A. "Saʿdallah Wannous: A Life in Theater." *Al-Jadid*, vol. 2, no. 8, June 1996, www.aljadid.com/content/sadallah-wannous-life-theater.

Updike, John. *Odd Jobs*. Random House, 1991.

Wannous, Saʿdallah. الملك هو الملك [Al-Malak huwa al-malak; *The King Is the King*]. 1997. Dar al-Adab, 2002.

———. *Four Plays from Syria*. Edited by Marvin Carlson and Safi Mahfouz, translated by Carlson, et al., Martin E. Segal Theatre Center Publications, 2014.

———. طقوس الإشارات والتحولات [Asharat wa'l Tahawalat]. Al-Adab, 1998. Translated as *Rituals of Signs and Transformations*.

———. مغامرات رأس المملوك جابر [Mughamarat ra's al-mamluk jabir]. Maktabat al-Usra, 2000. Translated as *The Adventure of the Mamluk Jaber's Head*.

———. "'Our Lot Is To Hope': Revisiting Syrian Playwright Saadallah Wannous' World Theatre Day Message." *Arabic Literature (in English)*, 27 Mar. 2016, arablit.org/2016/03/27/our-lot-is-to-hope-revisiting-syrian-playwright -saadallah-wannous-world-theatre-day-message/.

"World Lite: What Is Global Literature?" *n+1* vol. 17, Fall 2013, nplusonemag .com/issue-17/the-intellectual-situation/world-lite/.

Stephen Sheehi

Untranslatability, Discomfort, Ideology: Should We Teach Arabic Literature?

The revolutions and counterrevolutions in the Arab world since 2011 have challenged United States students of the Middle East to reach beyond the binary paradigms of neoliberalism, globalization, and illiberal democracies versus Islamism, liberals, and regionalism to make sense of our current global moment. This moment, therefore, demands that we develop pedagogical strategies to teach and learn about Arabic literature that transcend the normative dynamics in which *we* study, understand, sympathize, identify with, or learn about *them* through *their* culture.

This essay is an exploration of one potential pedagogical space, proposing an alternative methodology and theory for teaching Arabic literature in English translation in North American university classrooms. This proposal encourages academics—specialists, comparativists, and generalists alike—to reflect not only on the contexts of Arabic literary production (i.e., the context of the text, author, language, etc.) but also on the social relations in which educators, their students, classrooms, and institutions are enmeshed with the translation, circulation, deployment, and reading of Arabic texts within any given political moment.

The power-laden process of creating objects and others through knowledge production—brought to light decades ago by Edward Said's now canonical *Orientalism*—is regularly acknowledged today. It is recognized and integrated into university curricula and teaching methods, particularly in subjects related to the Middle East. Yet few have reorganized their teaching of Arab culture and literature around the awareness of the ways in which academics, students, classrooms, and universities occupy positions of privilege. We need to integrate into our very teaching an analysis of how we reproduce knowledge and ideology in larger national, class, and global formations that play an essential role in social and economic order (and disorder) in the United States and the Middle East.

Suggested here is not a pedagogy of revolution but rather, borrowing from Paula Allman, a revolutionary pedagogy of Arabic literature and culture. In the United States such a suggestion might sound scary, especially today, as we have seen special-interest groups, federal and local security apparatuses, and the Department of Defense publically target activists and scholars: Steven Salaita, Joseph Massad, Rabab Abdulhadi, Nadia Abu El-Haj, Wadie Said, and Norman Finkelstein are just a few.[1] We should understand this revolutionary pedagogy, long embraced by educational theorists, as transformative, because it opens up spaces in contact zones such as the classroom, where students, teachers, and texts are already interacting. This transformative pedagogy does not carry an agenda (carrying an agenda is a predictable criticism by certain elements in the North American political spectrum) but involves self-awareness so that we can inhabit an ethics of care in teaching Arabic literature in translation in a globalized world. By advocating such an ethics, I am not suggesting that teachers or students use the classroom to assuage the guilt and responsibility they feel about the privilege they have been given by their class, race, gender, or nation. To the contrary, a transformative pedagogy of Arab culture and literature insists on creating a third space of "care, responsiveness, and taking responsibility" in one's role in the very social relations that have brought students, educators, institutions, and writers to Arabic literature (Peta Bowden qtd. in Monchinski 46).

Should We Teach Arabic Literature?

Nineteenth-century Arabic writers, from their earliest encounters with the West, commented on the efforts of Europeans to learn Arabic, to read Arabic texts, and to learn about the rich intellectual heritage of Arabs. The journey of Europeans to learn Arabic in the modern era was always interlocked with and matched by Arab intellectuals' own desire to forge modern forms of writing and knowledge production in the context of the Ottoman reform and modernizing movement. From al-Jabarti and Hassan ʿAttar to Ahmad Faris al-Shidyaq to ʿAli Mubarak's fictional account of an Egyptian sheikh's accompanying an Englishman to Europe, modern pedagogy of Arabic language, literature, and culture was embroiled in asymmetrical and awkward power relations between, on the one hand, Arab teacher and Arab student and, on the other, Western student and Western teacher (El-Ariss; Tageldin). Subject position, agency, and power in the production of colonial knowledge—in this case, of Arabic literature—are now easily discernible in studying colonialism and postcoloniality. Yet the analogous relationship among students, teachers, and Arabic literature today is often absent from our pedagogical strategies. Our livelihoods and motivations for studying Arabic literature are themselves implicated in larger political, economic, and class configurations.

Administrators, educators, students, legislators, federal agencies, and civil servants are aware why enrollments in Arabic language and literature classes increased after 9/11. Courses in Arabic as a foreign language witnessed a seismic 126% rise in enrollments between 2002 and 2006 and then an additional 46% between 2006 and 2010, by far the largest gain among any of the foreign languages ("New MLA Survey"). We also know that enrollments in Arabic literature and culture classes have increased (Valosik). Christopher Stone reflects on the relation between a life-threatening attack on him in Egypt and teaching Arabic as a foreign language and on the relation between the United States Department of Defense and the growth, expansion, and funding of Arabic programs in the United States. In the popular attempt toward cultural sensitivity, he reminds us that the National Security Education Program (NSEP), which now funds large-scale Arabic instruction, "has broadened its definition of 'national security' to include fields such as 'international environment' and 'Human rights and humanitarian assistance.'"

A culturally informed approach to language acquisition is common *doxa* in Arabic-language pedagogy, but Karin Ryding notes that the "national need" for Arabic, not unlike the approach to Japanese during World War II, is "defined by fear and is tied to terrorism, crosses, and war"; consequently the focus on Arabic in higher education simultaneously "stigmatizes" Arabic speakers, as the focus on Japanese once did Japanese Americans (14). Arabic-language specialists, language departments, and universities—along with the State Department and Department of Defense—share this realization. Ryding also notes that Richard Brecht, the former director of the National Foreign Language Center and Center for Advanced Study of Language, funded by the Department of Defense, proposed "more effective coordination among legislation, educational policy initiatives, and academic efforts to create 'a coherent strategy for improving professional language competence in the US' as the best means to center cultural and language competency in the United States, especially 'critical languages' such as Arabic" (qtd. in Ryding 15). Stone is clear in reminding us that the primary intent and mission of the NSEP are "to develop a pool of language-capable professionals in various fields of study for employment with federal national securities agencies." Foregrounding Mary Louise Pratt's discussion of how Middle Eastern programs are enlisted to collaborate with the United States military ("Harm's Way"), Stone observes that "this collaboration is painted in positive terms" in order to "improve relations" between two seemingly exclusive but equivocal cultures, but "the context for this contact, though, is war and occupation."

The political turn over the past years toward a sensitivity to Arab culture is motivated not only by the "winning hearts and minds" strategy in United States interventionism, militarism, and diplomacy to enlist allies rather than provoke enemies. That is, it would be a misstep to interpret the rise in Arabic enrollments exclusively as a consequence of the security state and United States foreign interests. The rise is a consequence of neoliberal globalization, which has restructured higher education in the United States. Increased enrollments in Arabic literature and language classes are a consequence of the internationalization of higher education. The neoliberalism in the Arabic novel *Learning English* (ليرننغ إنجلش), by Rachid al-Daif, builds on a trope of the modern professor. The urbane life in Beirut and cosmopolitan desires of the professor contrast with the feudal life of his ancestral village, where his father just died. The narrator's story is a postmodern tale that cannot be understood without learning the new global language, English.

If *Learning English* contrasts the colonial language with Arabic and communicates that education in Lebanon is intertwined with global empire, in North America the internationalization of higher education is part of the professionalization of college students in order to equip them to participate in today's workforce.[2] The interest in Arabic literature and language is explicitly political and related to geopolitics. Teaching Arabic literature also participates in the corporatized shift in higher education that aims not to create informed and critical thinkers but to produce a professionalized workforce that has both the skills and ideology to reproduce and expand the mechanisms of the current global economic order.

If the relation between teaching Arabic literature and the security state has been recognized, its place in these larger shifts that began in the 1980s has been less noted. Scholars of critical pedagogy noticed the hegemonic arrival of a particular form of racial resentment (*ressentiment*) in the 1990s, where "the white middle class projects itself onto the contemporary age as the subject-object of history . . . at the expense of the urban underclasses, constituted in this media age as the primordial racial other" (McCarthy et al. 294). The racial shift in an era marked by the defeat of Communism was underscored by a naturalization of the middle-class paradigm that "declares there are no classes except itself, no ideology except its ideology" (205). In retrospect, it is not difficult to discern this swing as ideologically synchronized with the rise of the neoconservative right and the Clintonian democracy, which further dismantled the welfare state while championing the neoliberalization of the economies of North America.

All these shifts in United States social relations affect the classroom where Arabic literature is taught in translation. Indeed, the expansion of teaching Arabic literature beyond the confines of small classes of future Arabists is equally involved with changes in liberalization and depoliticization of race, education, and economy domestically.

The ideology of the white middle class became the triumphalist front man for a class hegemony that works in the service of corporate and international financial order.[3] It is this conflation of the middle class's educational and economic needs that has come to define the social and educational norm of the classroom at the institutional and pedagogical levels. The institutional structures that house the teaching of Arabic literature therefore changed, and many of us found ourselves lodged between the enthusiasm of teaching and the requirement of populating a corporate and functionary class to perpetuate the conditions about which many of the Arabic literary texts that we teach speak—directly and indirectly.

I have presented this overarching review to pose an often unarticulated, perhaps even taboo riposte to the question, "How do we teach Arabic literature in translation?" Let us ask ourselves instead, as Arabists and literary scholars of conscience, "Should we teach Arabic literature in translation at all?" This latter question is fraught with as much tension, self-righteousness, and pedanticism as the former. Let us answer not in techniques or even philosophies but through pedagogical strategies that center the positionality of the students, the course, and the instructor.

Those of us who teach Arabic literature can look to transformative learning to understand ourselves as "cultural workers" who "can contest dominant forms" of knowledge production "across a spectrum of sites where people shape their identity and their relations with the world" (Simon 39).

It is an ethical imperative for us to think more explicitly about how our pedagogies can work in a United States classroom whose specific object of study is Arabic literature in English translation. We need not espouse oppositional politics or become militants, as conservative and neoconservative pundits might warn. In a post-Saidian and globalized world, teaching Arabic literature can productively involve thinking about the positionality of the classroom in understanding the creation of that literature as an object of knowledge, about how that act of objectification, no matter how well-meaning or utilitarian, is informed by our own political privilege and subject (class, national, race, gender, and individual) position: "Our attempts to engage students are constructed within specific modes that we hope will provoke particular forms of communication, comprehension, and interest" (Simon 38).

Teaching Arabic literature in translation in the age of United States intervention, globalization, and neoliberalism gives us the opportunity to foster in students, in ourselves as teachers, and in academic institutions self-awareness and connectedness with the world. In adopting such pedagogical strategies, we locate the classroom, the student, the institution, and the specialist at sites adjacent to (i.e., separated from) the literary text and context but also in a shared but asymmetrical field of knowledge production and ideological reproduction. How to do this remains our challenge.

The Opaqueness and Durability of Stones

After my lecture dedicated to the Palestinian intifada, an uneasy student approached me after class. "The rocks in Israel are harder than here," he told me. "If you got hit, they'd cause serious injury. The [Israeli] soldiers are just defending themselves." He was one of those bright-eyed and sharp-minded freshman that we cherish as teachers. He was one of the best of my students in a course called Near Eastern Studies 101 or what I informally called From Gilgamesh to the Gulf War. Raised not too far from each other, we shared a sarcastic New Jersey sensibility. Before this lecture, he was particularly engaged in class when we studied the Torah and later Zionism, the history of the Haskalah, Judaism in Europe and the Arab world, and the writings of Theodor Herzl, Ahad Ha'am, Chaim Weizmann, David Ben-Gurion, Gershom Scholem, Martin Buber, and Ze'ev Jabotinsky. Despite the fact that at the time I was a fresh PhD known on campus for my pro-Palestinian, antiracist, and antiwar activism, acrimony never marred my classes. At the time, I attributed this lack of contention to the belief that we learn culture best through primary texts read in translation (or in the original, when possible). I still use primary texts but now see that my teaching practice was built on a critical blind spot: the assumption that they gave my students direct access to worlds, eras, and thoughtscapes directly through the voices that lived them.

Students in my classes, no matter the number of mutually respectful, decorous, and sincere conversations or the number of well-translated primary sources they could ever read, were not granted direct access. The mediated nature of translations read in a classroom itself imbued with ideology prevented it. My well-meaning, committed Zionist freshman in this space could not acknowledge (let alone believe) that the Israeli army, whose occupation of the West Bank and Gaza was internationally condemned, did not have the legal or ethical right, under any circumstances, to shoot children throwing stones. How can we speak through the barrier of ideology? Can translation ever bridge not only linguistic difference and semiotic distance but also subject positions and ideological positions, especially when those positions are clearly not equivocal? How can we speak through the barriers of First World privilege, complicity, and responsibility, through our ethical, political, and class investments?

Are rocks harder in Palestine than in the United States? Or, to use the metaphor of translation, are rocks harder in Arabic than in English? These are the questions of a teacher trying to mediate two seemingly irreconcilable sides of the hurled stone. I began by looking at the stone itself. What is this stone, this intent to harm soldiers enforcing an illegal occupation? As a way to think about these questions in teaching literature in translation, I turned to Mahmoud Darwish's famous poem "Those Who Pass between Transient Words" (عابرون في كلام عابر ; 'Abirun fi kalam 'abir). Using stones, words, and politics without apology, Darwish challenges us to think about what is translatable, to confront our own positionality and foreground it in teaching his poetry.

He locates the struggle for Palestine, indeed the claim to Palestine, in relation to the concrete, to history and identity, as opposed to those whose authority comes from the transience of words:

Oh, you who pass between transient words

. . . .

Take what you want from the blueness of the sea and the sands of memory
And take what you want from pictures so that you know all that you will
    not know
How a stone from our land builds the ceiling of the sky.

Oh you who pass between transient words
From you the sword—from us our blood
From you steel and iron—from us our flesh.
From you another tank—from us a stone. (my trans.)

أيّها المارون بين الكلمات العابرة

...

وخذوا ما شئتم من زرقة البحر وزملة الذاكرة
وخذوا ما شئتم من صور ، كي تعرفوا
أنّكم لن تعرفوا
كيف يبني حجر من أرضنا سقف السماء
أيّها المارون بين الكلمات العابرة
منكم السيف ـ ومنا دمنا
منكم الفولاذ والنار ـ ومنا لحمنا
منكم دبابة اخرى ـ ومنا حجر

Equating a stone to a tank returns us to Stone's and Pratt's concept of the weaponization of language. The possession, indeed occupation, of words by those with tanks, iron, and swords allows them to travel between borders and languages legitimately, a legitimacy that facilitates their (state's) "right to violence." Yet, in the hands of the occupied, from the perspective of the *munadil* (مناضل; "resister") and not the perspective of the occupier, the concreteness of the flesh and stone becomes embodied in those who struggle, who claim the right to their history and presence, which is distilled into their own corporeality. This poem is famous not because of its defiant tone or inspiring style but because Yitzhak Shamir quoted it when he was defense minister during the intifada "as proof that the Palestinians were not willing to compromise" (Lundberg).

This example is one of many that can recenter our discussion about teaching Arabic literature in translation not around language but around ideology. Many of us teach Palestinian literature in United States universities in part because it humanizes the Palestinian people, gives credence to their historical claims, and recognizes their human rights. For these same reasons, we face criticism from people who believe that this approach undermines Israeli, Zionist, and American truth claims or, most recently, that recognizing this humanity is an act of anti-Semitism. It is silly of course to argue whether or not Israeli-Palestinian stones are harder than American stones, as suggested by my former student, just as it is scholarly and morally irresponsible not to interrogate the assumption that the life of an Israeli soldier is more valuable than the Palestinian he shot. Working with a poem like Darwish's in a critical pedagogy allows us to face some of these issues head-on.

The poem does not deny that Israeli Jews feel affection for the land and sea, nor does it invalidate the memory of those who make claims to that land and sea, which were not Israeli in 1948. Rather, Darwish hurls a stone in order to say that the stones of that land are in fact harder, that they are Palestinian. If Arabic literature is taught in translation, it must be acknowledged that intersubjectivity and intertextuality in the classroom are structured by the hard stones of ideology and history and that these stones—in the texts and in their readers—are inescapably enmeshed in ideological reproduction. Sometimes to understand such positions and acknowledge the selfhood of otherness, we must recognize our cultural and political position and surrender it.

Untranslatability in the Classroom

Abdelfattah Kilito remarks that "the ancients not only disdained and ignored translation, it seems that they unconsciously endeavored to make their works untranslatable. They developed formulations, modes of expression, and styles difficult to translate" (17–18). Classical Arabic texts were similar to other great traditions, from Chinese to Latin, in which literature was a plastic surface on which to demonstrate the sublimity of the language and the awe-inducing mastery of the writer. The intent was never be transparent or to communicate; literature, a class and ideological enunciation, was created to stupefy and bludgeon the reader with a magnitude and *aletheia* of the language and the unique qualifications of the *adib* (أديب ; "litterateur") in representing that sublimity. This is not to romanticize Classical Arabic. I invoke Kilito's comments here only to show that, in literature, transparency and communicability of language are not self-understood goals.

For those who insist on the unbridgeable distance between us and them, the notion of the untranslatable confirms the otherness of Arabs and guarantees a perpetual and unresolvable clash of civilizations. But it is not intended to discourage those who long for harmony and understanding with their cultural others, who hope to find in literature the bridge that traverses political realities, power differentials, and history. The untranslatable, rather, is an ideological condition inherent in the parallax between an original work and its translation, especially when the work speaks to political, economic, and social conditions created by an asymmetry of power. In the classical era, translatability was a key to power and knowledge, a form of cultural capital that gave value to writers and their readers. In this current moment, the translatability and untranslability of Arabic literature in the United States cannot be divorced from the political and economic conditions that arise from the asymmetrical relation between the Arab world and the West, conditions that the modern Arabic novel often narrates and processes. Reading, then, must take place in the realm of contact zones, its positions actively structured and produced in the classroom and university by politics, investments, responsibility, and ideology.

Pratt wrote insightfully and ethically about the elephant in the North American classroom where non-Western, noncanonical literature is read. She speaks of the meeting between texts and people as a "contact zone" that is not an orderly space marked by an active reader who encounters a text that is passively waiting to be digested. Instead, the contact zone "invokes the space and time where subjects previously separated by geography and history are co-present, the points at which their trajectories now intersect." The zone "emphasizes how subjects get constituted in and by their relations to each other." In non-Western texts in translation, this coconstituency is not one of jubilant equity but marked by "radically asymmetrical" power and social relations (*Imperial Eyes* 8).

Pratt's development of the concept of the contact zone was not limited to her book *Imperial Eyes*, which developed the idea of a mutually constitutive, multidirectional literary space of interaction in the colonial encounter without decentering the disparities of power, violence, and history endemic to that encounter. Pratt had applied the concept to the teaching of colonial literature and to the reorganization of the curriculum to be inclusive of the non-Western canon, a project that began decades earlier. The classroom for her is an example of a contact zone "where cultures meet, clash, and grapple with each other, often in the contexts of highly asymmetrical relations of power," which should in turn force us to "reconsider the models of community that many of us rely on in teaching and theorizing . . ." ("Arts" 34). Although she roots her analysis in speech act theory, her work acknowledges the classroom as a space where different ideological positions converge. The teacher's role is to mediate this convergence without favoring one position at the expense of another.

The teacher therefore is not just an educator but also a negotiator and conciliator between positions that cannot be bridged without one side's surrendering privilege. Homi Bhabha speaks of this zone as the third space: "It is that Third Space, through the unrepresentable in itself, which constitutes the discursive conditions of enunciations that ensure that the meaning and symbols of culture have no primordial unity or fixity; that even the same signs can be appropriated, translated, rehistoricized and read anew" (37). The classroom as a contact zone for the meeting of the Arab world and North America allows us to think of the dynamism, politics, responsibility, and contingency of the text, its conditions of production, and our social relations to it. "By exploring this Third Space," Bhabha concludes, "we may elude the politics of polarity and emerge as the others of ourselves" (39). His optimism does not preclude a cold war of positions, historically and politically constituted, among students, teachers, and texts. Nor does the third space offer a voluntarism of tolerance that vacates cultural difference or refuse to "represent the relations of exploitation and domination in the discursive division between the First and the Third World, the North and the South" (20).

In her book *Against World Literature*, Emily Apter challenges the many camps, debates, and discussions unfolding around the ever-expanding fields of translation studies, comparative literature, and world literature. She unveils the unbreakable ontological and semantic kernel at the center of language, subjectivity, and literature that gives rise to the possibility or impossibility of a text to cross time, geography, language, context, and ideology. She reveals how ontological otherness and the semiotic disparities between reader and text are ineffectually mediated by language (as theorized from Wittgenstein to Agamben), not because of the vagaries of translation but because the untranslatable is the normative feature of a translated text.

Apter dialogues with Gayatri Spivak's notion of planetarity, expressed in *Death of a Discipline*, to displace the leveling effects of and cooptation inherent in globalization. Apter's work is a critique not only of translation studies and debates in world literature but also of the internationalized professionalization of higher education, which operates on the myth of the apolitical traversability, equivalence, and covalence between two literatures, two languages, two eras, and two peoples. Her thinking through the untranslatable rests on the ineffable intersection of ontologies, languages, semiotic systems, and selfhoods. The impossibility of translation (if not of communication, as Derrida and others posit) is a topographic feature of the political landscapes in and on which misunderstanding and inevitably mistranslation are built.

Admittedly, in an era that relentlessly poses the Arab and Muslim male and female as ineffably other, it is dangerous and irresponsible to celebrate the untranslatability of selves. We should not accept difference between the cultures of the invader and the invaded, between victim and terrorist, between free and oppressed, as if the two were separate but on an equal footing, historicized, contextualized, and subject to mutual empathy. Instead of sidestepping the juggernaut of semiotic untranslatability or, conversely, instead of becoming ensnared in the endless dog-chasing-tail circuit of defining what words like *jihad* really mean, we as educators should feature the production of culture, art, aesthetics, and politics in Arab culture alongside the reproduction of ideology and privilege in the American classroom. The untranslatable in the pedagogy of Arabic literature should take into account the weaponization of Arabic—the use of the language to appropriate, defang, domesticate, or enlist the Arab world.

Armed Struggle in My Classroom

Palestine offers the hardest stones when it comes to teaching Arabic literature. When those stones turn into Kalashnikovs or suicide bombers, the political division between conservative and liberal American students disappears in my classroom: they rally behind the predominant belief that conflates, as terrorism, all nonstate-sponsored violence and the violence of the oppressed. For example, my students regularly pick one quotation out of the autobiography of Leila Khaled, a Palestinian revolutionary. "As a Palestinian," Khaled wrote, "I had to believe in the gun as an embodiment of my humanity and my determination to liberate myself and my fellow men" (38). Class discussion ranges from unambiguous condemnation ("Violence breeds violence") to benevolent understanding but moral disapproval ("Desperate people do desperate things"). From this teaching experience, I have learned that the revolutionary imperative to armed struggle does not translate across eras and ideologies.

In the post-9/11 classroom in the United States, my students certainly can digest the desperation that compels people to violence. They understand the idea that desperate times call for desperate measures. What seems difficult for them to accept is that the use of revolutionary violence can be seen as a right and as a means to achieve genuine, systemic social transformation. Khaled's *My People Shall Live* is a narrative that stresses both. Khaled locates herself in the tradition of anticolonialist, liberationalist struggle:

> "[T]he supreme objective of the Palestine Liberation Movement is the total liberation of Palestine, the dismantlement of the Zionist state apparatus, and the construction of a socialist society in which both Arabs and Jews can live in peace and harmony. To achieve our objective we have adopted the strategy of people's war and protracted armed struggle. (106)

How does one translate this statement in an American classroom where the word *Palestine* is perplexing if not contentious, because in most American elementary and secondary-school geography books, not to mention local and cable news channels, Jerusalem is given as the capital of Israel?

The mainstream United States lack of sympathy for political violence in Third World resistance movements is not new. At the turn of the last century, Emma Goldman noted that, instead of understanding the social conditions against which men and women fight or the social conditions that compel them to violence, Americans look "upon the man who makes a violent protest against our social and economic iniquities as upon a wild beast, a cruel heartless monster, whose joy is to destroy life and bathe in blood; or at best, as upon an irresponsible lunatic" (86). The popular reaction to political violence today, including Islamist political violence, is similar. Yet we must foreground what Goldman dances around for her own rhetorical reasons. The misunderstanding or mistranslation of political violence does not come from a lack of knowledge; it is an ideological reaction and serves ideological positions.

The university classroom plays a role in the reproduction of ideologies—the war on terror, American interventionism, and cultural and economic globalization—that have brought students to study Arabic literature and culture in translation. The specter of political violence haunts even the most aesthetically oriented or apolitical course, not because of the inimical otherness of Arabs or Muslims or the putative imperial arrogance of the American academy but because the untranslatability of armed struggle arises from ideological positions.

I am not suggesting that we as teachers argue for or against political violence, whether it be Islamist, leftist, or state-sponsored. The job of teachers is not to transform complacent students into militants or merely to cultivate sympathy with struggles against oppression but to develop students' analytic, empirical, and aesthetic literacy, their skills and sensibilities in the process of respecting the text and fleshing out its history, context, and language. But we must link our discussion of violence in the Arab world to violence in our society, in a time when *terrorist* is marked almost always as Muslim, nonwhite, and usually Arab.

Arabic literature in translation allows us to explore the presence of violence on many levels: political violence, the violence of poverty, the violence associated with gender, terrorism, occupation, militarism. Learning about social conditions brings us back to social positions, to ideology, to economies that Arabic fiction, poetry, and autobiography so elegantly and complexly narrate. The challenge is that these social conditions often are not translatable and always are political. But we must teach them. The discomfort of facing this challenge when we bring Arabic texts into contact with American students needs to be foregrounded as part of the process of teaching and reading.

Ideological Bridges and Living with Discomfort

The untranslatable is the stone that calls attention to the ideological (class, gender, race, national) geology of the classroom. The ideologies in producing, circulating, translating, reading, and teaching the texts in the contact zone of the classroom are the stone, not the texts themselves. In that complex, multitiered, and multifaceted zone, teachers and students can identify the social relations that bring an Arabic text into the North American classroom while simultaneously probing the ideological positions that surround, inspire, and give meaning to the text's own cultural production in the Arab world.

Recognizing the cold war of positions that might initially structure an Arab literary text in a North American university does not mean that we are immobilized, that, to paraphrase Darwish, there is an irresolvable stalemate between the stones and the tanks. The best way to teach Arabic literature in translation is to anchor the class to the translated text and, if possible, to have that text be in conversation with the original. The attention to untranslatability is not a call for unreadability or unteachability. It is a decolonizing response to First World privilege and the ideology of American exceptionalism, not the result of an impenetrable language or Arab other. It is not a call for self-flagellation or self-indulgent soul-searching and not an excuse for ideological justification and absolution. The impenetrable surface of the Classical Arabic qasida (قصيدة) and *maqama* (مقامة) was a defining attribute of their aestheticism, their wonder, and their cultural currency, but that impenetrability did not keep many of us from reading them, translating them, circulating them, and teaching them. The pyrotechnical surface of Hariri's *Maqamat* makes that poem more profound than al-Hamadhani's far superior narrative. Medieval audiences, writers, and patrons relished the humility and wonderment that the untranslatable inspired and therefore accepted its concomitant discomfort.

Despite the ideological rigidity of the middle-class American classroom contact zone, in my years of teaching I have found much less hostility to the untranslatability of the Arabic text and much more anticonquest sensitivity, to draw again on Pratt. Pratt's notion of anticonquest refers to a writing strategy of innocence in European travel literature and colonial fiction, where characters sympathize or feel reciprocity with the colonialized and oppressed, as if to look through "imperial eyes" at colonialism while also being disconnected, disassociated, and indeed exonerated from any culpability in its system (*Imperial Eyes*). Evelyn Alsultany's study of representations of Muslims and Arabs in the media notes how sympathy is elicited and political engagements, positions, and representations are managed in order to negotiate what otherwise would be untenable and self-implicating dichotomies inherent to racist Islamophobia and Arab hating. The general current of sympathy in my classes, therefore, may be due not simply to the wonderful adeptness of the instructor or to the genuine curiosity of the students.

Anticonquest sentimentality often has the function of dissociating, so that American university students can feel compassion for the other in the safe confines of the classroom without accepting responsibility for the injustices perpetrated against that other. This dissociation operates in those same students' position vis-à-vis slavery and Native American genocide and dispossession. Anticonquest sympathies are also often the result of ideological identification. The North American university student is not required to interact through a liberal, humanist prism, but this prism indeed structures the Arabic novel more often than not. Liberal perspectives have shaped social and cultural visions, narratives, and thought since the rise of the nineteenth-century *adib*. These intellectual reformists offered an ideological isthmus across which the different classes could meet. Globalization has expanded that isthmus and the traffic on it. At the same time we must keep in mind that students' ability to empathize is the bedrock of a transformative pedagogy of caring, knowledge, self-awareness, and responsibility.

In 1998, Jenine Abboushi Dallal accused contemporary Arab and arabophone authors of writing for a foreign audience. Her accusation intuited an ideological current undergirding cultural and economic neoliberalism—Arabic literature's place in a shared and globalized marketplace. Authors writing in Arabic were speaking not simply to foreign audiences but also to shared ideologies that problematized or championed the liberal values that resurged after the fall of the Soviet Union and remerged as neoliberalism. The authors were interpellated into these ideologies as Arabs. For example, Muhammad al-Ashʿari's *al-Qaws wal-farashah* (القوس والفراشة ; "The Bow and the Butterfly") and Youssef Ziedan's *Azazeel* (عزازيل), nominees for the International Prize for Arabic Fiction (called the Arabic Booker), narrate virtually identical concerns of secularism, fanaticism, corruption, poverty, and the limits of liberalism and democracy, although the two works are very different in genre and form. Rajaa Alsanea's *Girls of Riyadh* (بنات الرياض ; Banat al-Riyadh) and Alexandra Chreiteh's *Always Coca-Cola* (دايما كوكا كولا ; Daʾiman coca-cola) articulate shared experiences of women's interactions in a globalized world despite the radically different social settings. Sonallah Ibrahim's *Zaat* (ذات) recalls not only the aesthetics of fragmented selfhood of al-Daif's *Learning English* but also the localized experience of society that is created by interlocking national, regional, and global economic and political forces that are in effect more oppressive than liberal.

It may seem counterintuitive in an argument about teaching Arabic literature as inevitably involving a confrontation with the untranslatable, but my students do not particularly warm to the works of Naguib Mahfouz, the Arab world's only Nobel laureate. They do not dislike his work, but it is never a favorite. *Palace Walk* (بين القصرين ; Bayn al-qasrayn), set in post–World War One Cairo, is filled with stock conflicts resulting from a patriarchal father. The hyperbolic character types in *Midaq Alley* (زقاق المدق ; Zuqaq al-midaq) invite the students to think about stereotyping, especially in terms of class. The sudden, tragic, and meaningless death of Abbas in the end remains a poignant fulcrum of discussion, yet the plot seems contrived and predictable. Mahfouz is digestible.

Mahmud Amin al-ʿAlim and ʿAbd al-ʿAzim Anis observed decades ago that Mahfouz's work "expresses the tribulations of the petit bourgeoisie in the second stage of the national struggle (the postcolonial era).

[Mahfouz] mobilizes his characters in the humanist paradigm and the framework of this social class, who carry its troubles and contradictions" (184; my trans.). Al-ʿAlim and Anis criticize his characters and stories as tepid and barren because they preclude the experiences beyond this middle-class worldview. Presenting familiar archetypes and dilemmas, Mahfouz's stories, al-ʿAlim and Anis note, are the travails of the middle class, identifiable across borders, referring to moral and political corruption, ignorance, superficiality, and lack of patriotic affiliation. These stories seem dull because they are familiar to my students, who prefer Alaa al-Aswany's *Yacoubian Building* (عمارة يعقوبيان ; ʿImarat yaʿqubian) over a work like *Miramar* (ميرامار), Mahfouz's 1950s counterpart novella, which is also about a boardinghouse. Mahfouz's tale of cosmopolitan Alexandrian boarders taking advantage of Zahra seems one-dimensional to contemporary American students, for whom the portrayal of a peasant housemaid is flat and robbed of agency.

Al-Aswany, on the other hand, fulfills the need for cosmopolitan urbanities; his work invokes the theme of a lost age, the betrayal of a meritocracy based on education and abilities, the degenerated dignity of the ruling classes, and the fragmentation of the national ethos and identity. Unlike Mahfouz's *Miramar*, which presents victimized women, victimizing men, and flat characters in the shadow of a failed revolution, al-Aswany's graphic handling of the fall of class archetypes offers a salacious exoticism. Petit bourgeois sensibilities do frame his novel, which can be read as a liberal morality play or national allegory, but at the same time there is enough sexual and social violence to ensure its otherness. Al-Aswany portrays Taha, a promising young man who turns to political Islam after being prevented from realizing his dream of joining the police force because of government corruption; depicts the sexual harassment and misogyny in the workplace that Buthaina faces before her fall; and, with the sexual othering of Hatim and the revelation of the false religiosity of Hajj Muhammad, confirms the differentness of Egyptian society.

The illustration of untranslatability in the classroom is often a shared position among class ideologies that might bind Arab and North American audiences, authors, teachers, and students more than it highlights their antagonisms. In other words, a détente in the cold war of positions is often built into the text, class, and instructor. This détente should be an opportunity for us not to celebrate the victory of liberalism throughout the world but to cross boundaries and understand the discomforting otherness created by our own privilege. We who teach Arabic literature should locate the ideological and historical positions of a text's trajectory into the class and be prepared not to alleviate the discomfort of our students. This discomfort has nothing to do with the perennial tension between the translated and original text, nor does it arise from the frustrated desire to capture the text's proleptic original semiotic and cultural force; it is inextricably bound to a myriad of political forces and effects from which even the most adept educator cannot escape. The discomfort comes from the incommensurability not of the Arab other but of the legacy and reality of political forces with the empathy and care that we otherwise feel toward Arabic literature.

How can we cross ideological lines to begin to digest other perspectives but also break our class solidarity and alliances with middle-class writers in order to recognize the class and political components that drive cultural production? Foregrounding discomfort as part of the process of teaching and reading begins to allow ourselves, others, violence, forgiveness, empathy, and guilt to all sit in the same room without displacing or undervaluing any of them.

When we talk about al-Hamadhani and his criticism of Abbasid proto-consumerist culture, we might simultaneously be talking about the imperial consumer in today's globalized context. When we read Khalil Gibran's *The Broken Wings* (الأجنحة المتكسرة ; Al-Ajniha al-mutakassira), we might also be linking the environmental destruction in North America with that of the Middle East. When we read Abdelrahman Munif's *Cities of Salt* (مدن الملح ; Mudun al-milh), we might think about petrocapitalism, geopolitics, and labor while also understanding how United States corporations and government relate to them. When we read Hanan al-Shaykh's *The Story of Zahra* (حكاية زهرة ; Hikayat Zahra), we might work to understand the complexities of women's liberation, sexuality, and the complicity of patriarchal violence in the United States war on terror. The white Western compulsion to save Muslim women can be read alongside this narrative of violence against women during the Lebanese civil war. This foregrounding of discomfort is a step toward righting the wrongs of the ways in which "worldwide class apartheid," as Spivak might say, is reproduced in our classrooms (*Other Asias* 20). More practically and perhaps less ambitiously, it develops a pedagogy of responsibility, where an ethics of care both imparts and reproduces knowledge while also using that knowledge as a shared space, a third space, for building genuine intersubjective community in the classroom and globally.

Notes

1. Groups like the David Project, Campus Watch, and, more recently, the AMCHA Initiative are examples of sustained, organized, and concerted campaigns to intimidate, harass, and threaten scholars who take public positions against United States foreign policy and Israeli human rights violations (Abunimah; Best et al.).

2. The utilitarian aim of making higher education more practical in order to equip students with the technological and practical knowledge they will need to become more competitive in today's global marketplace has been a centerpiece of discussion in the humanities and higher education for the past decade and a regular feature (Donoghue). For a critical discussion of the Governors Association Center for Best Practices publication on the best degrees for the marketplace, see Schneider.

3. My argument does not intend to reduce the complexities of neoliberal ideology into a stereotype figure of the white middle class. Rather, it shows how the ideology of the middle class was further reconfigured along racial and economic lines to fit with shifts in the global economy and the United States role in them. These shifts are discussed by scholars of neoliberalism, such as David Harvey and Kevin Doogan.

Works Cited

Abboushi Dallal, Jenine. "The Perils of Occidentalism: How Arab Novelists Are Driven to Write for Western Readers." *Times Literary Supplement*, 24 Apr. 1998, pp. 8–9.

Abunimah, Ali. "Zionist Group Publishes Target List of 'Anti-Israel' US Professors." *Electronic Intifada*, 14 Sept. 2014, electronicintifada.net/blogs/ali-abunimah/zionist-group-publishes-target-list-anti-israel-us-professors.

Al-'Alim, Mahmud Amin, and 'Abd al-'Azim Anis. في الثقافة المصرية [Fil-thaqafah al-misriyah; "On Egyptian Culture"]. Dar al-'Aman, 1989.

Al-Ash'ari, Muhammad. القوس والفراشة [al-Qaws wal-farashah; "The Bow and the Butterfly"]. Al-Markaz al-thaqafi al-'arabi, 2011.

Al-Aswany, Alaa. عمارة يعقوبيان ['Imarat Ya'qubian]. Madbuli, 2002. Translated as *The Yacoubian Building*.

———. *The Yacoubian Building*. Translated by Humphrey Davies, HarperCollins, 2006.

Al-Daif, Rachid. *Learning English*. Translated by Adnan Haydar and Paula Haydar, Interlink Publishing, 2007.

———. لير ننغ إنجلش [Lirningh Inghlish]. Al-Rayyes, 2007. Translated as *Learning English*.

Allman, Paula. *Critical Education against Global Capitalism: Karl Marx and Revolutionary Critical Education*. Bergin and Garvey, 2001.

Alsanea, Rajaa. بنات الرياض [Banat al-Riyadh]. Saqi Books, 2005. Translated as *Girls of Riyadh*.

———. *Girls of Riyadh*. Translated by Marilyn Booth, Penguin, 2007.

Al-Shaykh, Hanan. حكاية زهرة [Hikayat Zahra]. Al-Adab, 1984. Translated as *Story of Zahra*.

————. *Story of Zahra.* Translated by Peter Ford, Anchor, 1986.

Alsultany, Evelyn. *Arabs and Muslims in Media: Race and Representation after 9/11.* New York UP, 2012.

Apter, Emily. *Against World Literature: On the Politics of Untranslatability.* Verso, 2013.

Best, Steven, et al. "Teaching in a State of Fear: Middle East Studies in the Teeth of Power." *Academic Repression: Reflections from the Academic Industrial Complex,* edited by Steven Best et al., AK Press, 2010, pp. 262–79.

Bhabha, Homi. *Location of Culture.* Routledge, 1994.

Chreiteh, Alexandra. *Always Coca-Cola.* Translated by Michelle Hartman, Interlink Publishing, 2012. Print.

————. دايما كوكا كولا [Da'iman coca-cola]. Arab Scientific Publishers, 2009. Translated as *Always Coca-Cola.*

Darwish, Mahmoud. عابرون في كلام عابر ['Abirun fi kalam 'abir; "Those Who Pass between Transient Words"]. *Adab,* www.adab.com/modules.php?name=Sh3er&doWhat=shqas&qid=69470.

Donoghue, Frank. "Can the Humanities Survive the Twenty-First Century?" *The Chronicle of Higher Education,* 5 Sept. 2010, chronicle.com/article/Can-the-Humanities-Survive-the/124222.

Doogan, Kevin *New Capitalism? A Transformation of Work.* Polity, 2009.

El-Ariss, Tarek. *Trials of Arab Modernity: Literary Affects and the New Political.* Fordham UP, 2013.

Goldman, Emma. *"Anarchism" and Other Essays.* Mother Earth Publishing, 1910.

Gibran, Khalil. الأجنحة المتكسرة [Al-Ajniha al-mutakassira]. Hilal, 1912. Translated as *The Broken Wings.*

————. *The Broken Wings.* Translated by Juan Cole. White Cloud Press, 1998.

Harvey, David. *A Brief History of Neoliberalism.* Oxford UP, 2005.

Ibrahim, Sonallah. ذات [Dhat; Self]. Dar al-mustaqbal al-'arabi, 1992.

————. *Zaat.* Translated by Anthony Calderbank, American U in Cairo P, 2004.

Khaled, Leila. *My People Shall Live.* Edited by George Hajjar, Hodder and Stoughton, 1973. *Leila Khaled,* leilakhaled.files.wordpress.com/2011/10/my-people-shall-live-leila-khaled.pdf.

Kilito, Abdelfattah. *Thou Shalt Not Speak My Language.* Translated by Waïl S. Hassan, Syracuse UP, 2008.

Lundberg, John. "Why You Should Read Mahmoud Darwish." *Huffington Post,* 24 Aug. 2008, www.huffingtonpost.com/john-lundberg/why-you-should-read-mahmo_b_120470.html.

Mahfouz, Naguib. بين القصرين [Bayn al-qasrayn; "Between Two Palaces"]. Dar al-qalam, 1973. Translated as *Palace Walk.*

————. ميرامار Faggala, 1968. Translated as *Miramar.*

————. *Midaq Alley.* Translated by Trevor Le Gassick, American U in Cairo P, 1966.

————. *Miramar.* Translated by Fatma Moussa-Mahmoud, Doubleday, 1978.

————. *Palace Walk.* Translated by William Hutchins and Olive Kenney, Doubleday, 1989.

————. زقاق المدق [Zuqaq al-midaq]. Khayats, 1947. Translated as *Midaq Alley.*

McCarthy, Cameron, et al. "Danger in the Safety Zone: Notes on Race, Resentment, and the Discourse of Crime, Violence, and Suburban Security." *Power/Knowledge/Pedagogy: The Meaning of Democratic Education in Unsettling Times*, edited by Dennis Carlson and Michael W. Apple, Westview Press, 1998, pp. 274–95.

Monchinski, Tony. *Education in Hope: Critical Pedagogies and the Ethic of Care.* Peter Lang, 2010.

Munif, Abdelrahman. *Cities of Salt.* Translated by Peter Theroux, Random House, 1987.

———. مدن الملح [Mudun al-milh]. Al-muʾassasah al-ʿarabiya, 1984. Translated as *Cities of Salt.*

"New MLA Survey Finds That the Study of Languages other than English Is Growing and Diversifying at US Colleges and Universities." *Modern Language Association*, 8 Dec. 2010, www.mla.org/pdf/2009_enrollment_survey_pr.pdf.

Pratt, Mary Louise. "Arts of the Contact Zone." *Profession*, 1991, pp. 33–40.

———. "Harm's Way: Language and the Contemporary Art of War," *PMLA*, vol. 124, no. 5, 2009, pp. 1515–31.

———. *Imperial Eyes: Travel Writing and Transculturation.* 1992. Routledge, 2008.

Ryding, Karin C. "A Response to Mary Louise Pratt's "Building a New Public Idea about Language." *ADFL Bulletin*, vol. 36, no. 2, 2005, pp. 14–16.

Said, Edward. *Orientalism.* Vintage, 1978.

Schneider, Carol Geary, "'Degrees for What Jobs?': Wrong Question, Wrong Answers." *The Chronicle of Higher Education*, 1 May 2011, chronicle.com/article/Degrees-for-What-Jobs-Wrong/127328/?sid=at.

Simon, Roger I. *Teaching against the Grain: Texts for a Pedagogy of Possibility.* Bergin and Garvey, 1992.

Spivak, Gayatri Chakravorty. *Death of a Discipline.* Columbia UP, 2003.

———. *Other Asias.* Blackwell, 2008.

Stone, Christopher. "Teaching Arabic in the US after 9/11." *Jadaliyya*, 11 Apr. 2014, www.jadaliyya.com/pages/index/17286/teaching-arabic-in-the-us-after-9-11.

Tageldin, Shaden. *Disarming Words: Empire and the Seduction of Translation in Egypt.* U of California P, 2011.

Valosik, Vicki. "Arabic Is Blooming." *International Educator*, 2014, pp. 1–5, www.nafsa.org/_/file/_/ie_marpar14_arabic.pdf.

Ziedan, Youssef. *Azazeel.* Atlantic, 2013.

———. عزازيل (Azazil). Dar al-shuruq, 2008. Translated as *Azazeel.*

Philip Metres

Teaching (beyond) the Conflict: A Contrapuntal Reading

> There were no guns at the PLO Research Center, no ammunition, and no fighters. But there was evidently something more dangerous—books about Palestine, old records and land deeds belonging to Palestinian families, photographs about Arab life in Palestine, historical archives about the Arab community in Palestine, and, most important, maps—maps of pre-1948 Palestine with every Arab village on it before the state of Israel came into being and erased many of them. . . . You could read it in the graffiti the Israeli boys left behind on the Research Center walls: *Palestinian? What's that?* And *Palestinians, fuck you,* and *Arafat, I will hump your mother.* (Friedman 159)

At the heart of Palestinian narratives, to echo Edward Said, is the question of the "permission to narrate" itself ("Permission"). In other words, in light of the power of the Zionist narrative of Israel—articulated so effectively (and resembling the American settler-colonial story) and backed so fiercely by United States imperial interests and institutions—Palestinian stories seem to disappear. This erasure was made literal again in 2014, when Diane Sawyer reported that Israelis had been attacked by Palestinian bombs, while showing footage of Palestinians in Gaza being bombed by Israel (Khalek; "Outrage"). Yet even Thomas Friedman, long considered an imperial cheerleader by the political left, notes that the very fact of Palestinian history presented such a threat to Israel's narrative that the first place the Israeli Defense Forces headed, on invading Beirut in 1982, was to the PLO Research Center, in order to abscond with its archive.

This perverse situation animates my ongoing critical thinking and rethinking of how I teach Palestinian literature—and how this literature comes to be produced, circulated, and received. Since 2006, I have been teaching it in a contrapuntal fashion with Israeli literature, mostly in a course called Israeli and Palestinian Literatures but also in more recent courses: Peacebuilding and Literature, Studies in Postcolonial Literature. These experiences, and my reflection on the continued dispossession of Palestinians in Israel/Palestine, have led to my critical negotiation between the frames and aims of postcolonial theory, on the one hand, and peacebuilding theory, on the other. Although I began teaching Israeli and Palestinian Literatures with the purpose of highlighting the moral imagination evident in both literatures, I became increasingly uneasy that I was leaving students with the false impression that the conflict was as symmetrical as the authors' exercise in moral imagination. I found that I needed to foreground the tension between exploring the moral imagination and accounting for the vast asymmetry of power between Israel and the Palestinians. Not surprisingly, because of a keener attention to the asymmetry in sectors of the wider public, larger numbers of students are entering the class with knowledge of the Palestinian story.

This essay explores, first, the rationale for teaching Palestinian literature using a contrapuntal method and makes a case for a peacebuilding pedagogy that still accounts for the fact that Israel maintains almost complete hegemony over Palestinian life in Israel and the occupied territories. Second, I demonstrate the possibilities of contrapuntal analysis of Savyon Liebrecht's story "A Room on the Roof" (חדר על הגג ; Kheder al ha-Gag), told from the point of view of an Israeli woman who hires three Palestinians to build a room for her, alongside Ghareeb Asqalani's story "Hunger" (الجوع ; Al-juʿ), which tells the story of Saʿid, a Palestinian worker, from his point of view. Finally, I render explicit the promise and perils of teaching Palestinian literature in this way, highlighting the complication of "teaching while Arab" in the United States, which has itself changed since I began teaching (I began after 9/11). Through a critical reflection on my experience teaching this class and on the ways in which I have been situating myself in relation to the material, I hope to provide a resource to others who would like to teach Palestinian or Israeli literature from a framework that looks for and anticipates a transformation of the conflict and the establishment of a just peace.

Why Teach Palestinian and Israeli Literatures Contrapuntally?

Because I focus on Palestinian and Israeli literatures together in my class, I actively court cognitive dissonance—my own and the students'—enacting what Said, in *Culture and Imperialism*, calls "contrapuntal reading" (66). Contrapuntal reading requires a shift from the harmonizing ethos of the comparative literature model toward a cacophonous framing of literatures alongside each other—not necessarily in dialogue but in the context of both. In Said's words, "this global, contrapuntal analysis should be modeled not (as earlier notions of comparative literature were) on a symphony but rather on an atonal ensemble" (318), one that "emphasize[s] and highlight[s] the disjunctions, not to overlook and play them down" (146).

Said's contrapuntal reading represents a third way of reading postcolonial literature and the literature of empire, the first two being the politics of blame and the politics of colonial triumphalism. Said articulates a path that will enable us, reading the story of Palestine through Palestinian and Israeli literature, to see how "intertwined and overlapping histories" (19) already exist and to offer ways to begin imagining a just peace.

His contrapuntal reading rhymes well with John Paul Lederach's *The Moral Imagination*, whose subtitle is *The Art and Soul of Building Peace*. Lederach enumerates the moral imagination's four disciplines as

> the capacity to imagine ourselves in a web of relationships that includes our enemies; the ability to sustain a paradoxical curiosity that embraces complexity without reliance on dualistic polarity; the fundamental belief in and pursuit of the creative act; and the acceptance of the inherent risk of stepping into the mystery of the unknown that lies beyond the far too familiar landscape of violence. (5)

Lederach's emphasis on the need for cultivating empathy, curiosity, creativity, and courage might appear to be ineffectual liberalism, given the obstacles that Palestinians face. But his work reminds us that peace requires as much preparation as war. In fact, peacebuilding is probably more difficult, given the human propensity for exacting revenge and acting out of fear. Said's contrapuntal reading and Lederach's theory of the moral imagination meet at the intersection where we "imagine ourselves in a web of relationships that includes our enemies." Including one's enemies, of course, does not require one to accept their conditions. In contrast to the mainstream liberal discourse of peacemaking, Lederach argues that we should resist the assumption that peacebuilding is merely a balancing of perspectives, that there can be no normalization or reconciliation without justice:

> [W]e must understand and feel the landscape of protracted violence and why it poses such deep-rooted challenges to constructive change. In other words we must set our feet deeply into the geographies and realities of what destructive relationships produce, what legacies they leave, and what breaking their violent patterns will require . . . [and] we must explore the creative process itself, not as a tangential inquiry, but as the wellspring that feeds the building of peace. (5)

If we do not analyze fully and remorselessly the nature of destructive relationships, if we do not understand and address what has fueled the conflict and oppression, we risk moving too quickly to a false or unjust peace. To read contrapuntally is to hear with both ears, to see with both eyes, outside the frames offered by mainstream media or ideological propaganda. It does not mean, in the case of Israel/Palestine, to seek balance or coexistence at all costs; on the contrary, as Marcy Jane Knopf-Newman has explored in *The Politics of Teaching Palestine to Americans*, coexistence projects have tended to obfuscate the causes of Palestinian resistance, to undermine historical analysis, and to normalize oppression (66). Peacebuilding must define peace through prisms of both justice and security. Situating itself critically and empathically at the point of intersection of national frames, it must resist the binarism that wars and sectarianism require.

Background Research

Israeli and Palestinian Literatures, an introductory-level course, emerged from my study and teaching of war literature, postcolonial theory, and peace studies. Through a contrapuntal reading of literary and historical narratives of Israel/Palestine, with a special emphasis on works that activate or embody the moral imagination, I try to model for students how literature might contribute to a real peace process, one that addresses the crucial final-status issues, especially the plight of Palestinian refugees. I want to show that understanding the politics of representation can provide a way to see that conflicts are not eternal and inevitable but historically specific and therefore resolvable.

In my initial research, I was stunned by the cultural intervention of both Palestinian and Israeli literatures. Considered together, they offer critical insights into how the relationship between the Israeli state and the Palestinians has affected and is affecting both sides. Because my focus in this essay is on Palestinian literature, it is important for me to point to Israeli writers who have undergone unsparing self-criticism, bearing witness to the pain of Palestinian dispossession (beginning with the 1948 Nakba [النكبة ; "catastrophe"] and through the continuing occupation, particularly after the 1967 *naksa* [النكسة ; "setback"]), becoming voices of conscience that hark back to the Hebrew prophetic tradition. S. Yizhar (the pen name of Yizhar Smilansky) in particular merits attention for his *Khirbet Khizeh* (חרבת חזעה), an unvarnished portrayal of the destruction of a Palestinian village by Israeli forces in 1948. Other writers, such as Amos Oz and David Grossman, have explored the moral damage of the military occupation of the West Bank and Gaza Strip. At their best, they have not only represented the contradictions of Israeli society and the moral ugliness of occupation and dispossession but also, at moments, have challenged their own liberal Zionist (yet often orientalist) frames of reference.

I disagree with Elias Khoury's incisive but too quickly dismissive reading of Israeli literature's representations of Palestinians:

> How is the Palestinian represented? Either he doesn't speak because he is deaf and dumb and exists only in Hannah's dreams in [Amos Oz's] "My Michael"; or the Palestinians are part of the geography, as in Yizhar, or even for Oz in his short story "Nomad and Viper." In Yehoshua, the Palestinian is mute or a child, like Na'im in "The Lover." Even with David Grossman—the most open of the writers—in, say, "The Smile of the Lamb," the Palestinian is an insane character.

Khoury is largely correct but collapses the question of engaging otherness with the question of representing the other. Both "The Prisoner," by Yizhar, and "Nomad and Viper," by Oz, can be read easily as deconstructions of Israeli orientalist attitudes toward Palestinians. Khoury's reading of Khilmi in *The Smile of the Lamb* is only half reductionist; Khilmi may be half mad, but he's also a wise and loving proponent of nonviolent resistance (see Metres). Khoury also misses key authors who have engaged Palestinian reality in ways that are far more nuanced, and show far more solidarity, than Grossman's portrayal, such as Savyon Liebrecht (in "The

Road to Cedar City") and Aharon Shabtai (in *J'Accuse*). A contrapuntal reading of such works can be mobilized as part of an effort that goes beyond representing what has been called the beautiful soul of Zionism to explore the damage done by the racist othering of Palestinians.

Palestinian literature has struggled in its diverse locations against the dispossession, Israeli occupation, and the cultural, economic, and military siege that people have lived through since 1948. Palestinian writers such as Ghassan Kanafani, Emile Habiby, Mahmoud Darwish, Taha Muhammad Ali, and Sahar Khalifeh, when read alongside Israeli writers challenging the official Zionist myth-narrative of Israeli history, illuminate the human cost of the conflict to Palestinians (and the moral cost to Israelis) despite the ongoing erasure of Palestinian history. These writers help us see the predicaments of Palestinian lives increasingly hemmed in by what Jeff Halper has called the "matrix of control"—his term for the legal, economic, and military frameworks that suffocate Palestinian existence in Israel, the West Bank, and Gaza (ch. 6).

Palestinian writers dramatize how radicalism emerges from conditions of extreme privation and psychological humiliation. Kanafani's *Men in the Sun* (رجال في الشمس ; Rijal fi'l shams) and Khalifeh's *Wild Thorns* (الصبار ; Al-subbar), for example, confront how Palestinian politics has contributed to and complicated their suffering, how the struggle to satisfy personal desires or family needs can be in conflict with national aspirations. Finally, throughout the corpus of Palestinian writing—as Khoury has noted—we are witness to moments of the moral imagination in which the humanity of Palestinians and Israelis alike is represented.

Contrapuntalism in Practice

In the course, we alternate between Israeli and Palestinian texts and perspectives in specific periods: from the beginnings to 1948, 1948–67, 1967–93, 1993–2000, 2000 to the present. For the first period, we establish the complexity of the origins of the Israel-Palestine conflict, the problem of navigating radically different framings of that history. The first week, students read four brief accounts of Israeli history—a BBC article, an orthodox Zionist take, and that of Ilan Pappé, an anti-Zionist Israeli historian. They then read early Israeli patriotic war poems and Yizhar's story "The Soldier" and consider the debates in Israel regarding the narrative about what happened in 1948 and how Yizhar describes the Israeli soldier's treatment of Arabs. The following week, they read four Palestinian historical accounts of 1948, including the Web site complement to Walid Khalidi's *All That Remains*, a documentary history of the 1948 Nakba and the hundreds of destroyed villages of Palestine. This exploration, laying bare the contestedness of history itself, is followed by poems and a story, such as Kanafani's *Men in the Sun* or *Returning to Haifa* (عائد إلى حيفا ; 'A'id ila Haifa), which show how 1948 affected the lives of Palestinians.

Students often try to guess my political point of view and are surprised when they fail to figure me out: there is no easy way for them to find definitive answers (e.g., about who is right and who is wrong) or to predict what will happen next in a story. Reading contrapuntally and cultivating the moral imagination involve an ethos of openness and a willingness to refuse the fatalism of received narratives. Though the course admittedly employs an aspirational frame—the final unit is called "Prospects for Peace"—it suggests that history is fundamentally contingent, always in the making; further, it proposes that our positionality is never neutral and that our empowerment involves the loss of the invisibility of United States privilege.

The contrapuntal strategy is valuable because students learn more when they are challenged with contrary viewpoints. They are given greater agency to explore the complex longings and sufferings of Palestinians and Israelis as fellow human beings. Contrapuntal reading also provides inoculation against the virus of racism (whether it be anti-Arab or anti-Jewish), not only because literature activates the moral imagination but also because, at its best, it creates characters irreducible to ideology and stereotype. At the end of my course, students will know the hunger and desperation of Sa'id, from "Hunger," and the ethical uncertainty of the unnamed Israeli female narrator of "A Room on the Roof," who must confront her fantasies and fears about the Palestinian laborers whom she has hired. Students will know these characters better than they may ever know an actual Palestinian or Israeli.

A Case Study: The Post-1967 Occupation in "A Room on the Roof" and "Hunger"

In an article in *The New York Times* written nearly fifty years after the 1967 Arab-Israeli War, Jodi Rudoren explores the "double-edged sword" of Israeli jobs for Palestinian workers. If Palestinian laborers once helped build the state of Israel, now their labor supports the illegal settlement of the

West Bank. Hassan Jalaita, a mechanic, repairs jeeps for the Israeli army in the Mishor Adumim Industrial Zone inside the West Bank. According to Jalaita, "I feel like I'm not a human being—we are serving the occupation." This dilemma—between earning a living to support one's family and refusing to help an occupying power—has been an ongoing vexation for Palestinian workers. During the 1970s and 1980s, after the 1967 war and before the first intifada, according to Suha Sabbagh, who uses 1989 figures, about "120,000 laborers were bussed daily to work in Israel, 55% of whom work in construction, the rest in agriculture and industry. Unskilled day labor from the West Bank and Gaza represents 6.5% of the total Israeli work force" (71).

Given the asymmetrical power relationship in which Israelis and Palestinians find themselves, it is not surprising that encounters between them tend to confirm stereotypes and biases about the superiority of one's own culture and the inferiority of the other. Liebrecht's "A Room on the Roof" and Asqalani's "Hunger" both undermine these stereotypes and biases, staging two different encounters, intensely subjective and politically inflected, between Palestinian construction workers and Israeli overseers, in ways that explore how people are challenged by the complex humanity of the other. In both stories, there are crucial moments in which the moral imagination burgeons, but no false reconciliations take place and no panaceas are offered.

In "A Room on the Roof," set in Israel after 1967 during the period of a housing boom, an Israeli woman hires Palestinian workers to build a room on her roof while her husband, Yoel, is away. The central drama of the story, told from her point of view, concerns her struggle to maintain her authority over the workers, whom she feels she cannot trust, and her desire at the same time to be generous to them. Her sudden interest in one of the Palestinians, Hassan, teeters on the verge of (and nearly falls into) romantic love.

"A Room on the Roof" clearly alludes to Virginia Woolf's *A Room of One's Own*, and the story revolves around othernesses—the otherness of female subjectivity in a patriarchal society, the otherness of working-class Palestinians in bourgeois Israeli society. It's almost too easy to read the main character as an allegory for the Israeli state. After all, her independence requires the constant assertion of authority, yet she is an insecure, vulnerable person who has difficulty showing kindness and generosity. She swings between wanting to offer the workers coffee and the use of her kitchen or bathroom and refusing them the money they need to complete the job.

At one point, she has let them use the bathroom but begins to fear that they are readying a terrorist operation, because the knapsack is "the kind that Yoel used to extricate from the storeroom when his unit was called up for maneuvers" (52; מסוג התרמילים שהיה יואל פורק מן המחסן כאשר; יצאה יחידתו לאימונים [52]). It turns out that they are going to a wedding in nearby Tulkarem. For most American students, the narrator becomes a kind of medium by which they measure their own fear of and fascination with the other. They see, in Liebrecht's selectively omniscient exploration of the Israeli woman's thoughts, their own socially constructed thoughts about Palestinians.

The woman slowly shifts from seeing the three Palestinians as "a single person" (44) to being stunned by Hassan's gentleness with her baby son, Udi:

> She heard Hassan talking softly to the baby in Arabic, like a man who loves to talk to his child, in a caressing voice, the words running together in a pleasant flow, containing a high beauty, like the words of a poem in an ancient language which you don't understand, but which well up inside you. Udi, lying tranquilly on his chest, reached toward Hassan's dark face, and Hassan put his head down toward the little fingers and kissed them. She, stunned by the sight, stood where she was and looked at them, as the tremor inspired by fear gradually died down, and another, new kind of trembling, arose within her, seeing something that, even as it happens, you already yearn for from a distance, knowing that when it passes nothing like it will happen again. And, as though dividing themselves, her thoughts turned to Yoel, whose eyes examined his son with a certain remoteness. Since the baby's birth he had never clasped him to his body and was careful not to wet his clothes or have them smell of wet diapers. (53–54)

> . . . שמעה אותו מדבר אל תינוקה בערבית במלים רכות, כאיש אוהב המדבר אל ילדו,
> בקול מלטף והמלים נקשרות זו לזו בצלילים ענוגים, זורמים, אוצרים בתוכם יופי נשגב,
> כמילות שירה בשפה עתיקה אשר אינך מבין את פירושו, אך הן באות ומפכות בתוכך. אודי,
> שכוב רגוע בחיקו, שלח ידו אל הפנים השחומים וחסאן קרב פניו אל האצבעות הקטנות ונשק
> להן בשפתיו. והיא, נפעמת מן המראה עמדה והביטה בם ממקומה, הרעד שהוליך בה הפחד
> הולך ודועך בתוכה, ורטט אחר, חדש קם בה מול הדבר אשר כבר בהתרחשו אתה מתגעגע
> אליו כממרחקים, יודע כי כאשר יחלוף, לא ישוב כמוהו עוד. וכמתפצלות, הלכו מחשבותיה
> אל יואל שעיניו הנתונות בבנו בוחנות את נתונותיו בקפידה, ומאז שנולד לא אימץ אותו אל
> גופו ותמיד נשא אותו במרחק-מה נזהר שלא יתקמטו בגדיו ולא ידבק בו ריח החיתולים.
>
> (53–54)

The woman, utterly taken aback by Hassan's interaction with her baby, sees how the baby doesn't care about his background, just his gentleness. Then she is surprised to learn that Hassan can speak English better than she can, that he studied it at the American University of Beirut, and that because of difficulties in life he had to discontinue his studies (54–55). The "new kind of trembling" she feels is akin to the vulnerability of attraction. We sense that real change is possible in her, yet we are also aware of the distance that divides Hassan and her. Liebrecht, echoing the moral imagination of each of these characters, encourages the circle of humanity to widen, initiating possibilities of reconciliation.

Yet things go wrong. The Palestinian workers do violate some of her boundaries, and we never quite know if they've done it purposefully or, acting on their cultural codes, unconsciously. Are they cheating her, for example, or do they simply fail to understand her directions, or do they feel that she does not understand what the room addition requires? As she grows afraid of her own vulnerability and lack of authority, her distrust and hostility reemerge. Hassan, insulted by her treatment of him, leaves and doesn't return, and the story ends with the work finally done and the husband back but with her transformation incomplete. When Yoel comes home, she lies about having a "Jewish foreman" and hides the complexity of her feelings. She tells her husband about Hassan but doesn't name the man who "'spoke to [Udi] softly and kissed his fingers'" (63; דיבר אליו בשקט ונישק לו את האצבעות [61]).

Her feelings shock her:

> Suddenly she noticed the softness flowing into her voice, *betraying herself to herself*, and she added loudly, more stridently than she intended, "But once they made some trouble about the money and tried to trick me by putting iron rods that were too thin. Arabs, you know." (63; my emphasis)[1]

> לפתע הבחינה ברכות הזורמת בקולה, *מסגירה את עצמה לעצמה* והוסיפה בקול גבוה וצורם מכפי שהתכוונה: "אבל פעם עשו גם קצת בעיות בעניין הכסף וניסו לרמות אותי ושמו ברזלים דקים מדי בעמודים. ערבים, אתה יודע"
> (61)

Although she knows better, she reverts to the stereotypes about Arabs prevalent in her culture, to reestablish solidarity with her husband and hide her emotional self-betrayal. This poignant ending shows the subtle ways in which people betray themselves and one another when they perpetuate the ethnocentric mechanisms of othering, the machinery of colonial oppression. But such introspection should not be fetishized: it can be merely a typical operation of the colonial imaginary and a demonstration of the colonizer's inherent moral and intellectual superiority to the colonized. For that reason, it is necessary to read Liebrecht's story alongside a Palestinian story that deals with the same scenario. A contrapuntal reading allows us to dilate that moment of epistemological opening.

Whereas "A Room on the Roof" depicts the complex ambivalence of an Israeli woman's relationship with Palestinians, Asqalani's "Hunger" dramatizes the complexity of the experience of workers who struggle with their complicity in a state-building project that ensures the erasure of their people. By seeing the inner and outer lives of Saʿid, a desperately hungry Gazan construction worker who labors in Israel, we understand better the behavior of the workers in Liebrecht's story. We learn about their physical exhaustion and angry helplessness—their struggle just to get to work every day. Most of all, we become aware of the social and spiritual shame felt by Palestinians who must work in Israel to feed their families. We see in a new light the hidden lives of Hassan, Salah, and Ahmad, who remain ciphers untranslatable to the Israeli woman.

"Hunger" capitalizes on fiction's ability to explore a character's inner thoughts, which the translation emphasizes by italicizing Saʿid's inner monologue; it reveals that Saʿid has been in prison and has a revolutionary past but feels he must prostitute his revolutionary values in order to feed his children. The italicized monologue dramatizes the gap between the stoic exterior of its main character and the pain that seethes within him. Palestinians in Gaza, the story tells us, are imprisoned, behind bars, not only physically but psychically as well.

In contrast to the Israeli woman's slow recognition of a diversity of character among Palestinians in Liebrecht's story, Asqalani thrusts us into the conflicts in Palestinian society—for example, between those who suffer hunger, like Saʿid, and those with jobs or power in Gaza who ask "with distaste and condescension, 'Why don't you work in *Israel?*'" (381; لماذا لا تعمل في الداخل؟ [147]). Asqalani introduces us to complexity in Israeli society also: Saʿid is hired by an Israeli foreman and contractor named Shlomo, an Ashkenazi Jew, and later works with Azra, a Yemeni Jew who "speaks Arabic better than [he]" (385; يتكلّم العربية أحسن منك [150]). The cross-national identification between Saʿid and Azra suggests how Israeli society has suppressed its Arab roots both in the Palestinian community and in the Mizrahi communities, which emigrated from the

Arab world after the founding of Israel and often were treated as second-class citizens. Sa'id sees himself in Azra, whose pitiable, skeletal form feels like his own fate.

The skeleton motif, which weaves through the story, signifies both bodies and buildings, individuals and states. Avoiding the starvation of his children comes at an enormous cost for Sa'id: the building up of the state of Israel. When he recognizes Abu Mahmoud, a Palestinian foreman for whom he once worked, he feels the gulf between his ideals as a revolutionary and his reality as a father:

> *Abu Mahmoud, am I going to be sharing with you in the dressing up of this skeleton?* He remembered vividly the look of terror in the man's eyes the day he had torn up his work permit and thoughtlessly thrown it in his face. He had never attempted, that day, to hear his own stuttering, frightened words, nor had he sympathized with the terror he felt in his own heart. He had never realized, on that day, that the pain in children's eyes was stronger than a work permit and a measuring tape—stronger even than cement columns. (384; emphasis in the trans.)

فأنا اليوم معك يا أبا محمود نكسو عظام الهيكل. وارتسمت أمامه موجة الرعب في عيني الرجل يومها أن مزق بطاقة العمل و رماها في وجهه بر عونة. لم ينتظر يومها حتى يسمع كلماته المتعثرة الواجفة، و لا أحس بتيار الهلع الذي اجتاحه. و لم يتصور يومها أن الألم في عيون الصغار أقوى من بطاقة العمل، و مقبض المسطرين، بل أقوى من أعمدة الإسمنت العارية.
(150)

Sa'id understands that in order not to have a skeletal body and family he must put flesh on the skeletons of buildings, on the bigger skeleton of Israel. These Palestinian construction workers are making houses on their former homeland, houses that they will never own and that will lessen the possibility of their return. He makes and is unmade by his labor; in his making, "he himself [will] become a skeleton withered by the wind" (383; إذا اكتملت سيغدو هو هيكلاً تذروه الرياح [149].).

Interestingly, it is Azra who is the first to collapse from the work. Sa'id sees him as "this human skeleton" (385; هذا الهيكل الآدمي [150]) who labors as the building rises, in stark contrast to the "fields of Majdal spread out like a green carpet that is forbidden to you" وسهول المجدل تمتد من تحتك بساطاً أخضر محرماً عليك [151]). At the climax of the story, when the Yemeni Jew collapses, his body is "slumped over the cement mix, face downward" المتكوم على كوم الخلطة و قد انغرس وجهه في طين الإسمنت (387;

[152]). It is as if the building itself came to drown him. Saʿid reflects later that between him and Azra "there's no difference, no difference at all" (لا فرق، لا فرق). In this epiphanic moment, what binds the two men is not their language but their sharing in tormenting, oppressive labor, in which the workers literally are consumed in the process of building.

The story ends with Shlomo's firing of everyone—after his derisive comments about the crew and Saʿid's attempt to attack Shlomo physically in response to the insults. Yet, as in "A Room on the Roof," there is a glimmer of the moral imagination, and the possibility of a cross-national movement against economic and political oppression remains in the mind. Despite the smoke and dust that cover the workers from Shlomo's departing car—images of our greater human transience—Asqalani lays bare the pain of Palestinians living in statelessness—not without their humanity but with a keen despair.

Reading these two stories in a contrapuntal fashion compels students to engage critically with and feel empathy for the predicament of Palestinians and Israelis, through the irreducibly particular portraits of Asqalani's Saʿid and Liebrecht's unnamed narrator. It also reveals how the United States and Israel are connected by privilege (and by blind spots). My predominately white students often identify with the Israeli woman's fascination with and fear of her Palestinian workers. Encountering an analogous story from the Palestinian point of view makes them question the epistemological limits that inhere in political privilege.

The Perils of My Teaching Palestine as an Arab American

At the Radius of Arab American Writers conference in 2010, Michael Malek Najjar articulated the parallelism between the outing of queers and the outing of Arab Americans after the terrorist attacks of 9/11. Despite my own visible invisibility as a person who identifies as Arab but often is not recognized as such, I too felt exposed and vulnerable in those days in 2001. At the same time, 9/11 provoked me into action, into coming out publicly not just as a progressive but also as an Arab American who stands in solidarity with Arabs at a time when we have been the objects of suspicion and even hatred. My coming out was an experience both terrifying and empowering.

The level of fear that accompanied my entering the public sphere in the 1990s to protest the brutal economic sanctions against Iraq, and to decry house demolitions and land confiscations in Palestine, was considerable. I received a string of anonymous hate mail after being quoted in the local newspaper. Because of my personality, I dread the moment when an argument goes from a simmer to a boil or when a friend's face twists when I say something that disturbs his or her picture of the world or vision of me. I'm well aware of the deep division between my Jewish and Palestinian friends and of how the victims of history often don't feel saintly toward one another or toward themselves.

I bring together my personal, political, and pedagogical responsibilities through this course. I developed it despite my desire to run away and be invisible in my privilege of distance and unrecognizability—partly because, as Miguel de Unamuno once wrote, "Sometimes, to remain silent is to lie." I bring out this example of myself both because it may help others in an analogous position and because the challenges we face when writing about erased histories in the academy are shared beyond our specific positions.

A peace-building pedagogy fosters future peace builders and encourages academic honesty and openness. In developing my approach, I have benefited from the work of other scholar-teachers who work in this field, Knopf-Newman in particular. Knopf-Newman's strategies, articulated in *The Politics of Teaching Palestine to Americans,* differ from mine but have helped me sharpen my analyses. Her chapter "Separate and Unequal: On Coexistence" offers a valuable deconstruction of coexistence narratives that efface the radical asymmetries of power at the heart of the problem (65–102).

In 2007, I was e-mailed by a member of the local Jewish community to ask about my course, which was new then. This community is robust and diverse; Judith Butler, now a major Jewish voice for the Boycott, Divestment, and Sanctions Movement (against Israel), grew up and studied in it. The "concerned citizen" who contacted me must have accessed my online archive of resources and student projects. She wanted further information about the course but questioned its study of both Israeli and Palestinian literatures. She rejected my invitation to visit my class, arguing that there was no such thing as Palestinian literature or, for that matter, a Palestinian people. She sent a letter of complaint to my department chair and administrators at my university, accusing me of preaching anti-Semitism, teaching propaganda, and brainwashing my students. She demanded that the course be canceled.

I was heartened that the chair of my department immediately supported my course and me. After a careful vetting of the course and the correspondence, my dean did as well. Colleagues who teach similar courses have not always been so fortunate. Steven Salaita lost his tenured position at the University of Illinois in 2014, allegedly because of the "lack of civility" in his tweets during Israel's 2014 attack on Gaza (Moshman and Edler). His case was settled at the end of 2015 for almost one million dollars, but he was not reinstated in the position he was scheduled to take up at that university (Cohen). The concerned citizen was right about certain things—I am not a Torah scholar, for example—but she was wrong about the heart of the matter: my course offers students an opportunity to confront racism in themselves and their society, inviting them into imaginative empathy with the people on both sides of the wall, people who struggle under the burdens of fear and despair, terror and oppression. Though students of course always want answers, my course offers more questions than answers, but it provides them with resources to begin working out their own responses.

The concerned citizen caused a dark night of the soul for me, in which I questioned all the choices of my course as well as my ability to deal with such flammable material. I was painfully aware that although I know quite a bit about the Palestinian-Israeli conflict and the peoples in it, I will always be learning, not only about the subject of its literature but also about how ideology and trauma affect people. My introspection led me to consider from a new angle how the course, however subtly, invariably reflects my own perspectives on and framing of the conflict, on how the course concentrates on certain questions and not others—for example, the funding of terrorist groups by regional players or Hamas's failure to disavow the anti-Semitism of its founding charter.

I continue to revise the course to reflect my evolving understanding of the conflict. I believe that a historical wrong was perpetrated against Palestinians and continues in the form of occupation and dispossession. I also believe that Israelis have an important story to tell and that anyone interested in Palestinian rights must also be interested in the human rights of Israelis and fight anti-Jewish and anti-Arab hatred wherever it is found. I believe that a just peace is possible.

The personal and professional risks of teaching courses in North American university classrooms dealing with the Palestinian experience are worth taking. As teachers we must plant the seeds for critically engaged and empathetic global citizens who are not afraid to ask difficult questions about the future of Israel/Palestine and the United States relation to the conflict between Palestinians and Israelis. Simply reading the literary and historical narratives of Palestine and Israel and discussing them in class will not solve the conflict, but it will offer students an intimate window onto the geographies of violence and, more important, into the moral imagination. May fugitive moments of that imagination slip through the crevices of the walls promoted by ideologues and fundamentalists—all those who benefit from perpetuating this untenable yet seemingly intractable war.

Note

1. The author would like to thank Adam Rovner for providing the original Hebrew quotations. Rovner also offered an additional interpretation of the translation of the Hebrew that is of interest here. The verb *masgir* (מסגיר) is translated by Jeffrey Green as "betraying," which is accurate but carries different connotations in English. The verb in Hebrew indicates "handing someone over" but typically to a legal authority; the same verb is used for an extradition. It can also mean to "give oneself away" in the sense of exposing inner thoughts or feelings: this meaning is perhaps better than "betray" in the passage here.

Works Cited

Asqalani, Ghareeb. "Hunger." *Anthology of Modern Palestinian Literature*, edited by Salma Khadra Jayyusi, Columbia UP, 1992, pp. 380–88.

———. الجوع [Al-juʻ]. موسوعة الأدب الفلسطيني المعاصر [Mawsuʻat al-adab al-filastini al-muʻasir; Anthology of Modern Palestinian Literature], edited by Salma al-Khadraʾ al-Jayyusi, Al-muʾassasa al-ʻarabiya lil-dirasat wal-nashr, 1997, pp. 146–53. Translated as "Hunger."

Cohen, Jodi. "University of Illinois OKs $875,000 Settlement to End Steven Salaita Dispute." *Chicago Tribune*, 12 Nov. 2015, www.chicagotribune.com/news/local/breaking/ct-steven-salaita-settlement-met-20151112-story.html.

Friedman, Thomas L. *From Beirut to Jerusalem*. Macmillan, 1995.

Halper, Jeff. *An Israeli in Palestine: Resisting Dispossession, Redeeming Israel*. Pluto, 2010.

Khalek, Rania. "ABC News Tells Viewers That Scenes of Destruction in Gaza Are in Israel." *The Electronic Intifada*, 9 July 1014, https://electronicintifada.net/blogs/rania-khalek/abc-news-tells-viewers-scenes-destruction-gaza-are-israel.

Khoury, Elias. "A Boycott on Institutions Is a Good Thing for Israelis." Interview by Maya Sela. *Haaretz.com*, 5 June 2014, www.haaretz.com/jewish/books/.premium-1.597182.

Knopf-Newman, Marcy Jane. *The Politics of Teaching Palestine to Americans*. Palgrave Macmillan, 2011.

Lederach, John Paul. *The Moral Imagination: The Art and Soul of Building Peace*. Oxford UP 2005.

Liebrecht, Savyon. חדר על הגג [Kheder al ha-Gag]. תפוחים מן המדבר [Tapukhim min ha'midbar; *Apples from the Desert*], Sifriat Poalim, 1986, pp. 42–61. Translated as "A Room on the Roof."

————. "A Room on the Roof." Translated by Jeffrey M. Green. *Apples from the Desert: Selected Stories*, translated by Marganit Weinberger-Rotman et al. The Feminist Press at CUNY, 1998, pp. 39–64.

Metres, Philip. "Vexing Resistance, Complicating Occupation: A Contrapuntal Reading of Sahar Khalifeh's *Wild Thorns* and David Grossman's *The Smile of the Lamb*." *College Literature*, vol. 37, no. 1, Winter 2010, pp. 81–109.

Miguel de Unamuno. *Wikipedia*, 11 May 2016, en.wikipedia.org/wiki/Miguel_de _Unamuno.

Moshman, David, and Frank Edler. "Civility and Academic Freedom after Salaita." *JAF: AAUP Journal of Academic Freedom*, vol. 6, 2015, www.aaup.org/sites/ default/files/MoshmanEdler.pdf.

Najjar, Michael Malek. "Going It Alone: Arab American Drama and the Politics of Solo Performance." Radius of Arab American Writers Conference, 4 June 2010.

"Outrage Turns to Satire after ABC News Misidentifies Palestinian Victims." *Al- jazeera*, 10 July 2014, stream.aljazeera.com/story/201407101217–0023919.

Rudoren, Jodi. "In West Bank Settlements, Israeli Jobs Are Double-Edged Sword." *The New York Times*, 10 Feb. 2014, www.nytimes.com/2014/02/11/world/ middleeast/palestinians-work-in-west-bank-for-israeli-industry-they-oppose .html?_r=0.

Sabbagh, Suha, editor. *Palestinian Women of Gaza and the West Bank*. Indiana UP, 1998.

Said, Edward. *Culture and Imperialism*. Vintage, 1993.

————. *Orientalism*. Vintage, 1978.

————. "Permission to Narrate." *London Review of Books*, vol. 6, no. 3, 16 Feb. 1984, pp. 13–17.

Yizhar, S. חרבת חזעה [Khirbet Khizeh; "The Ruins of Hizeh"]. Sifriat Poalim, 1949.

————. *Khirbet Khizeh*. Translated by Nicholas de Lange and Yaacob Dweck, Far- rar, Straus and Giroux, 2015.

Michelle Hartman

Teaching Scandals: Gender and Translation in the Arabic Literature Classroom

Arabic Literature, Horizons of Expectations, and Gender-Race Thinking

A common frustration that we teachers of Arabic literature face in the North American classroom is the mismatch between the expectations of students about what they will learn and what we are trying to teach. The powerful and overwhelming stereotypes that students have about the Arab world accompany them into the classroom, no matter what their backgrounds are—racial, ethnic, gendered, sexual, and class—and no matter whether they actively agree with these stereotypes, vehemently oppose them, or fall anywhere in between. Most students, Arab and/or Muslim or not, including those who grew up in the Middle East, are not free of the stereotypes. Many if not most undergraduates in North America come to classes that deal with Arabic literature precisely because they were born and raised in what they themselves refer to as the post-9/11 era. They often situate their interest and engagement in the awareness that they have grown up in an environment saturated with overwhelmingly negative representations of the Arab world—Arabs, Muslims, and particularly Arab-Muslim women.

For the teacher of Arabic literature in translation, the English-language reception environment for Arabic literature shapes a horizon of expectations about what such texts will offer (Kahf). These expectations are a problem: in addition to carrying overt stereotypes, students arrive in the classroom with ideas about the Arab world that they are not always aware of, ideas deeply bound up in gendered assumptions about Arab men and women, particularly the idea that Arab masculinity, femininity, and sexuality are exotic, different, and dangerous. This attitude can be conceptualized as a kind of race thinking—that is, a deep interlocking between race and gender and other identity axes and categories (Razack 9–14). This essay looks at some possibilities for shaping an Arabic literature classroom that addresses mismatched student expectations and teacher desires while at the same time undermining the race thinking that structures the reading and reception of Arabic works.

We confront expectations and assumptions about gender whether we are teaching a seminar dedicated only to the novels of Naguib Mahfouz or a broad survey of Arab women's writing. The confrontation is brought into sharper focus for those of us who work with gender as a lens of analysis, who regularly highlight elements of gender expression in literature, and who question and probe the complexities of gender in literary works. This essay draws on my experiences teaching courses on Arab women's writing and Arab feminisms, in particular, as well as other classes on Arabic literature in translation. The reflections and suggestions I offer in this essay are meant for colleagues who teach similar courses and also for colleagues who teach other subjects but wish to delve into these issues.

I deal directly and explicitly in my classes with stereotypes and anti-Arab racism. North America is a world filled with negative stereotypes about Arabs and Muslims (Sheehi; Salaita). I have observed in my teaching over the last fifteen years that students are increasingly aware of stereotypes as stereotypes. They wish to confirm them, understand them, or break them down and fight against them. Engaging students on the level of their expectations is a more productive way to promote an ongoing critical engagement with the material than telling them that what they saw on CNN is wrong. But it is difficult work to unpack socially structured expectations underlying negative stereotypes, to work against the grain of the very discourses that students are often invested in as positive and liberatory—the two most important examples are liberalism and feminism. Many students who are drawn to the Arabic literature in translation classroom come because of a liberal or feminist impulse. As critical race feminists have pointed out, both liberalism and feminism stealthily prop up negative stereotypes, particularly that of the violent and dangerous Arab-Muslim man (Abu Lughod; Razack; Thobani). These discourses reinforce binaries such as *our* civility against *their* barbarism. Recent legislations tabled by governments where I teach (the Quebec Charter of Values proposal in 2013, banning headscarves and other conspicuous religious symbols by government employees, and the Canadian federal Zero Tolerance for Barbaric Cultural Practices Act, which passed in 2015) show that this discourse is central in the societies in which we teach.

The expectations that students have vary widely. Some come expecting to see Arab women portrayed as passive and oppressed and Arab men as misogynistic oppressors. Some expect magical and fantastic stories, like those from *One Thousand and One Nights*. Others expect Arabic literature to be religious and engaged with issues related to Islam, like why women wear hijabs. Still others expect to have confirmed what they were previously exposed to—a long tradition of poetic innovation, in particular by male poets glorifying Arab-Islamic history. These expectations often reveal themselves in classroom conversations.

Above all, students expect that Arabic literary texts will speak in a more or less unmediated way to explain the Arab world, how it really is; in other words, they expect a literary text to provide a door into a lived reality. The most frequent comment that students make to me is that they want to know what Arab authors—Arab women authors, in particular—are thinking about by reading works written in their own voices. The notion of an unmediated text has long been dismissed by literary critics, but in the Arabic literature classroom we cannot reject it out of hand. The very organization of literary texts by linguistic-national borders implies that there is something essentially Arabic about the works we teach. The insights of women-of-color theorists who have insisted that our location as writers and readers informs our literary critical practice are crucial here (Martin and Mohanty; Spivak).

Working with Gendered Translation Choices and Changes

From my more than fifteen years of teaching experience, mainly in Montreal but also in New York and Beirut, I am increasingly convinced that teaching Arabic literature through the problems of its translation is both an ethical imperative and a useful technique to expose English-speaking students to the complexities of Arabic literary texts. Using translation as a problem and concept to work our way into and through literary texts enables us to address larger contexts.

Gendered translation changes in Arabic literary texts abound, but they are not always easily or immediately identifiable. Those of us who teach Arabic literature mainly or exclusively in English tend to have the intuitive sense that many elements of the translations we use in our classes differ from those of the texts we have read in Arabic. We may feel uncomfortable with this difference, but even if we do, a line-by-line comparison of the original and the translation may not pinpoint the reason. Difference, of course, is inevitable in a work that has been edited-censored in the translation and publication process. Scholars and translators of Arabic literature who connect to the larger area of theoretical translation studies have shown that no translation is free of the ideologies that inform other elements of reception and horizons of expectations (Abdo; Amireh; Booth, "Translator" and "'Muslim Woman'"; Hartman, "Gender" and "My Tale"; Kahf).

It is not a coincidence that most of the scholarly work that has shown how English translations have changed Arabic texts focuses on texts by women writers and also on the gendered nature of the changes. The desire is strong to render Arab women's literary works in English legible in a very narrow and constrained range of meaning. The works investigated in detail flatten the specificities and nuances of Arab women's lives as represented in fiction or memoir in line with the stereotypes we are familiar with: Huda Sha'rawi's brother and father are excised from her memoir in English (Kahf), Nawal El Saadawi is concerned more with sexuality than economics (Amireh), Rajaa Alsanea's girls are stripped of their hybrid Arab-English joking (Booth, "Translator"), and the poetic genius of al-Khansa' is an exception rather than the rule because she is a woman (Hartman, "Arab Woman Poet"). The investment in controlling and changing Arab women's texts in conformity with certain ideas about Arab women might even be seen as parallel to the use of Arab and Muslim women's bodies for political purposes, as in Lila Abu Lughod's argument about how Muslim women are constructed as needing to be saved.

It is not only literary texts written by women that are distorted by translation. The operation of gendered logics in translating and reading Arabic literary texts, especially as they interlock with racial logics, is important to investigate for men writers as well. How gender roles and gendered elements of textual production are represented in translation is a site of tension and contestation. The control over the representation of gender is rooted in orientalist legacies as well as in those of colonialism, imperialism, and neoimperialism, whether we struggle against them or not in our translation and teaching practices. Therefore, in developing suggestions for classroom exercises and discussions, I connect the big picture of the gendered political and ideological situations in which we study, live, and work with how translators choose specific English words and expressions to render Arabic ones and how literary paratexts, material that falls outside the main body of the text (front and back covers of a book, for example), function in relation to these choices.

Teaching Scandals: Translation and Translation Choices

As Lawrence Venuti's recent book claims, "translation changes everything" (*Translation*). When texts are moved from one language system to another, they are changed. In a literary work, where the creative use of language is everything, it is difficult to understand such change as anything but a warping of, deformation of, or even violence enacted on the original. Many theorists have studied the negative effect of translation on a text (e.g., Boullata), but translation can also be seen as more than a necessary evil, as an attempt to produce some positive value, a gain rather than a loss. David Damrosch's recuperation of the concept of world literature, for example, claims that texts circulating in that domain are precisely those that "gain in translation" (281, 291).

Another useful concept, which I draw from an earlier work by Venuti, is the "scandals of translation" (*Scandals*). Thinking about change as scandal evokes a range of meaning in Arabic literary texts as they move into English-language reception environments. It is a scandal to read an Arabic text in English in the mode of interlocked gender-race thinking, and it is a scandal to realize that the changes made to these texts were made to stir students' interest and excitement. Here, I suggest, first, the use of critical writing that exposes such scandals; second, a comparison of original Arabic and English translation that shows changes. Even if we only know a little Arabic or no Arabic, short examples can be used in classroom teaching.

Drawing Examples from Scholarship

Teachers can assign scholarly articles on translation for students to use together with the study of a text or as a resource to develop ideas for classroom work. Productive classroom discussions about language and literature can emerge even when students work with English alone. Comparing two English words for senses, depth of meaning, and connotations is an exercise that students enjoy. Students with more language skills can draw on those. Moving from these understandings of language by using their own mother tongue and examples they are close to helps students then build analyses of materials with which they are less familiar.

Over many semesters, I have used two articles effectively in class: Amal Amireh's investigation of the works of El Saadawi and Mohja Kahf's study of the translation of Sha'rawi's autobiography, *Harem Years*. Both provide a framework, argument, and typology that students can be asked to identify and then apply to literary works and authors. I have rarely taught *Harem Years* but used, with Amireh's article, translations of works by El Saadawi, in particular *The Innocence of the Devil* and *Woman at Point Zero*. The articles by Amireh and by Kahf get students to think about what a faithful translation means and what making something accessible to a Western audience means. They also challenge the received notions of feminism that students have, particularly the notions that center on white women, by using persuasive scholarly arguments that highlight Arab feminist scholarship on Arab feminist writers.

Kahf's article identifies three roles that Arab women are made to conform to—victim, escapee, and pawn. An example is the change from the literal translation of the Arabic title "My Memoirs" (مذكراتي ; Mudhakkirati) to the provocatively orientalist *Harem Years*. The gendered layers that overcode this translation inform Kahf's argument. Amireh notes the change from the literal translation of the Arabic title of El Saadawi's classic work, "The Naked (Bare) Face of the Arab Woman" (الوجه العاري للمرأة العربية ; Al-Wajh al-'ary lil-mar'a al-'arabiyya), to *The Hidden Face of Eve*. In a reception environment obsessed with the hijab and niqab, the transformation from a woman's bare face to a hidden one is scandalous indeed.

The titles of books taught in a course on Arabic literature in translation are revealing even when the course is not focused on translation issues at all. Two modern literary works by Syrian women had their titles changed to foreground their female protagonists: Ulfat Idilbi's "Damascus: Smile of Sadness" (دمشق بسمة الحزن ; Dimashaq: basmat al-huzn) was changed to *Sabriya: Damascus Bitter Sweet*, and Siham Tergeman's "Oh Beautiful Damascus" (يا مال الشام ; Ya Mal al-Sham) was changed to *Daughter of Damascus*. The memoir of the Lebanese novelist Hanan al-Shaykh, which is also presented as an autobiography of her mother, uses a line from a folk tale as its title, "My Tale Is Too Long to Tell" (حكايتي شرح يطول ;

Hikayati sharhun yatul), which has more layered meanings than the English translation, *The Locust and the Bird*, because it alludes to the book's message in ironic ways (Hartman, "My Tale"). I have also written about the change to another work by al-Shaykh, full of gendered implications: the transformation of her novel titled "The Gazelle's Musk" (مسك الغزال ; Misk al-ghazal) into *Women of Sand and Myrrh* ("Gender"). There are many other examples. Roger Allen discusses the decision to render the titles of the books of Mahfouz's Nobel Prize–winning trilogy in orientalized translations of street names rather than use what Allen sees as a more productive way to name, which would undermine a *One Thousand and One Nights* gaze on them. He asks:

> The English translation of the *Cairo Trilogy*... inclines in the direction of domestication. For example, it includes virtual footnotes within the text itself in the form of the designation of a street in Cairo as "Shariʿ al-Nahhasin or Coppersmiths Street" (has anyone heard of a street in Paris called "Elysian Fields"?!)? (479)

Allen's question, to open a classroom discussion of titles and translation, is a productive way to tease out the interlocking categories of gender, race, and orientalism. Amireh's and Kahf's ideas can help students ask why a title is changed to emphasize women, what other strategies are used in these books to either foreground or minimize gendered elements, and how a woman writer's gender is highlighted as important to her authorship of the work.

Texts Reformed through Scandals: *Women of Sand and Myrrh*

Comparing the English-language reception of *Women of Sand and Myrrh* with the reception of the pre-Islamic poet al-Khansaʾ, I have shown how two Arab women writers with virtually nothing in common are read through the same orientalist feminist lens, which renders them and their work flat and stereotyped, ignoring their complexity and nuance ("Gender"). In other words, the same feminist lens that claims to give voice to Arab women writers draws on orientalist tropes that show them to be speaking in a desert, literally and metaphorically, exceptions to their culture. The reordering of the chapters of al-Shaykh's book gives it a different thrust: the Arabic novel, constructed with four women's equally represented voices in an order that emphasizes female empowerment and economic independence, becomes in English a narrator-and-frame story that emphasizes misery in the desert and an escape from it to civil war. This orientalist change insists on seeing Muslim and Arab women as voiceless and passive, always disempowered.

I have used *Women of Sand and Myrrh* many times in class and in many different ways. An effective technique I have used is to have half the students in the class read the novel in the order it was originally published in Arabic and the other half read it as published in translation. Discussion can then consider how the experience of reading and the narrative arc differ in the two different versions. Important issues raised by the changed order include the representation of female sexuality and same-sex relationships, the role of one woman's narrative voice being highlighted over four voices, and the representation of cultural, national, and linguistic difference.

Girls of Riyadh: Scandals of Language and Register

Another novel that deals with women in a desert society, this one openly rather than indirectly referring to Saudi Arabia, is Alsanea's *Girls of Riyadh* (بنات الرياض ; Banat al-Riyadh). I have used it in tandem with *Women of Sand and Myrrh* in classes devoted to women's literature, feminism, and translation. Three critical articles on the text address the problematic transformation of the Arabic original into its published English-language version. Marilyn Booth's essays about the translation are particularly useful, as an assignment or as a resource, to work through the gendered implications of linguistic change ("'Muslim Women'" and "Translation"). Vron Ware writes about the cultural politics of the book's circulation in the United Kingdom and encourages readers to connect their textual experiences to the larger imperial projects we are differentially implicated in today.

In my experience, teaching this book works well because students can be asked to think about specific translation changes and scandals, as discussed by Booth, in relation to their pleasure of reading a very different style of text that is purportedly translated with them in mind. My classes have never failed to develop opposing sides: some argue for the published version, which they find so accessible; others, for the unpublished version advocated by Booth. Sometimes, in a debate between a translation that is domesticating (bringing the text to the readers) and one that is foreignizing (bringing the reader to the text), they change their minds. Students may consider which strategy is better—or if either is effective—in our current English-reception environment, which holds Arabs and Muslims in disdain and places serious constraints on representations of gender.

The tension between colloquial and formal registers in the Arabic text of *Girls of Riyadh*, erased in the published translation but argued for by Booth, is an important feature. I work with this tension by asking students to write down expressions and phrases in English—usually I begin with those that elicit thinking about gender and sexuality. The result is usually a good number of examples in different linguistic registers. I then ask students to come up with words and expressions that they know but I do not or that their parents and grandparents use but the students do not; in these examples, intergenerational translation is needed. In the same way, we list words that I use in class regularly but that they would never use themselves. We also list words that men and boys use but women and girls do not and vice versa. We consider how people identified with certain groups are not allowed to use particular expressions but others are. We work through these sociolinguistic issues in English in order to connect them to those in Arabic.

These exercises explore layers, contexts, and registers of language while also showing how race thinking and gender thinking work together. We look for example at how racialized groups reclaim derogatory words and where the power but also the pain in these expressions is located. Discussing such matters in the classroom can be challenging and productive but also hurtful and difficult. Thus while this work can be empowering for students, it is not always empowering, and the effort that goes into such conversations should be acknowledged and considered in class planning and execution, and teachers should be aware that what hurts or helps students varies. These exercises teach that languages are never static and always change, that the intersection of spoken and written creativity produces meaning in a literary text, and that the English translation of an Arabic text is a refraction rather than a reflection.

Do Muslim Women Need Saving in Fiction?

In *Do Muslim Women Need Saving?*, Abu Lughod uses her years of field-work in Egypt and elsewhere to formulate her argument about how white Western women, as well as others, cast Muslim women as a disempowered monolithic community that can and should be saved from their religion, culture, and male relatives. Her work is easily used in the classroom to investigate how we read and consume Arabic literary works translated into English. Popular memoirs and fictional or fictionalized accounts of Muslim women who literarily need saving—the victim, the escapee, the pawn of a tabloid work by or about an imperiled Muslim woman—shape our horizons of expectations. M. Lynx Qualey writes:

> This genre doesn't concern us here except that it in many ways over-shadows, and shapes the reception of, Arabic literature (in translation). Its popularity alone is important. A quick search of random US public libraries will turn up far more Nonie Darwish than Mahmoud. The reason for the popularity is also important—these stories feed a particular hunger among French- and English-language reading publics, and some readers will also be looking to sate this hunger through fiction. ("Do")

The examples suggested by Amireh's and Kahf's criticism help students think about what techniques are used—cutting or shortening passages, changing the order of chapters, changing the names of characters—to make a book legible to different audiences. Students can reflect on which techniques they would find scandalous and which they would find acceptable. Is a sexier title acceptable but an orientalist one not? Is changing the title ethically different from reordering the book's chapters? What are the costs of making a book legible in these ways? The concepts of authorial ownership of a text and celebrity authorship, as discussed by Booth in relation to Alsanea ("'Muslim Woman'"), should be introduced into this conversation. Does it make a difference if an author likes the changes in a translation of her work? Is the author's opinion about these changes a confirmation of textual authenticity?

We might compare the idea of saving the Arab-Muslim characters of a text with the idea of saving the author and her work as she intended it or saving characters by Westernizing them. The simplification of a text deemed too different or exotic to be understood, so that it becomes "relatable," to use a favorite expression of English-speaking students today, raise vexed and important questions about gender and fiction, about who owns them and what frameworks we use to read, enjoy, and consume them. In another exercise, I ask students to develop their own ideas about saving Muslim women in relation to Arabic literary works in English translation. They can be assigned Abu Lughod's book or parts of it and asked to identify her argument and apply it to a translated text or one issue from a translated text. Dumbing down a literary work by translation—like eliminating from the *Girls of Riyadh* its local, Saudi specifics so that more people can understand it—is analogous to guaranteeing the women of Afghanistan a better life through the invasion and occupation of their land by the United States military. Students can consider this parallel in classroom discussions or assignments: If you remove your burka and look more like us, you will have a better life. If you change your book to make it more appealing to a United States audience, more people will read it.

These exercises can be controversial in the classroom, and the inexact parallel can lead to creative argumentation and deeper thought about what makes a text literary, especially in translation. Even if students don't know Arabic, they can also use this frame to do paratextual analyses. Covers, back-cover blurbs, titles, and so on can be analyzed with no linguistic knowledge. All students can then think in more depth about the changes that impact the reception of gender—for example, the downplaying or removal of male characters, as in the case of Shaʿrawi (Kahf), which is a direct parallel to "saving a brown woman" from the brown men in her life.

Translating for Bigots

Paratextual analysis is valuable for working with questions about translation for students who have little or no Arabic. A good example is the cultural work accomplished by a book cover, as Adam Talib observes. Talib reflects on the book covers used for Arabic fiction in relation to a post on African literature that was widely circulated on the Internet (Ross).

Fiction labeled African, as fiction labeled Arabic, is subject to flattening generalizations and unifying depictions: the proof is the similarity of images and colors even when works are very different. What is particularly striking about the book covers used for Arabic fiction is the gendered specificity and restricted femininity they evoke. We see again and again women wearing black veils, their heads turned and faces obscured, even when the images have nothing to do with or completely contradict what the book is about. In his talk, which is titled "Translating for Bigots," Talib speaks about the influence of the genre of Arab-Muslim women's memoirs in order to make larger points about the various constraints faced by a translator of Arabic literature into English, including pressures by publishers in creating books for the global English-language market.

As an exercise, students could compare a book that they read in class with its back cover copy, which often includes quotes about the book taken from reviews. The cover blurbs, often explicitly sexist, racist, and orientalist, can serve as a good example of how these stereotypings interlock. Booth and Ware both point to blurbs for *Girls of Riyadh*, and I have done the same for al-Shaykh's texts in the discussion of their reception ("Gender" 17 and "My Tale").

My translation of Alexandra Chreiteh's دايما كوكا كولا (Da'iman coca-cola), *Always Coca-Cola*, is a perfect example of how cover images can differ. The American edition shows a pop art close-up of a woman's face with lipstick; in the British edition, a woman's face is hidden in shadows. The original Arabic novel highlights the Coca-Cola bottle of the title, with a bottle cap below the words in a stylized font that looks like a logo, which is an inside joke developed throughout the work. But Iman Humaydan's *Other Lives* (حيوات أخرى ; Hayawat ukhra) has the same picture on the cover of the Arabic and English editions, and Chreiteh's more recent novel *Ali and His Russian Mother* (علي وأمه الروسية ; Ali wa ummuhu al-russiya) has a very similar picture on the Arabic and English covers, a similarity that as the translator I advocated.

Incorporating the study of translation into classroom practice, whether or not the teacher or students know Arabic, allows them to appreciate, analyze, and think about the politics of literary production and consumption. The approach of teaching scandals captures the attention of students and builds flexibility into the classroom. The use of paratextual elements and analyses drawn from comparative translation studies allows students with and without advanced Arabic-language skills to participate together and underlines the creation and perpetuation of stereotypes, orientalist discourse, and anti-Arab racism. This also helps make the connections in the interlocking nature of gender, racism, and orientalism. The discussions, exercises, and assignments that I have suggested here all make visible political issues that are inextricably linked to students' reading and consumption of Arabic literary texts, issues that so often are invisible to them before they come to class.

Gendered analysis in studying works of Arabic literature in translation as translations can bridge texts and contexts, politics and poetics. When we examine what goes wrong in a translation or what we do not like about it, we might sometimes even find not a loss but a gain. Student expectations may be challenged, and students may be asked to work against the grain of their expectations. In studying translation and gender and probing the kinds of questions they raise, we also may challenge ourselves as teachers, while at the same time working with the literary in multiple ways.

Works Cited

Abdo, Diya. "Textual Migration: Self-Translation and Translation of the Self in Leila Abouzeid's *Return to Childhood: The Memoir of a Modern Moroccan Woman* and *Ruju' Ila Al-Tufulah*." *Frontiers: A Journal of Women Studies*, vol. 30, no. 2, 2009, pp. 1–42.

Abu Lughod, Lila. *Do Muslim Women Need Saving?* Harvard UP, 2014.

Allen, Roger. "The Happy Traitor: Tales of Translation." *Comparative Literature Studies*, vol. 47, no. 4, 2010, pp. 472–86.

Alsanea, Rajaa. بنات الرياض [Banat al-Riyadh]. Saqi, 2005. Translated as *Girls of Riyadh*.

———. *Girls of Riyadh*. Translated by Marilyn Booth, Penguin, 2007.

Al-Shaykh, Hanan. حكايتي شرح يطول [Hikayati sharhun yatul]. Adab, 2004. Translated as *The Locust and the Bird*.

———. *The Locust and the Bird: My Mother's Story*. Translated by Roger Allen, Anchor, 2010.

———. مسك الغزال [Misk al-ghazal]. Adab, 1988. Translated as *Women of Sand and Myrrh*.

———. *Women of Sand and Myrrh*. Translated by Catherine Cobham, Anchor, 1992.

Amireh, Amal. "Framing Nawal El Saadawi: Arab Feminism in a Transnational World." *Signs*, vol. 26, no. 1, 2000, pp. 215–49.

Booth, Marilyn. "'The Muslim Woman' as Celebrity Author and the Politics of Translating Arabic: *Girls of Riyadh* Go on the Road." *Journal of Middle East Women's Studies*, vol. 6, no. 3, 2010, pp. 149–82.

———. "Translator v. author (2007): *Girls of Riyadh* Go to New York." *Translation Studies*, vol. 1, no. 2, 2008, pp. 197–211.

Boullata, Issa. "The Case for Resistant Translation from Arabic to English." *Translation Review*, vol. 65, no. 1, 2003, pp. 29–33.

Chreiteh, Alexandra. *Ali and His Russian Mother*. Translated by Michelle Hartman, Interlink Publishing, 2015.

———. علي وأمه الروسية [Ali wa ummuhu al-russiya]. Arab Scientific, 2009. Translated as *Ali and His Russian Mother*.

———. *Always Coca-Cola*. Translated by Michelle Hartman, Swallow Editions, 2011.

———. دايما كوكا كولا [Da'iman coca-cola]. Arab Scientific, 2009. Translated as *Always Coca-Cola*.

Damrosch, David. *What Is World Literature?* Princeton UP, 2003.

El Saadawi, Nawal. الوجه العاري للمرأة العربية [Al-Wajh al-'ary lil-mar'a al-'arabiyya]. Madbouli, 2006. Translated as *The Hidden Face of Eve*.

———. *The Hidden Face of Eve: Women in the Arab World*. Translated by Sherif Hetata, Beacon, 1982.

Hartman, Michelle. "An Arab Woman Poet as a Crossover Artist? Reconsidering the Ambivalent Legacy of Al-Khansa'." *Tulsa Studies in Women's Literature*, vol. 30, no. 1, 2011, pp. 15–36.

———. "Gender, Genre, and the (Missing) Gazelle: Arab Women Writers and the Politics of Translation." *Feminist Studies*, vol. 38, no. 1, 2012, pp. 17–49.

———. "My Tale Is Too Long to Tell: *The Locust and the Bird* between South Lebanon and New York City." *Journal of Arabic Literature*, vol. 46, 2015, pp. 1–25.

Humaydan, Iman. حيوات أخرى [Hayawat ukhra]. Arrawi, 2010. Translated as *Other Lives*.

———. *Other Lives*. Translated by Michelle Hartman, Interlink Publishing, 2014.

Idilbi, Ulfat. *Sabriya: Damascus Bitter Sweet*. Translated by Peter Clark, Interlink Publishing, 2003.

———. دمشق بسمة الحزن [Dimashq basmat al-huzn]. Dar Tlass, 1981. Translated as *Damascus Bitter Sweet*.

Kahf, Mohja. "Packaging 'Huda': Sha'rawi's Memoirs in the United States Reception Environment." *Going Global: The Transnational Reception of Third World Women Writers*, edited by Amal Amireh and Lisa Suhair Majaj, Garland Publishing, 2000, pp. 148–72.

Lynx Qualey, M. "Do Muslim Female Characters Need Saving?" *Arabic Literature (in Translation) Blog*, arablit.org/2013/11/25/do-muslim-female-characters-need-saving/.

———. "Translating for Bigots." *Arabic Literature (in Translation) Blog*, arablit.wordpress.com/2013/11/04/translating-for-bigots/.

Martin, Biddy, and Chandra Talpade Mohanty. "Feminist Politics: What's Home Got to Do With It?" *Feminisms: An Anthology of Literary Theory and Criticism*, edited by Robin R. Warhol and Diane Price Herndel, Rutgers UP, 1997, pp. 293–310.

Razack, Sherene. *Casting Out: The Eviction of Muslims from Western Law and Politics*. U of Toronto P, 2008.

Ross, Elliot. "The Dangers of a Single Book Cover: The Acacia Tree Meme and 'African Literature.'" Africa Is a Country, 7 May 2014, africasacountry.com/the-dangers-of-a-single-book-cover-the-acacia-tree-meme-and-african-literature/.

Salaita, Steven. *Anti-Arab Racism in the United States: Where It Comes From and What It Means Today*. Pluto, 2006.

Sha'rawi, Huda. *Harem Years: The Memoirs of an Egyptian Feminist, 1879–1924*. Translated by Margot Badran, Feminist Press, 1987.

———. مذكراتي [Mudhakkirati]. Dar Hilal, 1981. Translated as *Harem Years*.

Sheehi, Stephen. *Islamophobia: The Ideological Campaign against Muslims*. Clarity Press, 2011.

Spivak, Gayatri Chakravorty. "Can the Subaltern Speak?" *Marxism and the Interpretation of Culture*, edited by Cary Nelson and Lawrence Grossberg, U of Illinois P, 1988, pp. 217–313.

Talib, Adam. "Translating for Bigots." *YouTube*, 10 Nov. 2013, www.youtube.com/watch?v=aANKpO4zmGA.

Tergeman, Siham. *Daughter of Damascus*. Translated by Andrea Rugh, Center for Middle East Studies at the U of Texas, 1994.

———. يا مال الشام [Ya mal al-sham]. Alif-ba, 1998. Translated as *Daughter of Damascus*.

Thobani, Sunera. *Exalted Subjects: Studies in the Making of Race and Nation in Canada*. U of Toronto P, 2007.

Venuti, Lawrence. *The Scandals of Translation: Towards an Ethics of Difference.* Routledge, 1998.

———. *Translation Changes Everything: Theory and Practice.* Routledge, 2012.

Ware, Vron. "The New Literary Front: Public Diplomacy and the Cultural Politics of Reading Arabic Literature in Translation." *New Formations,* vol. 73, no. 1, 2011, pp. 56–77.

Part II

Engaging the Canon in Modern Arabic Literature

Rebecca C. Johnson

In Translation: Cosmopolitan Reading in the *Nahda*

Cosmopolitan Reading?

The inclusion of Arabic literature in the greater curriculum of literary studies is one of the spoils of the theory and culture wars of the 1980s and 1990s, so often pitched around the relevance of non-Western literatures, and is cause for approbation. Arabic fiction is no longer read solely to glean information about a region—in order to "comprehend how each text 'reflects' Arab reality," as Magda al-Nowaihi wrote in 2001 (28)—but is now read comparatively in a wide range of historical and literary contexts. Students might read Tayeb Salih in a course on the bildungsroman, Mahmoud Darwish in a course on comparative autobiography, or Ahmed Khaled Towfik in a global science fiction course. This development is what Martha Nussbaum advocated for in *Cultivating Humanity*—a "curriculum for world citizenship" that cultivates students' moral imaginations to "receive the voices of the excluded" (86, 98)—and what Kwame Anthony Appiah called a "cosmopolitan reading practice," where "we travel in books to learn 'mutual toleration,' even . . . sympathy and concern for others." Appiah provides a nuanced discussion of cosmopolitan reading practices and distinguishes between what he calls a "monological universalism," which he rejects as the normative act of imagining all human beings in a single image, and the "dialogical universality of cosmopolitanism," which displays "concern for our fellow humans without demanding of them that they be or become like ourselves" ("Cosmopolitan Reading" 202).

Yet even as American students receive more voices of the excluded, it is important to assess how they are receiving them, to uncover and analyze the at times hidden premises (both personal and institutional) that underpin their inclusion. Nussbaum argues:

> We need to learn more about non-Western cultures—above all for these reasons of good citizenship and deliberation in an interlocking world. But this learning is valuable for other reasons as well. It will enhance our self-knowledge as Americans. We will get a better picture of our own diverse nation by becoming aware of the many traditions, both Western and non-Western, that intermingle within it. And we will also understand the specifically Western aspect of our American origins, more precisely, "the Western tradition," by comparison with other ways and practices. (115)

Getting students to read more Arabic literature and giving instructors the tools to teach it are two of the goals of this volume. Another goal is to prompt students to think critically about the act of reading, from a work's political and institutional frameworks of reception to the particular processes of translation through which it passed to the ideologies—national, imperial, neoliberal—that guide our understanding of its inclusion in the "interlocking world" of literature. The mere presence of a non-Western text in a university course cannot itself further the goals of comparative study, such as to gain a critical understanding of the history of canon formation or to question the assumptions of generic definitions or literary periodization. Learning more about non-Western cultures can also serve the familiar purpose of learning what is Western about the so-called Western tradition; including non-Western texts in a curriculum can even reverse some of the theoretical innovations of the 1980s and 1990s, which problematized origins, authenticity, and the very border between the constructed categories of the West and non-West.

As inheritors of the expanded curriculum that Nussbaum and her contemporaries envisioned, students should be encouraged not only to read foreign literature in translation but also to examine the conditions under which they read it: the political and historical contexts in which they encounter it and the assumptions that they and their institutions bring to bear on it. If students are no longer expected to read Arabic literature only for the window it provides onto Arab societies, do they read it instead to gain insight into their own society, an insight that may primarily benefit them and their nation? As the American Academy of Arts and Sciences (AAAS) report on the state of the humanities in the university, *The Heart of the Matter*, recently stated, the humanities and social sciences should be defended for the sake of "a vibrant, competitive, and secure nation" (Commission on the Humanities and Social Sciences). For many students, cosmopolitan reading or world literature (a rubric under which Arabic literature is sometimes taught) is framed, implicitly or explicitly, as a process of self-discovery and national discovery. Seeing it as such has a long history. Goethe declared that "the epoch of world literature is at hand" after reading a French translation of a Chinese novel, in which he discovered that "[t]he people think, act, and feel almost exactly as we do" (Eckermann 92). For him, like in the AAAS report, reading foreign literature is good for the nation (it prevents "[us] Germans" from "pedantic arrogance") but only to a point: "[I]n such estimation of things foreign," he warns, "we must not cling to a particular work and regard it as ideal" (94). To see oneself in foreign literature sometimes requires one to resist the foreignness of the work itself.

Teaching nineteenth-century Arabic literature has made me acutely aware of the ways in which my students and I are interpellated by these projects, even as the texts we read challenge some of the Eurocentric underpinnings of cosmopolitanism. Arabic texts written in the nineteenth- and early-twentieth-century period called the *nahda* (نهضة ; "awakening") and sometimes referred to as the Arab Enlightenment often meditate on similar questions that their European Enlightenment contemporary, Goethe, asks—How does one live in the newly connected world? How does one understand another culture or make oneself understood to it? What is the proper or just relation to have with a foreigner?—but in radically different historical and political circumstances.

Whereas contemporary literature is more plentiful in translation and often more accessible to students, *nahda* texts ask them to contemplate ideas that were formed under colonial conditions, to see empire as a possible corollary to world citizenship, and to see the claims of power that are often hidden in cosmopolitan aspirations. Immanuel Kant's formulation of the cosmopolitan "right to the earth's surface" appears less hospitable when contemplated from the territory of the recently occupied (106). As Shaden Tageldin writes, teaching *nahda* texts "is fertile ground for pedagogies that might bring modern Arabic literature more squarely into the fold of empire and postcolonial studies, critical translation theory, and the resurgent fields of world and comparative literature," and study of the *nahda* is also a space for formulating new understandings of those fields and their intersections from the perspective of its authors ("Proxidistant Reading" 235).

Writing at the apex of high orientalism, and often with reading knowledge of at least one European language, many nineteenth-century Arab authors were acutely aware that their religious and cultural heritage, and even their social structures and material culture, were being translated for a European audience. Being travelers and translators themselves, they translated Europe for their audiences. To read these texts, which ask what it means to translate and be translated in a time of imperial consolidation, is to fundamentally change a course's perspective on cosmopolitan reading. Instead of asking students to understand these texts as examples of something called world literature, I ask them to examine some of the premises that constitute the concept: Which literature? Whose world? Under what conditions does another's word become available to us? What remains unavailable to us as readers? And how is the very we of reading determined by our approach to the text?

Nahda Studies

The relative neglect of nineteenth- and early-twentieth-century Arabic literary texts is not just the product of political exigencies. It is true that the anglophone translation market has largely passed over *nahda* works for ones that shed light on more recent events, but the scholarly field of modern Arabic literature has also favored the later texts. For many years, scholars saw the *nahda*—the root of the word signifies "to rise" or "to stand up"—as an enlightenment movement that had its main origins in the West and produced derivative literary works. Dating roughly to Napoleon's invasion and occupation of Egypt from 1798 to 1801, the period of reconfigured contact was once known as the Arab rediscovery of Europe, a phrase that refers to the innovations in communication and transportation (the opening of steamship routes, railways, telegraph wires, and printing presses) that coincided with the trade reforms and expansion of credit that opened the Ottoman Empire to new levels of foreign investment, trade, and immigration (Abu-Lughod).

For narrative literature, the result of this contact has long been described as modernizing. Scholars of the *nahda* have privileged forms of prose, such as the novel, over verse (Rastegar). Modern Arabic literature was characterized by "the introduction of unknown or barely known genres such as the theatre or the European-style novel," which brought that literature out of the so-called age of decline and "loosened the attachment of Arab societies to traditions reckoned inappropriate to modern civilization" (Tomiche 900). Narrative works, these scholars argued, strove to imitate Western forms and often failed, through a prolonged period of literary apprenticeship that culminated in the first decades of the twentieth century, when an "authentically" (Gibb 1) or "purely" (Moosa 256) Arab novel—most often identified as Muhammad Husayn Haykal's 1913 *Zaynab* (زينب)—emerges but still resembles the Western novel in its plot structures and formal devices.

In other words, Arabic literary modernity was itself seen as a translation project: authors working in Arabic tried to imitate Western narrative forms until they finally succeeded (Selim). This view meant that works that did not resemble those forms, instead following classical models or even combining the classical and the Western in innovative experimentation, were sidelined or seen as transitional curiosities—protonovels or intellectually frivolous and decadent displays of linguistic virtuosity. In recent years, however, scholars have looked at the production of the *nahda* as more ambivalent in its attitude toward Western literary, cultural, and even scientific models and less categorical in its rejection of indigenous ones (Barak; Elshakry). Studies of the *nahda* now tend to see experimentation in Western forms not only as admiring imitation of a dominant culture but also as a creative act of cultural resistance or indifference that "cared nothing for origins and genealogies" (Selim 38). These studies have renewed focus on the *nahda* in its variety and complexity and rigorously opened this century of literary history to new texts and methodologies of comparison, translation, and cultural exchange to see it as having a pluralistic genealogy and history (El-Ariss; Rastegar; Selim; Sheehi; and Tageldin, *Disarming Words*).

Nahda authors are now most often treated as ambivalent mediators among French, English, and Arabic influences; they are translators, cultural and otherwise, who are not, as Lawrence Venuti writes, "invisible" but deliberately and visibly manipulate the text (*Translator's Invisibility* 2). As Khalil al-Khuri, the author of *Alas . . . I Am Not a Foreigner* (وي... إذن لستُ بإفرنجي; Wayy . . . idhan lastu bi ifranji), another contender for the title of the first Arabic novel (1859), writes, "[T]he European tailor's shop isn't a school for civilization" (ليست دكانة الخياط الإفرنجي مدرسة التمدن [162]). Instead, al-Khuri advocates that Arabs "adapt" (اقتباس ; iqtibas; literally, "quote") foreign knowledge and arts in order to enliven "the Arab ummah" (الأمة العربية [163]; "community"). The denizens of the new age of the *nahda*, for al-Khuri as for scholars today, are seen not as passive receivers of foreign culture but as translators who actively select, interpret, transmit, and transform primary source material. Furthermore, although they responded to the same material conditions that underwrote the changes of the *nahda*—innovations in communications and transportation, increased cultural contact, the introduction of capitalist means of production and surplus accumulation, and the emergence of new classes, new elites, and new forms of governance—they did so in radically different ways.

Reading two canonical *nahda* authors with and against each other allows students to understand the diversity of modernist tendencies in the Middle East. The travel narratives of Ahmad Faris al-Shidyaq and of Rifaʿah Rafiʿ al-Tahtawi, both recently translated into English (in 2004 and 2013, respectively), are miscellaneous in form and incorporate elements of verse and expository prose. Neither is containable by the Western category of novel or epic, but both are instead part of a rich environment that includes poetry. Though both are long and therefore impractical to assign in their entirety in a survey course, even reading a few excerpts—especially alongside some of the few available examples of *nahda* poetry in translation—can help contextualize and circumscribe the role of European arts and sciences in the development of modern Arab thought. By focusing on these authors' methodologies of transmission and translation, students can uncover the different ways that these authors engage both European and classical Arabic arts and literature and see them as complex agents of modernity.

Both travel narratives were written by literary translators. Al-Tahtawi, who became the founding director of an Egyptian school for translation, translated François Fénelon's *Les aventures de Télémaque* (1867; "The Adventures of Telemachus") in addition to producing and supervising the production of numerous translations of scientific, historical, and legal texts. Al-Shidyaq headed the translation bureau of the Church Missionary Society press in Malta (which published translations of *Robinson Crusoe* and *Pilgrim's Progress*) and collaborated on a Protestant translation of the Bible. Aside from the authors' interest in European arts and sciences, the closeness of their years of departure (1826 for al-Tahtawi, 1828 for al-Shidyaq), and that both traveled to France by way of Alexandria, these two narratives bear little resemblance to each other. Al-Tahtawi's *The Extraction of Gold from a Brief Description of Paris* (تخليص الإبريز إلى تلخيص باريز ; Tageldin's translation retains the original's rhyming: *Extracting Pure Gold to Render Paris, Briefly Told* [113]) is a straightforward, factual travel narrative with direct ethnographic commentary on the traveler's experiences, while al-Shidyaq's *Leg over Leg Concerning That Which Is al-Fariyaq* (الساق على الساق فيما هو الفارياق) is a satirical narrative that is based on a fictionalized version of the traveler's experiences and that imitates and parodies many generic conventions, including that of the travel narrative.

The biographies of the authors account for many of the differences. Al-Tahtawi, classically trained in religious sciences and Arabic at Al-Azhar in Cairo, traveled to France as the religious adviser to a group of Egyptian students on a state-sponsored *mission scolaire*; later he was employed as an important state functionary in Egyptian higher education. Al-Shidyaq had a more idiosyncratic personal and professional career: he was a Lebanese Maronite Catholic who was trained as a scribe before working as a translator for the Protestant Church Missionary Society; he was an editor of the first Arabic periodical in Egypt, the state-owned *al-Waqaʾiʿ al-Misriyyah* (الوقائع المصرية ; "Egyptian Events"); and, after he converted to Islam, he served as the chief corrector of the Ottoman Imperial Press. Yet more important than biographical details is that the two men had very different orientations toward the act of translation. Whereas al-Tahtawi posited the equivalence of Arabic and French, emphasized common values and parallel concepts in the two cultures, and familiarized foreign customs, al-Shidyaq found incommensurability and singularity to be the ever-present companions of his translation practice. As he writes in one of his verse compositions:

> He who has missed out on translation knows not what travail is:
> None but the warrior is scorched by the fire of war!
>
> I find a thousand notions for which there is none akin
> Among us, and a thousand with none appropriate;
>
> And a thousand terms with no equivalent.
> I find disjunction for junction, though junction is needed.
> (qtd. in Sulh 144)

Extraction of Gold and *Leg over Leg* can be read as more than acts of cultural interpretation. Each work presents a theory of translation, displaying

different approaches to its fundamental questions, presenting different attitudes toward the status of the source material as well as toward the concept of literary and cultural equivalence. Each work postulates or criticizes
the existence of universal concepts and categories, implies a theory of how
meaning is produced, and comments on the material, social, and political
conditions of cultural contact. Above all, each asks this fundamental question: Under what conditions is culture, history, and literature translatable?

Al-Tahtawi: An Imam in Paris

The Extraction of Gold from a Brief Description of Paris, though published in 1834, when al-Tahtawi was employed as the chief translator of
an Egyptian military school, was first drafted before his departure from
Paris in 1831 and presented to the École Égyptienne de Paris as part of
the requirement for his certification as a French-Arabic translator. The
translation appears in *An Imam in Paris: Account of a Stay in France by
an Egyptian Cleric* (101–378), with an untranslated title, *Takhlis al-ibriz*
("The Extraction of Gold"). An eight-member committee that included
orientalists, clergy, and government officials evaluated the text and granted
al-Tahtawi his passing grade, deeming him "capable of translating those
works that will propagate instruction and civilization" in Egypt ("École
Égyptienne"). After revising the work shortly after his return to Cairo
(when he also added the epilogue), he published it to praise among his
home country's literary and political elite. Egypt's ruler, Viceroy Mehmet
Ali, had it translated into Turkish and distributed to government officials,
and its Arabic version was distributed to students and administrators in
the new government schools. Already, one could say, these mere facts of
reception and patronage begin to raise the central question of cosmopolitan reading as well as a fundamental issue of translation studies—that is,
what is broadly called a text's function in a receiving language and culture
(Venuti, *Translation Studies Reader* 4–6), the norms governing translation practice (Even-Zohar; Toury 51–62). What is the translation for, and
for whom?

Scholars of al-Tahtawi have addressed issues of translation in his work
(Tageldin, *Disarming Words* 108–51; Sawaie; and Salama-Carr). The preface, for example, shows how the author frames his translation, positioning
it for its intended audience or audiences. That al-Tahtawi wrote *Extraction*
as an educational text for an Egyptian audience is immediately clear:

When my name was entered among those of the travelers, and I made preparations to go, some relatives and well-wishers, especially our Shaykh al-'Attar . . . told me to observe in great detail everything that would take place on this trip, everything I saw and encountered that was strange and wondrous, and to write it down so that it could be useful to discover the face of this region, of which it is said that it is the bride among all regions, and in order for it to remain a guide for would-be travelers wishing to go there . . . I have adorned it with some useful digressions and convincing corroborations, and phrased it so as to urge Islamic countries to examine foreign sciences, the arts and the crafts. (105)

فلما رسم اسمي في جملة المسافرين وعزمت على التوجه أشار عليّ
بعض الأقارب والمحبين لا سيما شيخنا العطار فإنه مولع بسماع عجائب
الأخبار والاطلاع على غرائب الاثار أن أنبه عليّ ما يقع في هذه السفرة
وعلى ما أراه وما أصادفه من الأمور الغريبة والأشياء العجيبة و أن أقيده
ليكون نافعا في كشف القناع عن محيا هذه البقاع التي يقال فيها إنّها عرائس
الأقطار ، وليبقى دليلا يهتدى به إلى السفر إليها طلّاب الأسفار...ووشحتها
ببعض استطرادات نافعة واستظهارات ساطعة ، وأنطقتها بحث ديار
الإسلام على البحث عن العلوم البرانية والفنون والصنائع
(٤-٣)

We can see that the work's primary function was to educate al-Tahtawi's fellow Egyptians about the history and customs of France. Its opening pages frame its reception as occurring within identifiable social, religious, and political boundaries. The first sentences, praise of the Prophet Muhammad, situate the author in the community of the faithful or Muslim ummah; the paragraphs that follow, praise for Muhammad 'Ali as "the Benefactor," situate its reception in the political community of the Egyptian province of the Ottoman Empire; and the next paragraphs, praise for al-Tahtawi's teacher and head of Al-Azhar, Hasan al-'Attar, situate it in an intellectual community of classically educated elites whose geographic center is Cairo.

The preface answers many questions about the functions and norms of al-Tahtawi's work but raises others. Though al-Tahtawi announces his project by addressing himself to and positing himself in praiseworthy Ottoman and Islamic institutions of authority, he also writes that "perfection" in the arts and sciences is "found in the lands of the Franks . . . [and] lacking in Islamic kingdoms" (*Imam* 105; فإن كمال ذلك ببلاد الافرنج...وخلو ممالك الإسلام منه [Takhlis al-ibriz (being used in this essay instead of the beginning of the transliterated title, Hadhihi rihlat) 4]). Therefore he writes in order "to urge Islamic countries to examine the

foreign sciences, the arts and the crafts." At the same time he translates French culture into Arabic, that is, he translates Arab civilization into
French colonial frameworks: his wish to "arouse all Islamic nations—
both Arab and non-Arab—from their sleep of indifference" (106;
وأن يوقظ ب[هذا الكتاب] من نوم الغفلة سائر أمم الإسلام من عرب وعجم [5])
sounds surprisingly similar to Ernest Renan's "cercle de fer" ("iron ring")
that encloses the heads of Muslims and makes them "incapable of learning
anything or opening themselves to any new idea" (2–3). Assigning in class
Renan's "L'Islamisme et la science" ("Islamism and Science") with *Extraction of Gold* would yield fascinating intersections, especially consider-
ing Renan's puzzling indictment of al-Tahtawi's text as an example of the
Muslim intellectual's rejection of European reason and science (20).

Al-Tahtawi's ambivalence can also be seen at the level of form. In a few
short lines, al-Tahtawi describes his narrative in terms of classical Arabic
genres, identifying it as a travel in search of knowledge (رحلة ; *rihlah*) but
also explains that it is "presented in the way that the Franks use to record"
that knowledge (على طريق تدوين الإفرنج لها واعتقادهم فيها وتأسيسهم لها ;106
[4]). Again, a double translation is at work: French culture is translated
into an Arab generic norm, which is itself rendered into French norms of
recording facts.

Encouraging students to look for instances of cultural translation in
the text, where the author makes foreign material accessible to the reader,
can yield complex discussions of the relation between audience and source
material and of the role of the translator who mediates between them. The
book is divided into six *maqalat* (مقالات ; "essays"), which are subdivided
into discrete sections that take on distinct topics. Some essays narrate,
giving the reader an idea of the journey that al-Tahtawi and his students
took from Egypt to Paris and how they lived and studied in Paris; others describe French customs, history, or geography. Many if not all these
essays are structured by comparative observations: Marseilles resembles
Alexandria but with wider streets (156); the Nile is like the Seine in that
they both traverse a city, but their water is very different (173); Parisian
streets are lined with trees, as Shubra Street is in Cairo (175); French
stage performers resemble the *'awalim*, professional dancers and singers
of Egypt (229) except that they make references to philosophy and other
learned disciplines.

French cities, rivers, streets, and performers may be judged to have
more differences from than similarities to Egyptian ones, but the French
and the Egyptian are always seen as comparable, belonging to a higher or-

der of objects and experiences, to the general, even universal categories of cities, rivers, streets, and so on. As Myriam Salama-Carr argues, al-Tahtawi promotes a view of translation that is based on the ultimate commensurability of languages and cultures, a view not unlike empiricist concepts of language that one finds in European Enlightenment texts, where translation may vary the mode of expression but cannot change the meaning itself. (John Dryden referred to the translator's task as "to vary the dress, not to alter or destroy the substance" [20].)

Al-Tahtawi believes that while "each language has its own particular conventions of use" (*Imam* 188; فلكل لسان اصطلاح [Takhlis al-ibriz 56]), all are governed by the same rules. Arabic and French might have distinct conventions, but they are not incommunicable, being both governed by linguistic structures, a general category the author refers to as "rules" and of which "grammaire" and "the Arabic sciences" are two particular examples (see Tageldin, *Disarming Words* 125). Just as he finds Arabic books in French libraries containing "every field of science and language" (261; في أي علم كان بأي لغة كانت [125]) and the Arabic language to be one of the many "useful languages" studied in the Académie des Inscriptions et Belles-Lettres (269), Arabic is treated as one particular case among many.

Positing the inherent equality of French and Arabic under the conditions of coloniality in which al-Tahtawi learned French—as a language that his teachers believed would bring "the key to the arts and to science" (qtd. in Tageldin 112)—could be considered an act of resistance, an assertion of validity in the face of assumed inequality. But how do we reconcile that resistance with the goal that he states in his preface, of awakening his compatriots to the superiority of European arts and sciences? This question leads to another: Under what conditions does someone else's word become equivalent to our own? As Antoine Berman argues, translation is always an ethical encounter or "experience of the foreign" with an irreducible other. Tageldin argues that this encounter is grounded in the colonial context. She suggests that the "seduction of translation" undergirds colonial power: it "lures the colonized to seek power *through* empire rather than against it, to translate their cultures into an empowered 'equivalence' with those of their dominators and thereby repress inequalities between those dominators and themselves" (*Disarming Words* 10).

To look more closely at al-Tahtawi's assertions of commensurability, I select one, in section 7 of the third essay, "On the Entertainments of Paris," which describes the variety of theatrical arts to be found in Paris:

Then there are also spectacles where horses, elephants and other animals perform shows. There is a theater called the Théâtre Franconi, where there is a wonderfully trained elephant famous for performing extraordinary tricks. Just as the Opera is the biggest theater, the smallest is called Théâtre de Monsieur Comte (tiyatir al-Kumt). This serves to amuse children, like the hawi in Egypt. "Comte" is the name of the manager of this spectacle. All the actors and actresses are young people. In this theater, you can see sleight of hand, magic and other things like that. . . .

I do not know of an Arabic word that renders the meaning of spectacle or "theater." The basic meaning of the word spectacle is "view," "place of recreation" or some such, whereas "theater" originally also meant "game," "entertainment," or the venue where this takes place. And so it may be compared with those actors called "shadow players." More appropriately, shadow play is a form of theater, as both are known by the Turks as komedya. However, this denomination is too restrictive, except if it is used in a broader sense. There is no objection to translating "theater" or "spectacle" as khayali [imaginary] if you enlarge the meaning of this word, as a result of which it comes close to the idea of "spectacle." (230–31)

و هناك أيضاً سبكتاكلات أخرى يلعبون فيها الخيل والفِيَلة ونحوها ومنها
التياتر المسماة تياتر فرنكوني ...وفيها فِيل مشهور بالألعاب الغريبة معلم
تعليماً عجيباً وكما أن أعظم التياترات الأوبرة فأصغرها تياتر تسمى تياتر
الكمت وهي معدة لنزاهة الصغار كالحاوى في مصر والكمت اسم معلم
هذه السبكتاكل وكل اللاعبين واللاعبات صغار السن وهذه التياتر يوجد بها
كثير من الشعبيثيات والسيم ونحوها...

لا أعرف اسماً عربياً يليق بمعنى السبكتاكل أو التياتر غير أن لفظ سبكتاكل
معناها منظر أو منتزه أو نحو ذلك ولفظ تياتر معناه الأصلي كذلك ثم سمى
بها اللعب ومحله ويقرب أن يكون نظيرها أهل اللعب المسمى خيالياً بل
الخيالي نوع منها وتشتهر عند الترك باسم كمديه وهذا الاسم قاصر إلا أن
يتوسع فيه ولا مانع أن تترجم لفظه تياتر أو سبكتاكل بلفظ خيالي ويتوسع
في معنى هذه الكلمة ويقرب من تصوير السبكتاكل
(88–89)

Describing the spectacle, an operation that requires both literal and cultural translation, leads al-Tahtawi into a series of comparisons. The Théâtre de Monsieur Comte is like *al-hawi* (الحاوي ; "a snake charmer") and the spectacle like shadow players. Yet even as he makes these comparisons, he struggles with the problem that none of the terms he uses are exactly equivalent. *Spectacle* may literally translate to "view" or "place of recreation," but that solution is unsatisfactory; *spectacle* may be like a shadow play, but shadow plays are just one subset of theater and so would be too narrow a term. *Komedya*, a term translated into Turkish and already altered in its receiving context, is "too restrictive." Each Arabic equivalent is rejected as too particular, not general enough. As Tageldin argues, al-Tahtawi had a "conviction that French ways of knowing are more properly 'universal' than Arabic ones" (*Disarming Words* 129). The terms on which commensurability is established are French, not Arabic; Venuti would call them "foreignized" (*Translator's Invisibility* 15–16), because they need to be modified in order to be properly equivalent.

Al-Tahtawi encourages his Arabic readers to enlarge their vocabulary so that they can read French culture in translation; the meanings of Arabic words must be altered to accommodate French cultural concepts, and Arabic neologisms must be invented to serve as French equivalents (Sawaie 401–03). He asks his readers to enlarge or modify cultural concepts, such as honor or eloquence, to accommodate French definitions. For example, he advises them to still consider French men honorable even though they are not jealous of their women (*Imam* 365). He would have his readers reevaluate Arabic eloquence to exclude poetry with homosexual themes: "Among the good qualities of their language and poetry is that [the French] refuse to extol homosexual love. . . . As a result, when one of them translates one of our books, he changes the words" (181–82;

ومن الأمور المستحسنة في طباعهم الشبيهة حقيقة بطباع العرب عدم ميلهم إلى حب الأحداث والتشبب فيهم أصلا فهذا أمر منسي الذكر عندهم...فلذلك إذا ترجم أحدهم كتابا من كتابنا يقلب الكلام إلى وجه آخر [Takhlis al-ibriz 52]). The creation of transcultural categories requires the modification of Arabic expression. What appears at first as a zone of equivalence in which Arabic and French poetry, though different, are essentially equal subsets of a general category called poetry (in which each language allows poetry under its own rules of versification [339]) becomes less neutral: Arabic is an often deviating (and deviant) subset of a universal category that closely resembles French. Equivalence can be achieved only by enlarging, censoring, or transforming Arabic. As translation theorists working in postcolonial contexts have repeatedly pointed out, translation norms are also sources of discursive power, and a translator's efforts with a foreign text can be understood as a confrontation with alien usages that threaten the receiver's linguistic and cultural norms (Cheyfitz; Niranjana; Appiah, "Thick Translation"). "One does not translate between equivalents," Lydia Liu writes, "rather, one creates tropes of equivalence in the middle zone of translation between the host and guest languages" (137). By reading al-Tahtawi's tropes of equivalence closely and critically, we see that the "middle zone of translation" is not neutral and that, despite his assertions of equality, world literary space is colonized.

Al-Shidyaq: *Leg over Leg*

Al-Shidyaq displays very different ideas about equivalence in his narrative *Leg over Leg Concerning That Which Is al-Fariyaq* (الساق فيما هو الفارياق على الساق; Al-saq ʿala al-saq fi-ma huwa al-Fariyaq).[1] As he writes in an early chapter:

> In addition, I have imposed on the reader the condition that he not skip any of the "synonymous" words in this book of mine, many though they be (for it may happen that, on a single road, a herd of fifty words, all with the same meaning, or with two meanings that are close, may pass him by). If he cannot commit to this, I cannot permit him to peruse it and will not offer him my congratulations if he does so. I have to admit that I cannot support the idea that all "synonyms" have the same meaning, or they would have called them "equi-nyms."

ثم إن شرطي على القارئ أن لا يسطر شيئا من الألفاظ المترادفة في كتابي
هذا على كثرتها. فقد يتفق أن يمر به في طريق واحدة سرب خمسين لفظة
بمعنى واحد أو بمعان متقاربة. إلا فلا أجيز له مطالعته ولا أنّوه به.
على أني لا أذهب إلى أي الألفاظ المترادفة هي بمعنى واحد وإلّا لسموها
المتساوية

(1.1.7)

Al-Shidyaq points out here that the Arabic root for "synonym," *r-d-f* (ف د ر), does not connote equivalence. The verbs derived from it can mean "to pile up in layers," "to flock," or "to form a single line"—all meanings that are invoked in the image of a herd of words. The image might serve for the text as a whole, which contains extensive lists of synonyms and near synonyms, some as long as 250 words, which the author insists are not equivalents. An index to the lists appears at the end of the fourth volume and is itself eight pages long in its original printing.

Leg over Leg is equal parts travel narrative and linguistic treatise, and the link between cultural and linguistic translation is apparent at every juncture. The subtitle, "Days and Months and Years Spent in Critical Examination of the Arabs and Their Non-Arab Peers," contains wordplay that could result in a second translation—for example, "critical examination" could also be translated as the "linguistic mistakes" (عجم ; ʿujm) of the Arabs; "Non-Arab Peers" could be literally rendered as "barbarians"

(الأعجام ; al-'ajam; those whose speech is unintelligible to Arabic speakers). The complete title makes clear that al-Shidyaq and al-Tahtawi share a broad intellectual project: both authors put "leg after leg" (another alternative translation of *al-Saq 'ala al-Saq*) in order to write a critical examination of Arabs and Europeans that puts linguistic interpretation at its center.

But if al-Tahtawi compares Europe with Egypt by constructing a zone of correspondence between French and Arabic, al-Shidyaq is skeptical about the very existence of linguistic or cultural equivalence. In this respect they lie at opposite poles of translation studies. Al-Shidyaq shows an affinity to what has been called a "hermeneutic model" of translation (Venuti, "Genealogies" 6). He stresses the interpretive function of translation and notes that the interpretive role of the translator is often unreliable. He shows how translations are, as Walter Benjamin argued, "a somewhat provisional way of coming to terms with the foreignness of languages [each foreign to the other]," which can never be fully reconciled (257). For al-Shidyaq, communication in intercultural and interpersonal interactions is imperfect, hindered by misinterpretation and mistranslation. Al-Tahtawi emphasizes translation's role in facilitating communication, spreading knowledge, and creating universal categories—his model of translation is "instrumental" (Venuti, "Genealogies" 6)—whereas al-Shidyaq emphasizes the ever-present possibility that translation can create communication breakdown and spread misinformation, fracturing the world into fragments of insurmountable difference, into "untranslatables" (Apter 31–44).

Leg over Leg was published in Paris in 1855, while al-Shidyaq was employed by the Society for Promoting Christian Knowledge and living now in France, now in England. It comes between the publication of his two other travelogues, *al-Wasitah fi Ma'rifat Ahwal Malta* (1836; الواسطة في معرفة أحوال مالطة ; "Description of the Known Conditions of Malta") and *Kashf al-Mukhabba' 'an Funun Uruba* (published in 1863 but composed earlier; كشف المخبأ عن فنون أوروبا ; "Uncovering the Hidden Arts of Europe"). *Leg over Leg*, unlike these and also unlike *Extraction*, is a fictional version of his travels. Its protagonist, al-Fariyaq (a condensation of the author's given and last names, Faris al-Shidyaq), closely resembles the author, and the wife of al-Fariyaq, al-Fariyaqiyyah, closely resembles the author's wife. These characters, whose names can be translated as "he who distinguishes" and "she who distinguishes," act as cultural and linguistic interpreters for the reader.

Reading *Extraction* and *Leg over Leg* together helps make sense of al-Shidyaq's difficult text, because it is written in dialogue with travel narratives like al-Tahtawi's and makes reference to (and fun of) their conventions of representation. *Leg over Leg*'s comparisons, for example, are not often binary, not performed between the two opposite and mutually exclusive poles of France and Egypt, but instead take place among and in cities and cultural groups. The Lebanese are compared not only with the English but with the Egyptians and the Turks; in Europe, the English are compared with the French, the Parisians with the people of Marseille, Oxford residents with Cambridge residents, and so on. Each comparison, leading to another, more minute one, serves to make comparison itself difficult.

Descriptions are never allowed to settle into the stable categorizations that readers expect of travelogues. Al-Shidyaq in fact, mocks such expectations, calling the standard descriptions of travelogues, like "I saw such and such a city and beheld its wide clean streets, spacious homes, fine ships, magnificent markets, beautiful horses, wonderful women, and hosts of soldiers," nothing but "what's called in chaste Arabic prating, prattling, nonsense . . . " (قد رأيت مدينة كذا وشاهدت شوارعها النظيفة الواسعة‟ وديارها الرحيبة ومراكبها الحسنة واسواقها البهيجة وخيلها المطهمة ونساءها الرائعة وعساكرها الجرارة..فذلك كله يسمى في العربية هَذرا وهراء ... [4.1.12]). And he mocks travel writers who idealize European customs at the expense of Arab ones, listing claims similar to al-Tahtawi's in rapid succession (14) before admonishing readers that "countries with many virtues also have many vices and everyone has some fault, or indeed faults" (إن البلاد التي تكثر فيها الفضائل تكثر فيها الرذائل أيضًا [15]). By contrast, his own "Description of Cairo" chapter begins with generalizations so vague as to be comical—"Cairo is one metropolis among metropolises, one city among cities, one settlement among settlements . . . " (فأقول أنها مصر من الأمصار أو مدينة من المدن أو مَدَرة من المَدَر... [2.5.1])—but then enumerates curiosities so particular as to be representative of nothing other than the author's imagination. In the absence of stable categories, a description of Cairo is nearly impossible to render.

If students are asked to compare the translation techniques of al-Tahtawi and al-Shidyaq, they will probably observe that the general categories al-Tahtawi invokes never go unchallenged in *Leg over Leg*. In one scene of cross-cultural understanding, when al-Fariyaqiyyah witnesses an Englishman kissing an unmarried young woman in greeting, she not only questions its propriety but also rethinks the very definition of *kissing*:

Kissing among us is always accompanied by panting, sighing, sucking, smelling, and the closing of the eyes. But this fellow seems to me to be doing no more than delivering a light puff of breath, devoid of any feeling, as one might if one had no regard for the matter at hand . . . to kiss the brow, as the Franks do, is meaningless.

فإن القبلة عندنا لا تكون إلا مع زفير وتنهّد ومصّ وشمّ وتغميض العينين.
فأمّا هذا فإني أراه يزّف خلّوا من إحساس فعل المستخفّ بما تحت يده... فإن
تقبيل الجبين كما يفعل هؤلاء لا معنى له.

(3.6.3)

Such a kiss is not a kiss—it does not translate. Al-Fariyaqiyyah in effect illustrates the untranslatability that many philosophers of translation have posited as underlying all linguistic and cultural exchange (Apter; Kilito; Ricœur; Weber). For them, translation expresses not only the "innermost kinship of languages" but also the inability of humankind to attain their commensurability—that "inaccessible realm of reconciliation and fulfillment of languages" (Benjamin 255, 257). "At every moment," as Jacques Derrida writes, "translation is as necessary as it is impossible" (372). Even though al-Fariyaqiyyah's husband replies by giving her no less than seven other words in Arabic for kissing (making the total synonyms used for the word in this passage ten!), al-Fariyaqiyyah doubts that they are reconcilable. As al-Shidyaq explains, synonyms are not "equi-nyms." Resemblances can proliferate without creating equivalences.

Looking for instances of interpretation in *Leg over Leg* yields scenes, like the one above, that highlight the uncertainty of translation. Al-Fariyaq and al-Fariyaqiyyah never simply record their experiences; they also actively and sometimes lengthily decipher and debate them. This commentary can make reading the text laborious—the main characters interrupt the action in order to reflect on it, opening digressions and disquisitions on related themes—but it makes clear one of the basic assumptions of translation studies: "A translation always communicates an interpretation, a foreign text that is partial and altered" (Venuti, *Scandals* 5). Scenes of translation in *Leg over Leg* underline their partiality—for example, al-Fariyaq deliberately mistranslates poetry (4.11.3), English preachers mispronounce Arabic (2.3.2), and travel writers misinterpret song lyrics (3.3.4). "How could the English swallow everything vomited down their throats by a stranger holding a sword with tassels and buttons?" readers are asked (ازّاى يبقى
الإنكليز يبلعوا كل شى يستفرغه في حلقهم الغريب اللى عنده سيف بأزرار وحمايل

[3.3.5]). They are never under the illusion that they receive narratives, experiences, or even words as they were originally spoken. Translation, even though it is necessary, is represented as difficult, laborious, and often erroneous, so readers are warned to employ a hermeneutics of suspicion. They should not receive knowledge, even from sources that seem authoritative, uncritically.

For al-Shidyaq, translation is ultimately inseparable from claims to authority and power. His narrative asks the same questions that I ask of my students: On whose terms does another's language become available to us? On whose terms does my language become available to others? The objects of translation in many of *Leg over Leg*'s anecdotes are Arab, not European, and the interpreters are French or English (Johnson et al.). Al-Fariyaq is acutely aware of his position as an object, not a subject, of translation. Like al-Fariyaq, al-Shidyaq was ill received by orientalists; his poem praising Paris was translated and published in the journal of the Société Asiatique as a literary curiosity (4.18.11), but he was turned down for a teaching position at both Cambridge and Oxford. The closest he came to being employed as an expert in his field of Arabic literary studies was to tutor a Frenchman in Arabic. Perhaps in response, he includes an appendix of errors in Silvestre de Sacy's translation of the *Maqamat* of al-Hariri, which was corrected by two other respected French scholars of Arabic. Of Sacy's commentary (his interpretation of the *Maqamat*), al-Shidyaq simply states that the errors are "too numerous to count" (5.5.1). His scathing criticisms of European translations of Arabic speak not only to both personal disappointments but also to structural conditions of power. Al-Shidyaq disrupts their objective claims to representational authority by undermining their role as translators, by poking not-so-gentle fun at them, and by delivering direct attacks on them.

Al-Tahtawi's insistence on creating linguistic equivalence despite translation's difficulties and al-Shidyaq's skepticism toward translators form just two responses to the challenge of interpreting Europe during the *nahda*. In each is embedded an ethics of reading: one seeks common ground with the foreign, and at the same time one complicates it and even refuses it. Both texts therefore provide models for and challenges to students' own reading practices. This ethics is especially important to attend to in *nahda* texts, which students typically find a chore to read—full of commonplaces or stereotypes, unnecessarily wordy descriptions, and convoluted plots. Al-Shidyaq, anticipating this response, forbids his readers to skip over seeming redundancies. *Leg over Leg* forces students to read every word, to leave their expectations of narrative style and submit to al-Shidyaq's style. Both authors ask their readers to imagine other readers still, other styles, and other linguistic conventions. That is, they ask their readers to recognize "a summons to translation at the very threshold of all reading-writing" (Derrida 366) and to read in translation themselves. They do not merely "receive the voices of the excluded" but also recognize the many layers of interpretation—political, institutional, literary, and personal—that have intervened in order to make those voices heard.

Note

1. In my citation from the bilingual edition, the numbers given are for volume, chapter, and paragraph.

Works Cited

Abu-Lughod, Ibrahim A. *Arab Rediscovery of Europe: A Study in Cultural Encounters.* Princeton UP, 1963.

Al-Khuri, Khalil. ‏وي ... إذن لستُ بإفرنجي‎ [Wayy . . . idhan lastu bi ifranji; Alas . . . I Am Not a Foreigner]. Al-majlis Al-ʿaʿla lil-thaqafah, 2007.

Al-Nowaihi, Magda. "Unheard in English." *The MIT Electronic Journal of Middle East Studies,* vol. 4, 2004, pp. 23–29, dome.mit.edu/bitstream/handle/1721.3/177975/MITEJMES_Vol_4_Fall2004.pdf?sequence=1.

Al-Shidyaq, Ahmad Faris. *Leg over Leg; or, The Turtle in the Tree: Concerning the Fariyaq, What Manner of Creature He Might Be.* Translated by Humphrey T. Davies, New York UP, 2013–14. 4 vols.

Al-Tahtawi, Rifaʿah Rafiʿ. ‏هذه رحلة الفقير إلى الله تعالى رفاعة رافع الطهطاوي إلى‎ ‏ديار فرنسا المسماة بتخليص الابريز إلى تلخيص باريس أو الديوان النفيس بإيوان باريز‎ [Hadhihi rihlat al-faqir ila Allah Taʿala Rifaʿa Rafiʿ al-Tahtawi ila diyar Faransa al-musammat bi takhlis al-ibriz ila talkhis Bariz, aw al-diwan al-nafis bi iwan Baris; This Is the Journey of the Poor Servant of God the Exalted Rifaʿa Badawi Rafiʿ al-Tahtawi to the Provinces of France, Entitled The Extraction of Gold from a Brief Description of Paris, or the Precious Diwan on the Arcades of Paris]. Dar al-Tibaʿa al-Khidiwiyya, AH 1250 (1834). Translated as *An Imam in Paris.*

———. *An Imam in Paris: Account of a Stay in France by an Egyptian Cleric, 1826–31.* Translated by Daniel L. Newman, Saqi, 2004.

Appiah, Kwame Anthony. "Cosmopolitan Reading." *Cosmopolitan Geographies: New Locations in Literature and Culture,* edited by Vinay Dharwadker, Routledge, 2001. pp. 197–228.

———. "Thick Translation." *Callaloo,* vol. 16, no. 4, Autumn 1993, pp. 808–19.

Apter, Emily S. *Against World Literature: On the Politics of Untranslatability.* Verso Books, 2013.

Barak, On. *On Time: Technology and Temporality in Modern Egypt.* U of California P, 2013.

Benjamin, Walter. "The Task of the Translator." *Selected Writings, Volume 1: 1913–1926*, Harvard UP, 1996, pp. 253–63.

Berman, Antoine. *The Experience of the Foreign: Culture and Translation in Romantic Germany*. State U of New York P, 1992.

Cheyfitz, Eric. *The Poetics of Imperialism: Translation and Colonization from the Tempest to Tarzan*. Oxford UP, 1991.

Commission on the Humanities and Social Sciences. *The Heart of the Matter: The Humanities and Social Sciences for a Vibrant, Competitive, and Secure Nation*. American Academy of Arts and Sciences, 2013, www.humanitiescommission .org/_pdf/hss_report.pdf.

Derrida, Jacques. "What Is a 'Relevant' Translation?" Translated by Lawrence Venuti. Venuti, *Translation Studies Reader* pp. 65–88.

Dryden, John. "On Translation." *Theories of Translation: An Anthology of Essays from Dryden to Derrida*, edited by Rainer Schulte and John Biguenet, U of Chicago, 1992, pp. 17–31.

Eckermann, J. P. *Conversations with Goethe*. Edited by Hans Kohn, translated by Gisela O'Brien, Frederick Ungar Publishing, 1964.

"École Égyptienne—Retour de plusieurs des élèves dans leur patrie." *La revue encyclopédique*, vol. 48, 1830, pp. 521–23.

El-Ariss, Tarek. *Trials of Arab Modernity: Literary Affects and the New Political*. Fordham UP, 2013.

Elshakry, Marwa. *Reading Darwin in Arabic, 1860–1950*. U of Chicago P, 2013.

Even-Zohar, Itamar. "The Position of Translated Literature within the Literary Polysystem." *Poetics Today*, vol. 11, 1990, pp. 45–51.

Gibb, H. A. R. "The Egyptian Novel." *Bulletin of the School of Oriental Studies*, vol. 7, 1930, pp. 1–22.

Johnson, Rebecca Carol, et al. "*The Arabian Nights*, Arab-European Literary Influence, and the Lineages of the Novel." *Modern Language Quarterly*, vol. 68, no. 2, 2007, pp. 243–79.

Kant, Immanuel. *Kant: Political Writings*. Edited by Hans Siegbert Reiss, Cambridge UP, 1991.

Kilito, Abdelfattah. *Thou Shalt Not Speak My Language*. Translated by Waïl S. Hassan, Syracuse UP, 2008.

Liu, Lydia. *Tokens of Exchange: The Problem of Translation in Global Circulations*. Duke UP, 1999.

Moosa, Matti. *The Origins of Modern Arabic Fiction*. Lynne Reinner, 1997.

Niranjana, Tejaswini. *Siting Translation: History, Post-structuralism, and the Colonial Context*. U of California P, 1992.

Nussbaum, Martha C. *Cultivating Humanity: A Classical Defense of Reform in Liberal Education*. Harvard UP, 1997.

Rastegar, Kamran. *Literary Modernity between the Middle East and Europe: Textual Transactions in Nineteenth-Century Arabic, English, and Persian Literatures*. London: Routledge, 2007.

Renan, Ernest. *L'Islamisme et la science*. 1883. *Internet Archive*, archive.org/details/lislamismeetlas00renagoog.

Ricœur, Paul. *On Translation*. Routledge, 2006.

Salama-Carr, Myriam. "Negotiating Conflict: Rifaʿa Rafiʿ al-Tahtawi and the Translation of the 'Other' in Nineteenth-Century Egypt." *Social Semiotics*, vol. 17, no. 2, June 2007, pp. 213–27.

Sawaie, Mohammed. "Rifaʿa Rafiʿ Al-Tahtawi and His Contribution to the Lexical Development of Modern Literary Arabic." *International Journal Middle East Studies*, vol. 32, no. 3, 2000, pp. 395–410. *JSTOR*, www.jstor.org/stable/259515?seq=1#page_scan_tab_contents.

Selim, Semah. "The People's Entertainments: Translation, Popular Fiction, and the Nahdah in Egypt." *Other Renaissances: A New Approach to World Literature*, edited by Brenda Deen Schildgen et al., Palgrave Macmillan, 2006, pp. 35–58.

Sheehi, Stephen. *Foundations of Modern Arab Identity*. U of Florida P, 2004.

Sulh, ʿImad. آثاره وعصره أحمد فارس الشدياق: [Ahmad Faris al-Shidyaq: Atharuhu wa ʿasruhu; Ahmad Faris al-Shidyaq: His Work and His Period]. Beirut: Dar an-Nahar, 1980.

Tageldin, Shaden. *Disarming Words: Empire and the Seductions of Translation in Egypt*. U of California P, 2011.

———. "Proxidistant Reading: Toward a Critical Pedagogy of the Nahdah in U.S. Comparative Literary Studies." *Journal of Arabic Literature*, vol. 43, nos. 2–3, 2012, pp. 227–68.

Tomiche, Nada. "Nahdah." *The Encyclopaedia of Islam*, edited by P. J. Bearman, 2nd ed., vol. 7, Brill, 2008.

Toury, Gideon. *In Search of a Theory of Translation*. Porter Institute for Poetics and Semiotics, 1980.

Venuti, Lawrence. "Genealogies of Translation Theory: Jerome." *Boundary 2*, vol. 37, no. 3, 2010, pp. 5–28.

———. *The Scandals of Translation: Towards an Ethics of Difference*. Routledge, 1998.

———, editor. *The Translation Studies Reader*. Routledge, 2000.

———. *The Translator's Invisibility: A History of Translation*. 2nd ed., Routledge, 2008.

Weber, Samuel. *Benjamin's -abilities*. Harvard UP, 2008.

Maya Kesrouany

The Joke's on Me: Teaching
Emile Habiby's *The Pessoptimist*
in Translation

> *I am acquainted with the Western tradition of satire from Boccac-*
> *cio to Mark Twain . . . the tradition of irony and sarcasm in al-*
> *Mutanabbi, and* The Arabian Nights. . . . *I also like Voltaire very*
> *much, to the degree I feel his direct influence on me and my writing.*

> —Emile Habiby

Emile Habiby's 1974 novel الوقائع الغريبة في اختفاء سعيد أبي النحس المتشائل
(Al-Waqaʾiʿ al-gharibah fi ikhtifaʾ Saʿid Abi Al-Naḥs Al-mutashaʾil; *The Se-*
cret Life of Saeed the Ill-Fated Pessoptimist, translated by Salma Khadra Jayyusi and Trevor LeGassick in 1985) presents several challenges in a world
literature classroom, even when most of the students are native Arabic
speakers. The novel engages a history of cultural as well as military occupation and interlaces it with the tragic reality of nonreturn in the context of
Palestine. The main themes of the novel are interrelated with its complex
formal texture, which incorporates references to classical Arabic literature
and modern Arabic poetry as well as Hebrew literature; appropriates the
French novel *Candide*; and implicitly rewrites the *maqama* (مقامة), best
defined as "a prose genre in Arabic literature combining verbal virtuosity
with a picaresque portrayal of society" (Allen, *Arabic Novel* 11). Lital Levy

118

describes how the novel "symbolically invert[s] discursive power through deliberate moments of communicative slippage that result from mistranslation and misinterpretation," relating such inversion directly to bilingual wordplay between Hebrew and Arabic (108–09, 115). As Jonathan Scott puts it, "Habiby's singular style, crystallized in his choice of form and structure, is always conscious of the translation issue" (114).

I have taught this novel in translation in postcolonial and world literature classes at the American University of Beirut and the American University of Sharjah, mainly to native Arabic speakers who have some familiarity with Arabic literature from their high school education. In all these courses, I have treated the difficulties of Habiby's novel paradigmatically as a problem of translation. In this essay, I address three attributes of the novel that could frame class discussions in relation to translation. On the formal level, the novel is made up of forty-five vignettes (letters) addressed by Saeed to an anonymous person, who communicates their content to the readers. Thus the novel relies on frame narration, underlining the theme of witnessing, and it engages the *Arabian Nights* (referenced repeatedly), the *maqama*, and the hadith. It interrogates transmission in its main character, the fool and spy, a figure who combines the comic character of the *maqama* as well as the literature of al-Jahiz, who wrote on such diverse comic topics as donkeys, fools, and penny-pinchers, most notably in his كتاب البخلاء (Kitab al-bukhala'; "Book of Misers").

The Pessoptimist also speaks to the French novel, explicitly in its reference to *Candide* (a whole chapter is dedicated to it) and implicitly in its response to the obsession of the *nahda* (نهضة; "Arab Renaissance") with the translation of French sentimental, Romantic, and realist novels. During the *nahda* there were several enthusiastic waves of translation of Western literature into Arabic. The first wave features a preoccupation with didactic literature, as exemplified by Rifa'ah Rafi' al-Tahtawi's translation of *Les aventures de Télémaque* ("The Adventures of Telemachus"); the second involves entertainment and detective fiction; and the third shows a remarkable investment in the imitation of realist, Romantic, and modernist styles, as represented by Ahmad Hassan al-Zayyat's translation of Goethe's *Werther*. For this reason I have found it useful, in teaching Habiby's novel, to assign parts of critical works on the *nahda* by Taha Badr, Sabry Hafez ("Transformation"), and Yusuf Najm. The *nahdawi* writers and translators were particularly interested in the bildungsroman. *The Pessoptimist* comically rewrites that account of teleological development by making its hero a fool and inserting him into a narrative that does not progress toward any resolution. Because the return to the homeland remains impossible, the only way out of the endless cycle of occupation is to resort to a man from outer space. As a failed bildungsroman, *The Pessoptimist* parodies the inheritance of a European novel form that deals with the maturation of a character in a strictly Western frame of progress.

The Pessoptimist converses both with classical Arabic narrative and with the *nahdawi* translation of European literature, and it sees translation, on the levels of form and content, as ultimately impossible: in form, there can be no encounter between the European novel and the *maqama* in occupied Palestine; in content, literary and cultural references cannot be rendered. The novel makes impossible translation the condition of return: authentic representation of a foreign text is as impossible as a return to a preoccupation Palestine. This is not to say that literature is fundamentally untranslatable; rather, the complexities of the translation process are emphasized. To read what is lost in translation helps us understand the modern Arabic novel in relation to both its Western counterpart and its classical inheritance. Habiby empties classical forms into the modern novel and mocks the premise of the bildungsroman, but he also displays a paradoxical desire for an absent original in the names of his female characters, Yuaad and Baqiyya, as well as in the return of similarly named characters, the second Saeed and the second Yuaad.

Reading *The Pessoptimist* together with nineteenth-century texts uses translation to expose students to the difficult inheritance of the modern Arabic novel, drawing together the complexities of old and new. This novel is a particularly vibrant example of interaction with older traditions, because it builds on the figure of the comic character in traditional Arabic storytelling, uses references to Arabic poetry, and narrates the story of two impossible dreams of return: the first to a virgin, unoccupied homeland; the second to a tradition of Arabic narrative untainted by the European novel.

I frame the discussion of the untranslatable by having my students read selections from Paul de Man, Jacques Derrida, and Emily Apter. Then I discuss the names of the female characters and connect them to the impossibility of translation as a correlative of the impossibility of return. Then I take up the novel's relation to *Candide*. Finally I address Habiby's rewriting of the *maqama* as stunted bildungsroman in an effort to produce a more authentic Palestinian novel.

The Untranslatable

Walter Benjamin saw the translated text as a separate entity that has as much claim to meaning as the original. I give my students brief excerpts from de Man's "Conclusions" and Derrida's "Des Tours de Babel," two different readings of Benjamin's essay "The Task of the Translator." I introduce the general ideas behind deconstruction and their relevance to the project of Habiby in *The Pessoptimist*. De Man staunchly argues against approaching meaning as fixed and instead emphasizes the randomness of signification in all languages. Translations, both literal and for sense, fail to produce meaning as categorical and unified. Literal translation assumes that what is said in one language can easily be said in another, since all languages reflect objective meanings that exist in the world outside language. Translation for sense implies that all languages can produce a meaning, just in different ways. In either case, a translation fails when it cannot convey a meaning that was always there in the original (36).

In Derrida's reading of Benjamin's essay, the task of translation is an ethical imperative: both a debt and a responsibility to the other. Like de Man, Derrida recognizes that the translation points to a failure in the original, because the original "was not there without fault . . . complete . . . and identical to itself" (222). The translation leaves the original intact and presents itself as original in its own right.

In teaching Habiby's novel in translation and as a text that repeatedly invokes various forms of translation, I find that de Man and Derrida help in setting up the original novel's difference from its translation. I remind the students of the novel's use of *Candide*, the *Arabian Nights*, the *maqama*, and the bildungsroman and of how some of those resonances are lost in the English translation and can be retrieved only by remembering that the Arabic and the English texts are both originals. The Arabic text owes a debt to a history of translation that violently imposes the modern as teleological progress on Arabic narrative. *The Pessoptimist* remembers that story of translation and bears traces of it in the loss, in English, of some of the original cultural references. If the *maqama* is a parody of the hadith, then *The Pessoptimist* is pastiche at best, having no singular original to parody. Roger Allen has shown how the length of the novel's title and its wordplay are reminiscent of both the *maqama* and the *saj'* (Allen, "Intertextuality" 5–6).

My discussion of the untranslatable in the novel is also informed by the arguments in Apter's recent book *Against World Literature: On the*

Politics of Untranslatability (2013), whose "aim is to activate untranslatability as a theoretical fulcrum . . . with bearing on approaches to world literatures." I refer to the untranslatable in the many senses that Apter lists: "'lost in translation,' the mistranslated, unreliable translation and the contresens, an impassive condition that would seem to nest in language; sometimes discernible as a pull away from language norming" (introduction). The English translation suffers from loss, errors, and "contresens" despite being very accurate. One example I use is from chapter 19: the repetition of the sequential *fa-* in front of verbs (،فابتعدت عني، فتشبثت بها ففرت إلى غرفتي، فوقعنا على السرير ... فسمعنا...فانخلع ضلعي...فاغلقت الباب [78]).[1] The point is for the students to understand that the English text should not be taken as a replication of the original, that each benefits from being treated as a separate entity, especially when Habiby uses translation as a paradigm to represent Arabic literary history.

Apter's category of the untranslatable is set up not "as pure difference in opposition to the always translatable" but "as a linguistic form of creative failure," and it can "come off as non-sense" (ch. 1). The ramifications of this definition for teaching *The Pessoptimist* are enormous because the untranslatable also becomes tied up with the politics of occupation. The violence of the occupation is an ineffable but powerful presence in the story of the Palestinians, located in Habiby's text in the ways that its language testifies to cultural and military imperialism in the twentieth century. In class we discuss the untranslatable in particular moments of loss between the original and the English text but also on a larger formal level, by focusing on the names of the women in nontranslation and by comparing the novel with the traditional *maqama* and contextualizing its self-presentation as a failed bildungsroman.

Naming the Untranslatable

The names of the novel's female characters, which remain untranslated in English, Yuaad, Baqiyya, and the second Yuaad, are intertwined with the fantasy of return. The female becomes a metonymic extension of the land: she does not metaphorically replace it, according to the logic of a faithful translation, but becomes annexed to it, according to the logic of the untranslatable. Peter Heath has similarly described the names as symbols (63). I urge my students to go through the sections where the women are named and described in relation to occupied Palestine and to focus on their presentation and representation as constitutive of the impossibility of return. I supplement the discussion with a brief excerpt from Fredric Jameson's *Postmodernism* on parody and pastiche and argue that although the novel seems to be parodying other forms, it is better described as pastiche, given the absence of an original text, just as the original land is absent, to be parodied (Heath 167).

The name of the first woman, Yuaad, Saeed's first love, means "to be repeated" or "to be returned." Baqiyya, his second love, means "she who has remained." The second Yuaad, daughter of the first, is a brave woman who sneaks into Israel in search of her brother. The women's names are not translated, but their meanings are given in English, because the translation includes the explanations that appear in the original. Saeed falls in love with the first Yuaad in Mandatory Palestine; Israeli soldiers forcibly evict her in 1948, condemning her to a life in diaspora; she gives birth to the second Yuaad and a son, whom she names Saeed and who is a heroic resistance fighter; the first Saeed meets this second Saeed in an Israeli prison after the defeat of 1967.

Baqiyya, who remains in Israel after 1948, gives birth to Saeed's only son, Walaa, which means "loyalty" or "fidelity," and Walaa becomes a *fida'i* (فدائي ; "freedom fighter before 1967"). Baqiyya is in possession of a secret treasure that her father left her near the shores of Tanturiyya, where she is from. Before we learn her actual name, she is referred to as the Tanturiyya, the woman from that town, and, much like Yuaad, she becomes a metonymic extension of the land. Walaa retrieves the treasure and uses it to fund his fight against the Israelis. He and his mother are eventually discovered and surrounded by the Israeli army, and they disappear into the sea.

The motif of impossible return is played out in the names of characters. Jacob, an Israeli who was formerly Saeed's guardian, asks Saeed, "If you are innocent, why was it 'Yuaad' you loved, 'Baqiyya' you married, and 'Walaa' you had as a son? All these names are highly suspect to the state" (Habiby, *Secret Life* 122; ويستعيد الرجل الكبير أصلك وفصلك أدلة على أنك تتغابى ولكنك لست بغبي. فلماذا لم تعشق سوى يعاد ولم تتزوج سوى باقية ولم تنجب سوى ولاء؟ ([Al-Waqa'i' 158]). When in jail, Saeed jokingly quotes Shakespeare in his attempt to placate the Israeli guards with humor, saying, "'What's in a name?' as Shakespeare put it" (124; وما يهم الاسم' كما قال شكسبير ؟ وقلتها بالإنجليزية. [160]).

The female characters embody this logic of naming in which they become metonymic extensions of the land and are erased in that metonymy, made to disappear as if they were never there, much like occupied

Palestine. For instance, Baqiyya is originally referred to as Tanturiyya, after the village she comes from. She shares her secret of a hidden treasure with Saeed and their son, Walaa, and in the final scene of the second part of the book, she and Walaa disappear into the sea.

The first Yuaad is described as an open wound when in chapter 20 she is associated with a "repeated promise of [her] return" (65). In the Arabic, the line reads: إحياء الوعد بعودة يعاد (ihya' al-wa'd bi 'awdat yu'ad [32]). Metonymically connected to the fantasy of a Palestine before its occupation, she embodies an empty repetition: as often as she returns, she will continue to be exiled; as long as she is exiled, she will be compelled to return. The doubling of her character and Saeed's in chapter 38 (133) suggests a faint promise of liberation from this tyranny of the logic of naming.

When Saeed and the second Yuaad escape and are on the run from the Israelis, they end up in a little town that also bears a secret, that of harboring a refugee. Yuaad explains to Saeed where they are:

> She told me we were in the village of Salakah, in the plain. This name is not on the map, not because it has ceased to exist, although this does happen, but because it never existed. The fact is that I invented this name for the village that gave us shelter to preserve its curious secret which, although known to many, has been kept from the authorities for twenty years. (139)

> فأخبرتني بأننا في قرية 'السلكة' المرجية. وهذا الاسم غير ظاهر على الخارطة لا لأنه زال من الوجود، ومثل هذا الأمر موجود، بل لأنه غير موجود. فقد استعرت لهذه القرية، التي آوتنا، اسم السلكة، أم سليك بن السلكة، الذي 'طاف يبغي نجوة/ من هلاك فهلك/ فالمنايا رصد/ للفتى حيث سلك'، وذلك حفاظاً على سر هذه القرية العجيب.
> (183)

Saeed's secret of the aliens, Baqiyya's secret of the treasure, and the village's secret are all connected to the theme of the untranslatable name. The village's name, according to the translator's note, refers to al-Sulaik ibn al-Sulkah, "a pre-Islamic vagabond poet famous for the quickness of foot and thorough knowledge of the Arabian terrain that enabled him to evade capture by the authorities" (169). That Salakah could have never existed, poetic as its name is, points to the loss of an origin, which is a familiar condition in Palestine and does not come as a shock to the student. But it is interesting that a name erases the thing to which it points: Yuaad is an always failed promise of return, Baqiyya does not remain but disappears into the sea, and the second Yuaad is driven into exile. I refer my students to chapter 43, in which Saeed awaits a third Yuaad, after wanting to marry the second, so he could start over. This ironic reference to a pure beginning, a blissful state that he never really had with the first Yuaad, is telling of the cyclical nature of this narrative and of the futility of return.

Saeed and Candide

The untranslatable also manifests in the novel's chapter on *Candide, ou l'optimisme* (1759; "Candide; or, Optimism"). The title of *Pessoptimist* clearly rewrites the French title, reinscribing the optimist in Palestinian history. I explain to my students the differences and similarities between the two texts. *The Pessoptimist*, like *Candide*, has three parts and politically motivated vignettes that respond to historical events, such as the Nakba (النكبة) of 1948, for Habiby, and the Seven Years' War (1754–63), for Voltaire. Ahmad Harb's detailed comparison of the two works is helpful in thinking through which sections to present in the classroom. Both novels reject optimism: *Candide* concludes that "we must cultivate our garden," having rejected the Leibnizian belief that "all is for the best in the best of all possible worlds" (88); *The Pessoptimist* insists that under occupation there is no garden to cultivate. It rewrites Voltaire's novel by using multiple narrative voices (first and third) and having its main narrator speak from an alien space that radically disables any notion of development.

Habiby reworks Candide's optimism into a contextualized sense of coping, wherein good is only good insofar as it is not the worst-case scenario. Chapter 22 of the translation is entitled "The Unique Resemblance between Candide and Saeed." Saeed declares that life has not changed much since the time of Candide, except that now El Dorado exists on this planet (72 in the translation; 95 in the Arabic), sarcastically pointing to the parallel between the vengeful war of retaliation (mostly through rape and murder) on the people of Abares by the Bulgarians (chapter 2 of *Candide*) and Israel's response to the September 1972 attacks on Israeli athletes in Munich by attacking women and children in refugee camps in Syria and Lebanon. (I generally focus on the connections the novel makes between the two events and refer students to several accounts of Operation Wrath of God and its representation in the media and film, noting that many aspects of it are not known, but that it took place from 1972 to 1988 and so overlapped with the invasion of Lebanon in 1982. I refer them to Klein.) Candide describes a horrific battle in detail to emphasize the disproportionate and excessive use of violence, and Saeed uses the description to make his point in this chapter.

The alternation between first- and third-person narrative in Habiby's novel, according to Harb,

> raises the possibility that *Sa'eed the Pessoptimist*, unlike *Candide*, is a novel of intention rather than realization, for the protagonist is not involved in a process of development or realization. Neither his age (he is an old man), nor the "above-the-ground" narrative position . . . makes such involvement possible, and therefore the theme of realization is rendered impossible in Habiby's novel. (99)

Saeed speaks from above the earth while pointing earthward to El Dorado, but the reality of El Dorado, like that of Salakah, remains uncertain. Maher Jarrar believes that Habiby is presenting Israel sardonically as El Dorado (21). Harb writes that "Sa'eed . . . combines the naiveté of Candide, the foolish optimism of Pangloss, and the deep pessimism of Martin." This combination makes possible the "metaphorization of [his] character rather than his development as might be grounded in its own reality" as representative of the life of Arab Israelis (100). This interpretation works well with 'Attiya's reading of the novel as a political treatise that fully documents the lives of Arabs in the state of Israel since 1948 (198–99).

At the end of chapter 22, the man from outer space asks Saeed to explain the basic difference between himself and Candide, and Saeed answers that whereas Candide used to insist that all is well with the world, Saeed cannot "so much as raise a groan" of complaint (75; أما أنا فحتى الأنين لم يكن متيسراً لي [99]), and the next chapter is entitled "Saeed Changes into a Cat That Meows" (76; كيف تحول سعيد إلى هرة تموء [100]). Because of the burden of his secret affiliation with the men from outer space, Saeed can speak only from a place of disappearing and in a pessoptimistic voice.

I introduce my students to the bildungsroman and describe its popularity in the Arab world during the *nahda*. I encourage them to read Boutros Hallaq's study of the Arabic bildungsroman. We discuss the interesting interaction between the *maqama* and the bildungsroman during the Arabic literary renaissance and contextualize the stunted growth of Saeed in the rewriting of *Candide* as well as in the rewriting of the *maqama*. I point out the significant movement of translation of European literature into Arabic during the *nahda* and devote time to al-Tahtawi's translation (1867) of François Fénelon's *Les aventures de Télémaque* (1699). As *Candide* itself is a parody of Fénelon, this connection is especially important. By bringing together the *maqama* and the bildungsroman, Habiby produces an untranslatable form that circumvents the progressive narrative of the European novel and grounds it in the particular Palestinian aesthetic of nonreturn.

Recycling the *Maqama*: Appropriating the Novel

The correlation between the colonial enterprise of the novel form as representative of a superior European culture and the colonial occupation of Palestine is anchored in the untranslatable. After concluding the class discussion on the reuse of Voltaire's *Candide* and its relevance to the context of occupied Palestine, I discuss the role that the translation of European literature played in establishing a national identity for the intellectual elite of Egypt, Greater Syria, and Palestine. I direct students to supplementary readings (e.g., Badr; Hafez, *Genesis*; and Najm), then explain the formal attributes of the *maqama* with brief reference to its history and development. We focus on specific moments in *The Pessoptimist* that recall the *maqama* and on the ways in which the novel rewrites it.

In the tradition of the *maqama*, *The Pessoptimist* relies on frame narration. The first chapter of the novel opens with a third-person narrator explaining that Saeed has written to him, asking him to "please tell [his] story" (3). The Arabic is كتب إلي سعيد أبو النحس المتشائل ، قال (13). This framing device, with the verbs "to write" and "to say or tell," is a staple of the *maqama*. I direct students unfamiliar with *maqama* traditions to readings (e.g., Beeston; Omri; and Stewart). I give them excerpts from al-Hamadhani's *Maqamat* to emphasize the significance of the form as a mode of parody in Arabic narrative, using W. J. Prendergast's translation *The Maqámát of Badí' al-Zamán al-Hamadhání*. I ask them to consider James Monroe's comment in relation to their readings:

> The whole point in this extravagant diction is that it serves to draw attention to an ironic contrast, on the linguistic level, between what is being said by the characters, and what is being done by them . . . the many allusions to the Koran and the Hadith [being] perverse, inasmuch as a holy text is being invoked in support of deceitful practices. (96)

Framing distances the narrator from Saeed and us and from the novel; it is a means of questioning realistic representation in fiction. Since the novel is preoccupied with issues of witnessing (after all, Saeed is a spy), the framing device adds to the uncertainty of the account. The episodic quality of the novel makes it difficult for the reader to create a teleological narrative.

According to Allen, Habiby's work "evokes the maqama at almost every turn, not least in its use of irony and humor, but without actually imitating it" (qtd. in Abisaab 1). Habiby is not imitating the *maqama* but referencing it, and the result is a clever pastiche that brings together the *maqama* and the French novel to make a stunted bildungsroman. Thus even before the novel is translated into English, it is already recycling and rehashing its origins.

Instead of trying to make sense of the events of the novel, it's more productive for the reader to understand the discontinuity in the telling of the tale as formative of the content. I bring up Muhammad al-Muwaylihi's *Hadith 'Isa ibn Hisham* (حديث عيسى بن هشام), translated by Allen as *A Period of Time*. In *The Arabic Novel*, Allen writes, "Sa'id's claim to have encountered extra-terrestrial beings sets up precisely the same narrative-distancing based on either time or space which had been used as a device by , , , al-Muwaylihi" (67). We discuss primarily the opening pages of the *Hadith* and the grave scene as a statement on the discontinuity of linear time: the text literally speaks from the grave, thus challenging the tyranny of linear novelistic time (Allen, *Period* 50–58). *Hadith* foregrounds the conflict between the Islamic worldview and the concept of modern time. Anshuman A. Mondal's "Between Turban and Tarbush" can be assigned as supplemental reading on this issue. In showing my students the similarities between *Hadith* and *The Pessoptimist*, I demonstrate the significance of the *maqama* form in resisting the imposition of the novel on Arabic narrative. Mohamed-Salah Omri categorizes *The Pessoptimist* as an implied *maqama*, which involves a "defamiliarization of the Western novel" that promises "resistance" and "mediation" (255). Rula Jurdi Abisaab finds this *maqama*esque resistance in the inadequate translation of ثيابي الباطنية (thiyabi al-batiniya) as "underwear," erasing the meaning of باطن (batin; "what is hidden from sight") and therefore the secret of Saeed's resistance (4).

Habiby's major contribution in recycling the *maqama* is to create a cyclical rather than progressive account. Saeed identifies 1948 as the time when his life became stunted. In chapter 14, he "takes refuge in a footnote" (سعيد يلتجئ لأول مرة إلى الحواشي). The footnote, standing outside the text, destroys the inside of the frame tale: "You used to assure us, honored sir, that history, when it repeats itself, does not reproduce itself precisely. If the first occurrence were tragedy, the second would be farce" (وحيث أنكم كنتم تؤكدون لنا، يا محترم، إن التاريخ حين يكرر واقعة، لا يعود على 44; نفسه بل تكون الواقعة الأولى مأساة حتى إذا تكررت كانت مهزلة، فإني أسألكم: وأيهما المأساة، وأيهما المهزلة؟ [58]). The footnote interrupts the story to point to

11 December 1948, "that unforgettable date [that] marked both the end and the beginning of successive eras of my life" (53; فأنا لا أنسى هذا التاريخ الذي أصبحت، فيما بعد، أؤرخ به حياتي ما قبل وما بعد [69]). The cyclical repetition of historical events and the thwarting of the movement of time become inextricable from the recycling of the *maqama* in the bildungsroman, turning the bildungsroman into a farce, a consequence of empty repetition. The footnote is an empty commentary outside the time of the novel (بأن التاريخ عندما يعيد نفسه يعيدها متقدماً أماماً [60]; "When history repeats itself, he repeats her moving forward" [my trans.]), and the only progress made here is made outside of the time of any possible resolution.

Habiby's novel embodies the untranslatable in a world literature classroom, materializing Apter's insistence on complicating the comparative gesture. By successfully reinscribing the *maqama* in the bildungsroman and placing this reinscription in an occupied Palestine, *The Pessoptimist* represents a characteristically Palestinian aesthetic that enriches students' comprehension of both Arabic literature and the political present of Palestine. The novel does not offer a utopian resolution at the end: Saeed disappears, and we get his account after the fact. However, from that position of distance, the novel leaves the reader hanging precisely in that truly alienating comparative gesture, and no comforting return home is promised.

Note

1. In Arabic, *fa-* affixed to the beginning of a verb signals a relation of sequence and causality, so that one action is the next one or an inevitable result of the preceding verb.

Works Cited

Abisaab, Rula Jurdi. "*The Pessoptimist*: Breaching the State's Da'wâ in a Fated Narrative of Secrets." *Edebiyat*, vol. 13, no. 1, 2002, pp. 1–10.

Al-Hamadhani, Badi' al-Zaman. *The Maqámát of Badi' al-Zaman al-Hamadhani: Translated from the Arabic with an Introduction and Notes, Historical and Grammatical*. 1915. Translated by W. J. Prendergast, Routledge, 2015.

Allen, Roger. *The Arabic Novel: An Historical and Critical Introduction*. Syracuse UP, 1982.

———. "Intertextuality and Retrospect: Arabic Fiction's Relationship with Its Past." *Intertextuality in Modern Arabic Literature since 1967*, edited by Luc Deheuvels and Barbara Michalak-Pikulska, Manchester UP, 2010, pp. 1–12.

———. *A Period of Time: A Study and Translation of Hadith 'Isa ibn Hisham by Muhammad al-Muwaylihi*. Ithaca Press, 1992.

Apter, Emily S. *Against World Literature: On the Politics of Untranslatability.* London: Verso, 2013. E-book.

'Attiya, Ahmad Muhammad. الرواية السياسية العربية الرواية في دراسة :السياسية الرواية [al-Riwaya al-siyasiyya—dirasa fi al-riwaya al-siyasiya al-arabiya; The Political Novel: A Study in the Arab Political Novel]. Maktabat Madbuli, 1981.

Badr, 'Abd al-Muhsin Taha. (۱۸۷۰ ـ ۱۹۳۸) مصر في الحديثة العربية الرواية تطور [Tatawwur al-riwaya al-'Arabiya al-hadithah fi Misr, 1870–1938; The Development of the Modern Arabic Novel in Egypt, 1870–1938]. Dar al-Ma'arif, 1963.

Beeston, Alfred F. L. "Al-Hamadhani, al-Hariri, and the *Maqamat* Genre." *'Abbasid Belles-Lettres*, edited by Julia Ashtiani et al., Cambridge UP, 1990, pp. 125–36.

Benjamin, Walter. "The Task of the Translator." *Illuminations*, translated by Harry Zorn, Pimlico, 1999, pp. 70–82.

de Man, Paul. "Conclusions: Walter Benjamin's 'The Task of the Translator.'" *Yale French Studies*, vol. 69, 1985, pp. 25–46. Messenger Lecture at Cornell U, 4 March 1983.

Derrida, Jacques. "Des Tours de Babel." 1985. *Acts of Religion*, edited by Gil Anidjar, Routledge, 2002, pp. 102–34.

Habiby, Emile. المتشائل النحس أبي سعيد اختفاء في الغريبة الوقائع [Al-Waqa'i' al-gharibah fi ikhtifa' Sa'id Abi Al-Nahs Al-mutasha'il]. Dar ibn Khaldun, 1974. Translated as *The Secret Life of Saeed, the Ill-Fated Pessoptimist.*

———. *The Secret Life of Saeed, the Ill-Fated Pessoptimist.* Translated by Salma Jayyusi and Trevor LeGassick, ARRIS Publishing, 2003.

Hafez, Sabry. *The Genesis of Arabic Narrative Discourse: A Study in the Sociology of Modern Arabic Literature.* Saqi Books, 1993.

———. "The Transformation of Reality and the Arabic Novel's Artistic Response." *Bulletin of the School of Oriental and African Studies*, vol. 57, no.1, 1994, pp. 93–112.

Hallaq, Boutros. "Bildungsroman, Individual and Society." *Sensibilities of the Islamic Mediterranean: Self-Expression in a Muslim Culture from Post-classical Times to the Present Day*, edited by Robin Ostle, IB Tauris, 2008, pp.149–62.

Harb, Ahmad. "Invisibility, Impossibility: The Reuse of Voltaire's *Candide* in Emile Habiby's *Sa'eed the Pessoptimist.*" *Arab Studies Quarterly*, vol. 32, no. 2, 2010, pp. 92–106.

Heath, Peter. "Creativity in the Novels of Emile Habiby with Special Reference to *Sa'id the Pessoptimist.*" *Tradition, Modernity, and Postmodernity in Arabic Literature: Essays in Honor of Professor Issa J. Boullata*, edited by Kamal Abdel-Malek and Wael B. Hallaq, Cambridge UP, 2000, pp. 158–72.

Jameson, Fredric. "The Cultural Logic of Late Capitalism." *Postmodernism: or, The Logic of Late Capitalism*, Duke UP, 1990, pp. 1–54.

Jarrar, Maher. "A Narration of 'Deterritorialization': Imil Habibi's *The Pessoptimist.*" *Middle Eastern Literatures*, vol. 5, no. 1, 2002, pp. 15–28.

Klein, Aaron J. *Striking Back: The 1972 Munich Olympics Massacre and Israel's Deadly Response.* Random House, 2005.

Levy, Lital. *Poetic Trespass: Writing between Hebrew and Arabic in Israel/Palestine.* Princeton UP, 2014.

Mondal, Anshuman A. "Between Turban and Tarbush: Modernity and the Anxieties of Transition in Hadith 'Isa ibn Hisham." *Alif: Journal of Comparative Poetics*, 1997, pp. 201–21.

Monroe, James. *The Art of Badi' az-Zaman al-Hamadhani as Picaresque Narrative*. American U of Beirut P, 1983.

Najm, Muhammad Yusuf. (١٩١٤ ـ ١٨٧٠) الحديث العربي الأدب في القصة [Al-qissa fi al-adab al-'arabi al-hadith, 1870–1914; The Story in Modern Arabic Literature, 1870–1914]. Al-Maktaba al-Ahliya, 1961.

Omri, Mohamed-Salah. "Local Narrative Form and Constructions of the Arabic Novel." *Novel: A Forum on Fiction*, vol. 41, nos. 2–3, Spring-Summer 2008, pp. 244 –63.

Scott, Jonathan. "The Miracle of Emile Habiby's *Pessoptimist*." *College Literature*, vol. 37, no. 1, 2010, pp. 110–28.

Stewart, Devin. "*Maqama*." *The Cambridge History of Arabic Literature in the Post-classical period*, edited by Roger Allen and D. S. Richards, Cambridge UP, 2006, pp. 145–58.

Voltaire. Candide *and Other Stories*. Translated by Roger Pearson, Oxford UP, 2006.

Rula Jurdi

Arabic Poetics through a Canonical Translation: Teaching Tayeb Salih's *Season of Migration to the North*

Readers and critics continue to be drawn to Arabic novels' exploration of colonial legacies, all the more so as the realities of American imperial politics today in Arab African and Middle Eastern societies echo those legacies. How the novels move into English translation is also deeply shaped by politics, history, and current events. My decision to teach Tayeb Salih's *Season of Migration to the North* as part of two courses, Literature as History at Skidmore College (1996–98) and The Middle East through Literature at the University of Akron (1998–2004), was undeniably influenced by this context. Both courses were offered in history departments, although my training, multidisciplinary, was in anthropology and modern Arabic literature as well as in history. Therefore I needed to explain in historical terms why I was basing my courses entirely on modern Arabic and Iranian novels, short stories, and poetry. In this essay, I discuss some of my motivations and techniques for teaching Salih's text.

The Courses

"Literature as History" is an arguably reductionist course title. Throughout the course, I worked to deconstruct its title and also problematize the study of Arabic fiction in translation so that students would be able to treat these works as new spaces for exploring the artistic production of modern Arab societies. In this way, *Season of Migration to the North* was not a supplement to a historical narrative or text but rather an alternative to it. My hope was to provide an approach to the Middle East and the Arab world that was radically different from what was offered by a standard survey textbook in Middle East history. I wanted to give students an intimate experience of the creative labor that goes into the production of Arabic fiction, an experience that would take them to uncomfortable and ambiguous spaces, which many historical texts do not. I did not want to provide them with either coherent summaries of what happened or tidy answers about the major achievements and upheavals of the twentieth century.

I also hoped that an appreciation of *Season of Migration*'s artistry would in and of itself decenter orientalist and colonial narratives about Third World literature. If students could appreciate the distinct literary allusions and symbolism of this work of fiction, I believed, they might better understand its African Arab writer and creator. Teaching the novel in this way for me was a path toward normalizing Arab novelists and demonstrating their creative brilliance as on par with that of their American and European counterparts. I employed a set of methodological tools that allowed undergraduate students to appreciate the deeper artistic texture of this novel and what lies in the shadows of its factual, historical data.

In both courses I faced the challenge of how to make the point that no novel can function as a guide to understanding encounters or clashes between East and West, not even a novel, like *Season of Migration*, that has been lauded for its attention to a violent series of East-West encounters (Amyuni; Hassan, "Gender" and *Tayeb Salih*). The classroom exercises I designed therefore aimed to show that Salih's novel offers multifaceted insights into British colonialism in Sudan. In addition, I developed a set of interventions to help the students explore the poetics of this novel in translation.

Poetics through Unequal Languages

The classroom dynamic in both my courses recalled the famous debate between Fredric Jameson and Aijaz Ahmad over Third World literature. As Michelle Hartman discusses in the introduction to this volume, the terms of that debate often spark students' attention: Must all Third World literature be a national allegory? If the main literary value of the Arabic novel is as a national allegory, according to Jameson, *Season of Migration* is precisely the kind of text he had in mind (81–86). Certainly, a vast array of historians, political scientists, and other Middle Eastern studies scholars use this novel to explain the displacements and violence caused by colonialism and the encounter between colonized and colonizer (Abdul Jabbar; Davidson; El-Enany; Elsheshtawy; Geesey). My course presented this view but also deployed theoretical issues, methods, and tools in class to destabilize the idea that this Arabic novel should be understood primarily as either a national allegory or a political commentary.

I drew a parallel between literary and cultural translation, which sees a novel as an ethnography of a society, groups, and individuals (Hammersley 50–51). Cultural translation is not uncontroversial in the teaching of Arabic literature in English; many contributors to this volume seek to unseat it. Thus I explained to my students that ethnography is not merely a correct representation of social reality but also a critical representation of it, shaped by the ethnographer's experiences and sensibilities. Ethnography can embody many different ways describing a society. I drew on Grant Banfield's Marxist conceptualization of critical ethnography as something that changes the world instead of just interpreting it (62).

In establishing the course's parameters, I resisted the dichotomy between politics and poetics, by refining the meaning of *political* and by emphasizing the unique and complex relation between Salih, the novelist, and the Arabic postcolonial literary tradition. We examined the techniques that Salih uses in depicting his female characters, especially Bint Majzoub and Hasna, which opened up new questions about his gender politics and his challenges to the topoi of love and manhood in classical Arabic literature. Students were encouraged to think in new ways about gendered colonial constructions in African Arab societies. In this essay, I focus on a more complex example of the poetic and aesthetic world of موسم الهجرة الى الشمال (Mawsim al-hijra ila al-shamal; *Season of Migration to the North*): the exploration of the themes of *'udhri* (عذري) poetry (love poetry), Sufi, and carnal love and how Salih weaves them into his novel along with classical Arabic poetry and literature.

To teach these issues in a United States classroom, I had to decide how to handle the novel as a translated text. By the late 1990s, *Season of Migration to the North* had become one of a very few canonical works of Arabic fiction regularly taught in English translation. I decided to delve into the translation choices made by Denys Johnson-Davies, not to criticize or undermine them but to imagine alternative ones. Although Johnson-Davies's well-respected translation clearly has allowed students to appreciate some of the aesthetic qualities of the original work, I supplemented it with my own elaborations and alterations, and these were discussed in class. I used an Arabic proverb that was omitted from the published translation to help students see some of the subtle classical and colloquial aspects of the novel.

Translating Language versus Translating Culture: Fiction and Anthropology

As a poet and historian who also studied anthropology, I encouraged my students to explore how the translation of Salih's novel intersected with ethnography. At the same time I was cautious about this approach, aware that the knowledge we gain through reading literature in this way can be problematic and because there are other lenses through which a society can be viewed. But Rachel Newcomb, an anthropologist and novelist, writes:

> Novels can be useful in teaching because, like good ethnography, they humanize the struggles of people one might not hear from otherwise. The Sudanese author Tayeb Salih's *Season of Migration to the North*, for example, offers an excellent portrayal of post-colonial malaise and hybridity. Alaa Al-Aswany's *The Yacoubian Building* is another novel I use in class to illustrate topics such as urbanization, sexuality, and social class in Cairo.

I reminded my students that ethnography itself is a form of translation, of rendering another language and its sets of meaning comprehensible to us. Claire Chambers notes that the ethnographer confronts different levels of translation in attempting "to explain another culture" and that the most immediate level "is the literal translation of the other culture from 'the languages it really lives in' to 'our own'" (3). When a literary work moves between languages, many levels of translation are activated, not just of content and context but also of form. Both ethnographers and translators must search for terms and expressions between source and target languages, enriching both. The enrichment of the target literature is clearly evident in the translation of *Season of Migration*.

More than linguistic equivalence is at stake. Talal Asad notes how social anthropologists have depicted their activity as one of translation but that they have rarely examined translation as "a process of power" (142–43, 148). Just as the translation of culture reflects inequalities between Sudan and Britain and between Sudan and the United States, so does the translation of a text from Arabic into English. My students were able to offer their own examples of power difference, pointing to gendered inequality in the translation and reception of European fiction in North America, noting how men's texts become canonical whereas women's rarely do.

Aesthetics and Poetics of *Mawsim al-Hijra*

My students, in their focus on the political, tended to echo most of the critical works in English on *Season of Migration*. They were reluctant to turn to its language—its aesthetics, poetics, the questions that the consideration of style would bring to a conversation about the text. My role as a teacher was to show them how style, revealing ambiguities and contradictions, can deepen their experience of the political.

It was immediately evident to students that temporality in the novel was not simple: the plot moves between two or three distinct times. They also saw the importance of the use of voice: the recurring declarations made in the first person by Mustafa Saʿeed give the effect that he is talking directly to the reader. Some students noted the clever pairing of prayers and sexual scenes and the implications of this pairing. These observations were a starting point for them to collaborate as a class in examining how *Season of Migration* builds on and breaks with central themes in Arabic literature and poetry. We explored the connotations, allusions, and symbolism tied to Saʿeed's sexual encounters with Ann Hammond and Jean Morris and his eventual murder of Morris. The students considered specific questions in small groups (three to four students each), then shared their findings with the whole class.

The students read the chosen scenes carefully and wrote down any ideas they had about both the literary form and the language used. In the passage about Ann Hammond, for example, they noted the reference to the poetry of Abu al-Nuwwas. I then gave an overview of the ongoing debate among Arab scholars about Abu al-Nuwwas (Farid) and asked them to gather all references in the novel to him and his poetry. I highlighted questions about his complex sexuality and his themes of love and wine drinking. Students were already drawing important connections between Abu al-Nuwwas and the imagery of love and death in *Season of Migration*. They noticed a reference to his Sufism and tried to understand that (many did not know what Sufism was).

This example is instructive. In the novel, the protagonist Saʿeed gives his own autobiography and in one passage refers to a lecture he delivered to leading British scholars on Abu al-Nuwwas:

وقلت في المحاضرة أن أبا النوّاس كان متصوفًا، وأنه جعلَ من الخمرِ
رمزًا حمّله جميع أشواقه الروحية، وأنّ توقه إلى الخمرِ في شعره كانَ في
الواقع توقًا إلى الفناء في ذات الله...كلام ملفق لا أساس له من الصحة،...

(*Mawsim* 144)

In the lecture I said that Abu Nuwas was a Sufi mystic and that he had
made of wine a symbol with which to express all his spiritual yearnings,
that the longing for wine in his poetry was really a longing for self-
obliteration in the Divine—an arrant nonsense with no basis of fact.
(*Season* 143)

Sa'eed argues that Abu al-Nuwwas was more important than 'Umar al-
Khayyam and that his mention of wine in fact signifies the desire for annihilation in God. But then Sa'eed adds wickedly that he fabricated this
entire theory.

I asked my students to consult introductory works in English on
Sufism and work out the connection between Sufism and a supposedly
libertine poet like Abu al-Nuwwas (al-'Aqqad). Are similar connections
made in other places of the novel? Our quest to unravel the allusions and
symbolism generated a great deal of excitement among the students. They
noted how in the Sufi context truth and lies are treated as symbols: truth
is transcendental reality; lies, this world and its sensory experiences, which
only appear to be real.

My students now saw the complexity of Salih's style of representation,
that Sa'eed may not have been lying even though he claimed to be. That
the similes and comparisons that Abu al-Nuwwas uses to express his love
for wine, youthful boys, and women have a unique texture suggests to
some critics that they hint at transcendental love. Wine, a central symbol
for divine love in Sufi literature, can be seen as part of the dialectic between carnal and universal love.

I introduced my students to the theme of mystical versus carnal love
by having them read selections from the *'udhri* poetry of Jamil Buthayna
and the Sufi poetry of al-Hallaj. They were able to make informed comments and took imaginative steps to unpack Salih's expansive use of literary themes and symbolism. They discussed his interweaving of *'udhri*
love and sacrifice. They also looked at death and its symbolism in the
scene of Jean Morris's murder. We then discussed Salih's treatment of
love, sacrifice, and death in the context of the poetics of the Arab literary
tradition.

Al-Hallaj's sexual references to death as a virginal, ecstatic experience and the notion that death is the door to the truth became extremely

significant in the murder scene. Salih depicts Saʿeed's killing Jean Morris while ravishing her sexually:

رفعتُ الخنجر ببطء فتابعتْ حدّه بعينيها. واتسعت حدقتا العينين فجأةً
وأضاء وجهها بنور خاطف كأنه لمع برق. لبثتْ تنظر إلى حدِّ الخنجر
بخليط من الدهشة وَّالخوفِ والشبق. ثم أمسكتْ الخنجر وقبّلته بلهفة. وفجأةً
أغمضّت عينيها وتمطّت في السرير رافعةً وسطها قليلًا فاتحةً فخذيها
أكثر......

وقالت لي: أحبكَ، فصدقتها. وقلت لها أحبكِ وكنت صادقا.....والكون
بماضيه وحاضره ومستقبله اجتمع في نقطة واحدة ليس قبلها ولا بعدها
شيء.
(166–67)

> Slowly I raised the dagger and she followed the blade with her eyes; the pupils widened suddenly and her face shone with a fleeting light like a flash of lightning. She continued to look at the blade-edge with a mixture of astonishment, fear and lust. Then she took hold of the dagger and kissed it fervently. Suddenly she closed her eyes and stretched out in the bed, raising her middle slightly, opening her thighs wider. . . . "I love you," she said to me, and I believed her. "I love you," I said to her, and I spoke the truth . . . the universe, with its past, present and future, was gathered together into a single point before and after which nothing existed. (165)

Some students had first interpreted this scene as a clever linking of colonial violence, sexuality, East-West fatal attraction, and the plight of colonized subjects. Others saw it as an elaboration on the theme of exoticization of the colonized subject, the oriental object who fascinates the occidental subject. All these ideas can be extrapolated from the novel, but our reading in class allowed the poetic and aesthetic dimensions of this scene to shine through and not be buried by an overdetermined political analysis.

My students were now recasting their notions of lies and truth in interpreting Saʿeed's statement that his sexual union with Jean Morris was a moment of truth. Others stressed the longing for death expressed in the dramatic monologue by her and the concept of death through sexual rapture. I supplied terms like *desire* and *intoxication* as equivalents to *rapture*, terms used elsewhere in the novel in similar scenes. The students explored the Sufi aspect of the scene: the lie-truth dialectic, death symbolism, and intoxication. Death overcomes dualisms; it can deliver a person from the agonies that the senses, time, history, and politics create.

We turned to the section where Saʿeed discusses the wine poetry of Abu al-Nuwwas (*Mawsim* 144–55; *Season* 143–46) and recites it to

Ann Hammond (or Sausan). The references to "virgin," "wine," "cup," and "kiss" and the imagery of the "lamp of heaven" create significant links among carnal desire, intoxication, and heavenly delight:

أما يسرُّك أنَّ الأرضَ زهراء والخمرَ ممكنةٌ شمطاء عذراء
(145–46)

Does it not please you the earth is awaking,
That old virgin wine is there for the taking? . . . (144)

وكأسٍ كمصباح السّماء شربتُها على قبلةٍ أو موعدٍ للقاء
(146)

Full many a glass clear as the lamp of heaven did I drink
Over a kiss or in promise of tryst we'd keep. . . . (145)

Sa'eed recites another poem by Abu al-Nuwwas to Ann Hammond as well. He uses this imagery to draw a parallel between men who join the battle beating their war drums and wine drinkers who play the lute and carry lilies in their hands, which are stretched like bows:

إذا ما ضربوا الطّبل ضربنا نحنُ عيدانا
لفتيانٍ يرَوْنَ القتلَ في اللّذة قربانا
(146)

When on their drums they beat, we on our lutes do play
To young men who death in pleasure count a sacrifice divine. . . . (145)

Wine drinking becomes intertwined with desire (لذّة ; ladhdha), death or being killed (قتل ; qutil), sacrifice (قُربان ; qurban), and divine love. Students saw clear links to the metaphors in the Sufi poetry of al-Hallaj. We looked again at the passage in the novel preceding Sa'eed's recitation of Abu al-Nuwwas's poetry. Sa'eed appears to reciprocate, against his will (as if he is intoxicated), the love expressed by Ann Hammond. He declares:

ورغم إدراكي أنني أكذب، فقد كنت أحسّ أنني بطريقة ما أعني ما أقول، وأنها هي أيضاً رغم كذبها فإنّ ما قالته هو الحقيقة. كانت تلك لحظة من لحظات النشوة النادرة التّي أبيع بها عمري كلّه
(145)

Though I realized I was lying, I felt that somehow I meant what I was saying and that she too, despite her lying, was telling the truth. It was one of those rare moments of ecstasy for which I would sell my whole life. (144)

By losing control over his own lying, he finds the truth.

Through the same classroom activities, students saw another level of metaphorical and allegorical meaning in the scene of Jean Morris's celebration of her own death in the moment of fulfilled desire. Annihilation (فناء ; fana'), the extinguishing of the individual self for the beloved, is offered as a path toward universal truth and universal beauty. Salih toys with the idea that through Sufism one can overcome the dualism between the colonizing West and colonized Africa. This Sufi vision may seem politically defeatist or fatalistic, but in a Sufi framework it can imply a radical transformation, a rebirth. In Sufi theory, death is often an allegory for a drastic alteration in one's state of consciousness, a transcendence of the contradictions in life set up as binary oppositions: pain and pleasure, colonizer and colonized, master and servant. Jean Morris and Sa'eed, as they experience this kind of Sufi death, realize that the contradictions pushing them apart are merely a veneer behind which is hidden the universal truth of love. My students examined how Salih challenges the dichotomy between carnal and 'udhri love, a dichotomy often drawn in the Arabic literary tradition. They also were able to see how this writer could make use of a Sufi tradition without thinking of Sufism as an esoteric field.

Class time is always limited, and it might seem unfeasible to bring elements of classical literature, history, politics, religion, and so on into a discussion of a modern novel by Salih, but I found that introducing Sufism was an effective way to break down the divide between past and present, history and literature, and prose and poetry.

Who Is the Translator? Why Does It Matter?

Part of the success of *Season of Migration* in English can be attributed to the translator's vivid engagement with the original text. I presented to the class a short biography of Johnson-Davies, who was born in Vancouver, Canada, to English parents and spent his childhood in Sudan, Egypt, Uganda, and Kenya. At the age of 12, he was sent to school in England. Having studied oriental languages at Cambridge University and lectured on translation and English literature at several universities across the Arab world, Johnson-Davies experienced the other side of the colonial encounter depicted by Salih. He had read many of the colonial texts that Salih's novel referenced and was familiar with European colonial literature as well. This personal and political background contributed to the pleasure he derived from translating this Arabic work into English.

The novel was first published in 1966 in Arabic in the bimonthly cultural magazine *Hiwar* (حوار ; "Dialogue"), so the Arab readers of *Hiwar* originally read *Mawsim al-Hijra* one chapter at a time. *Hiwar* was edited by the Palestinian poet Tawfiq Sayigh and received support from the Congress for Cultural Freedom, an American political organization formed in 1950, which consisted of over a hundred European and American intellectuals opposed to Communism and Stalin. The Congress for Cultural Freedom later was exposed as having been secretly funded by the CIA, and *Hiwar* was discontinued after five years (Johnson-Davies 71–72; Coleman 190, 223). Johnson-Davies writes in his autobiography that the head of the Congress for Cultural Freedom, John Hunt, had informed him in the early 1960s that he intended to found an Arabic literary journal and would appoint Yusuf al-Khal, a Lebanese poet and pioneer in the free verse movement, as its chief editor. Johnson-Davies suggested instead Sayigh, who had taught Arabic at Cambridge (71–72).

Thus even before *Season of Migration* was published in *Hiwar*, Johnson-Davies was rubbing shoulders with American imperial politicians. He grew critical of their policies a few years later. From the beginning, then, the novel was located in a mixed Arab-Western intellectual and political context. It represented a type of literature that was sanctioned by both British imperial officials and a diverse group of orientalist scholars consulted by them, scholars who expressed neither support of or resistance to their Middle East policies.

The short time it took between the appearance of the original serialized novel and its translation (1969), as well as its positive reception by academics and university students in the United Kingdom and North America to this day, gives *Season of Migration* a special place among works of postcolonial fiction in the Arab world. Its success in the West enhanced its authority for Arabs. In contrast, Sonallah Ibrahim's تلك الرائحة (Tilka al-ra'iha; *That Smell*) also appeared in 1966, only to be confiscated by the Egyptian government under Nasser. It was republished and distributed only in 1986. Ibrahim's novel weaves together a narrative based on his experiences of imprisonment under Nasser's regime. Johnson-Davies translated it in The Smell of It *and Other Stories* (1971), before it started to circulate in Arabic. It was retranslated by Robyn Creswell and released under the title *That Smell* (2013; see Starkey). One would think that, given Nasser's anti-British and anti-American stance, *The Smell of It* would have stirred as much interest as *Season of Migration* in the West, but it didn't. Ibrahim was a leftist Arab activist and scholar and therefore avoided by a journal like *Hiwar*. During the 1960s, Ibrahim did not belong to the kind of intellectual-political network that Salih enjoyed, a network that might have facilitated Western readers' access to and appreciation of his novels.

Translation Choices, Organization, and Linguistic Style

The translation choices made in *Season of Migration* were discussed in class. Salih's novel, for example, had ten chapters, but Johnson-Davies's English version removed the numbering from the chapters and added section breaks within them. The breaks appear to have been designed to give the English-language novel a coherence that the translator felt was needed. The sentence وأنا أشرب قهوة الصباح (99; "I drink the morning coffee" [96]) marks the start of a new section of the chapter, perhaps because it serves as a prelude to the important conversations that follow.

The characters in the translation, especially Saʿeed, speak a highbrow British English. For example, Johnson-Davies uses the term "prefects" instead of "heads" of boardinghouses (Mawsim 55; *Season* 51). The use of such British expressions accentuates Saʿeed's connection with upper-class society. Salih's dialogues between Sudanese locals like Bint Majzoub, Wad Rayyes, and Mahjoub, written in Standard Arabic, are translated into Standard English. Making these conversations colloquial would have given them a different flavor.

Translation choices can be particularly important for sexual images, metaphors, and allusions. In Salih's Arabic, I found the language to be stronger, even intentionally raw, than in the translation. At first I was unsure whether my judgment was affected by the fact that Arabic was my first language but on reflection decided that different wordings would have conveyed the Arabic original better. The term ضاجعتُها (daja ʿatuha; "had sex with her") is not really the same as نمتُ معها (nimtu ma ʿaha; "slept with her," as Johnson-Davies renders this phrase). It is a Standard Arabic term but more explicit. For أفحشتُ التَّخيُّل (afhashtu al-takhayyul [Mawsim 44]), which Johnson-Davies translated as "I exceeded all limits in my imagination" (*Season* 41), I would have preferred a more emphatic translation, "I exceeded all limits in my sexual fantasy" or even "I verged on the licentious in my sexual fantasies." Cruder sexual lexicon and imagery are more in keeping with the artistic and thematic concerns of *Mawsim*.

Reading *Season of Migration* with a Proverb Reinserted

One translation choice that I dwelled on in class was the deletion of a sentence from the book. The sentence, which appears twice, is a creative alteration by Salih of the well-known Arabic proverb وافق شنٌّ طبقة ("—Tabaqa was a perfect match for Shannun"). Tabaqa stands for a female, and "Shannun" (or "Shanna," as it appears in the novel) for a male, and the story behind the proverb stresses their compatibility. Johnson-Davies removed it from the novel altogether, perhaps because it was too difficult to make the expression accessible to an English-speaking readership. But this line adds a clever and artistic touch to the novel.

The proverb is commonly used in colloquial Arabic, and the accounts of it appear in medieval Arabic sources, such as أخبار الأذكياء (Akhbar al-adhkiya'; "Stories of Intelligent Men"), by Ibn al-Jawzi (d. 1201), a medieval jurist and literary critic (see Seidensticker). Shannun was an Arab maverick who traveled the world to seek out a woman who matched him in intelligence. He rode his horse until he found a man who was going to the same village, so they rode together. Shannun asked the man, "Will you carry me, or should I carry you?" The man said, "You ignorant man! How can one person riding a horse carry another?" Later they saw crops that had been harvested. Shannun asked, "Do you think someone has eaten from this harvest or not?" The man replied, "You ignorant man! Can't you see it standing there?" When they passed a funeral, Shannun asked, "Is the person for whom the funeral is being held alive or dead?" The man answered, "I've never seen anyone more ignorant than you. Do you think they buried someone alive?" When the man reached his house, he told his daughter Tabaqa the story of Shannun.

Tabaqa proceeded to unravel all the allusions and metaphors in what Shannun had said, thereby revealing the true meaning behind his questions. She explained Shannun's question:

> "Will you carry me or should I carry you?" meant: "Will you start a conversation, or should I do it, so we can pass the time on the road?" As to his question about whether or not the food of the harvest had been eaten, he meant: "Did its owners sell it before it had been harvested and take the money to buy food, therefore not using the crops, or were the crop's owners so rich they didn't need it?" As for his statement about the dead man, he wanted to know if the man had left behind any children through whom his memory would live on. (Ibn al-Jawzi 140)

Tabaqa's father then went to Shannun and gave him the correct answers to his questions. When Shannun learned that it was Tabaqa who provided the answers, he married her and took her to his family. Hearing about how clever she was, they said, "Tabaqa is a perfect match for Shannun." In another version of this proverb, Shannun tells a friend that he never married because he couldn't find a woman in his community who had the intelligence that would agree with his character. He therefore left to seek this woman elsewhere.

Taking a closer look at idiomatic expressions, popular sayings, and local customs showed students how ethnographic details travel with difficulty from language to language and geography to geography. They then were able to explore how Salih made use of the proverb.

The proverb in the original text reads:

> جذبها عالمي الجديد عليها. دوَّختها رائحة الصندل المحروق والند، ووقفتْ
> وقتًا تضحكُ لخيالها في المرآة، وتعبث بعقدِ العاج الذي وضعتُهُ كأنشوطة
> حول جيدها الجميل. دخلتْ غرفة نومي بتولا بكرًا، وخرجت منها تحمل
> جرثوم المرض في دمها. ماتت دون أن تنبس ببنت شفة. ذخيرتي من
> الأمثال لا تنفذ. ألبِسُ لكلّ حالةٍ لبوسها، شنّى يعرف متى يلاقي طَبقة.
>
> (Mawsim 38; emphasis mine)

> It was my world, so novel to her, that attracted her. The smell of burning sandalwood and incense made her dizzy; she stood for a long time laughing at her image in the mirror as she fondled the ivory necklace I had placed like a noose around her beautiful neck. She entered my bedroom a chaste virgin and when she left it she was carrying the germs of self-destruction within her. She died without a single word passing on her lips—my store of *hackneyed phrases* is inexhaustible. For every occasion I possess the appropriate garb. (*Season* 35; emphasis mine)

Sa'eed is describing Sheila Greenwood, a rural waitress who commits suicide after her relationship with him ends. I offered a different translation and interpretation of the last three lines, stressing that the proverb is anything but a "hackneyed phrase":

> She died without uttering a single word. My ammunition of proverbs is inexhaustible. For every occasion I possess the appropriate garb. Shannun, the proverbial shrewd man, knows when to meet Tabaqa, his true match among women.

Salih manipulates the Arabic proverb to bring out the idea that Sa'eed, a man with extraordinary intelligence, like the proverbial Shannun, has the right words for every occasion. But unlike Shannun, he plots to get Tabaqa, is calculating. Salih suggests that Arabic proverbs can be fitted to any situation, justify any act, and be used as a linguistic and cultural tool to dazzle and hunt down the colonizer.

The same proverb is repeated later in connection with Isabella Seymour. Johnson-Davies omits it again in his translation:

الطائر يا مستر مصطفى قد وقع في الشرك. النيل، ذلك الإله الأفعى، قد فاز بضحيّة جديدة. المدينة قد تحوّلت إلى امرأة. وما هو إلّا يوم أو أسبوع، حتّى أضرب خيمتي، وأغرس وتدي في قمة الجبل. أنت يا سيدتي قد لا تعلمين، ولكنك مثل "كارنافون" حين دخل قبر توت عنخ آمون، قد أصابك داء فتّاك لا تدرين من أين أتى، سيودي بك إن عاجلًا وإن آجلًا. ذخيرتي من الأمثال لا تنفد. شنّي يعرف متى يلاقي طبقة. وأحسست بزمام الحديث في يدي، كفنان مهره مطواع، أشدّه فتقف، أهزّه فتمشي، أحرّكه فتتحرك وفقا لإرادتي، إن يمينًا وإن شمالًا.

(43; emphasis mine)

Here, Sa'eed talks to himself as if he were an Englishman. There is a reference to the Nile, the serpent god, the city transformed into a woman, and the Western scholar who entered the tomb of Tutankhamun. After giving these comparisons, which evoke magic, disease, and the gods' wrath, he repeats, "My ammunition of proverbs is inexhaustible. Shannun, the proverbial shrewd man, knows when to meet Tabaqa, his true match among women." Salih stresses that Sa'eed's stories—much like Shahrazad's—are the source of his power, a power that allows him to pursue his victims (the victim in this case is Isabella Seymour). The proverb is followed by this statement: "I felt that the reins of the conversation were in my hands. . . ." Arabic proverbs, exoticizing him, trap the British woman.

Jean Morris turns out to be the exemplary Tabaqa of the novel, the ultimate match for Sa'eed. He, who refers to himself repeatedly as a pathological liar, describes her:

كانت تكذب حتّى في أبسط الأشياء. تعود إلى البيت بقصص غريبة عن أشياء حدثت لها وأناس قابلتهم لا يمكن أن يصدّقها العقل. ولا استبعد أنّها عديمة الأهل، كأنها شهرزاد متسوّلة.

(157–58)

She used to lie about the most ordinary things and would return home with amazing and incredible stories about incidents that had happened to her and people she'd met. I wouldn't be surprised if she didn't have a family at all and was like some *mendicant Scheherazade*. (*Season* 155; emphasis mine)

He and she compete in storytelling, Shahrazad's weapon, in a process that leads to her death as well as the end of his career and escapades in Britain. In our classroom discussions, the students used my retranslations and interpretations of the text in remarkable ways. Without knowing Arabic, they successfully engaged the original and translation to draw out important connections with other sections of the novel and suggested different ways of handling the proverb of Tabaqa and Shannun.

It is important to give a broad and deep contextualization to a translation like *Season of Migration to the North* when teaching North American undergraduate students, who are largely unfamiliar with Arabic and Arabic literary traditions. Spending time on a short passage in this way can help students engage a literary text—especially in a history course or department. They greatly benefit from knowing the contexts in which both the original text and the translation were created and how the two are connected. Too often, Salih's work has been read solely in its translated version.

My approach has allowed students to delve into the literary contributions of this text in the larger context of the Arab literary tradition generally and fiction specifically. It allowed them to explore the complex relation between the political and the poetic, which transcends simple dichotomies, and to avoid reducing the poetic to the political.

Note

Translations from the Arabic are mine, unless otherwise indicated.

Works Cited

Abdul Jabbar, Wisam Khalid. "The Mimetic Discourse in Tayeb Salih's *Season of Migration to the North*." *Rocky Mountain Review*, 2012, pp. 130–43.

Ahmad, Aijaz. "Jameson's Rhetoric of Otherness and the 'National Allegory.'" *Social Text*, vol. 17, 1987, pp. 3–25.

Al-ʿAqqad, ʿAbbas Mahmud. أبو نواس الحسن بن هانئ [Abu al-Nuwwas: Al-Hasan b. Hani']. Dar Nahdat Misr li-al-Tibaʿa wa-al-Tawziʿ, 1980.

Amyuni, Mona, ed. *Tayeb Salih's* Season of Migration to the North: *A Casebook.* American U in Beirut P, 1985.

Asad, Talal. "The Concept of Cultural Translation in British Social Anthropology." *Writing Culture: The Poetics and Politics of Ethnography: A School of American Research Advanced Seminar*, edited by James Clifford and George E. Marcus, U of California P, 1986, pp. 141–64.

Banfield, Grant. "What's Really Wrong with Ethnography?" *International Education Journal*, vol. 4, no. 4, 2004, pp. 53–63.

Chambers, Claire. "Anthropology as Cultural Translation: Amitav Ghosh's *In an Antique Land*." *Postcolonial Text*, vol. 2, no. 3, 2006, pp. 3–4.

Coleman, Peter. *The Liberal Conspiracy: The Congress for Cultural Freedom and the Struggle for the Mind of Postwar Europe*. Free Press, 1989.

Davidson, John E. "In Search of a Middle Point: The Origins of Oppression in Tayeb Salih's *Season of Migration to the North*." *Research in African Literatures*, vol. 20, no. 3, Autumn 1989, pp. 385–400.

El-Enany, Rasheed. *Arab Representation of the Occident: East-West Encounters in Arab Fiction*. Routledge, 2006.

Elsheshtawy, Yasser. "The Mythical East: Architectural Metaphors in Tayeb Salih's *Season of Migration to the North*." *Built Environment*, vol. 31, 2005, pp. 21–30.

Farid, Mahmud Kamil, editor. ديوان أبي النواس: تاريخه، رأي الشعراء فيه ، نوادره، شعره [Diwan Abi al-Nuwwas: Tarikhuhu, ra'i al-shu'ara' fihi, nawadiruhu, shi'ruhu; The Poetry Collection of Abu al-Nuwwas: His Biography, How Other Poets Viewed Him, His Anecdotes, and Poems]. Al-Maktaba al-Tijariyya, 1937.

Geesey, Patricia. "Cultural Hybridity and Contamination in Al-Tayyib Salih's *Mawsim al-hijra ila al-Shamal* (*Season of Migration to the North*)." *Research in African Literatures*, vol. 28, no. 3, Autumn 1997, pp. 128–40.

Hammersley, M. *What's Wrong With Ethnography?—Methodological Explorations*. Routledge, 1992.

Hassan, Wail S. "Gender (and) Imperialism: Structures of Masculinity in Tayeb Salih's *Season of Migration to the North*." *Men and Masculinities*, vol. 5, no. 3, January 2003, pp. 309–24.

———. *Tayeb Salih: Ideology and the Craft of Fiction*. Syracuse UP, 2003.

Ibn al-Jawzi. أخبار الأذكياء [Akhbar al-Adhkiya'; "Stories of Intelligent Men"]. Edited by Muhammad Mursi al-Khawli, Matabi' al-Ahram al-Tijariyya, 1970.

Ibrahim, Sonallah. *That Smell and Notes from Prison*. Translated by Robyn Creswell, New Directions, 2013.

———. *The Smell of It and Other Stories*. Translated by Denys Johnson-Davies, Heinemann, 1971.

Jameson, Fredric. "Third-World Literature in the Era of Multinational Capitalism." *Social Text*, vol. 15, 1986, pp. 65–88.

Johnson-Davies, Denys. *Memories in Translation: A Life between the Lines of Arabic Literature*. American U of Cairo P, 2005.

Newcomb, Rachel. "Fiction and Anthropology." *Savage Minds: Notes and Queries in Anthropology*, 1 Sept. 2013, savageminds.org/2013/09/01/fiction-and-anthropology/.

Salih, Tayeb. موسم الهجرة إلى الشمال [Mawsim al-hijra ila al-shamal]. Dar al-'Awda, 1969. Translated as *Season of Migration to the North*.

———. *Season of Migration to the North*. Translated by Denys Johnson-Davies, Three Continents Press, 1993.

Seidensticker, T. "Ibn al-Jawzi." *Encyclopedia of Arabic Literature*, edited by Julie Scott Meissami and Paul Starkey, vol.1, Routledge, 1998, pp. 338–39.

Starkey, Paul. "Capturing the Spirit." Review of *That Smell and Notes from Prison*, by Sonallah Ibrahim. *Banipal*, www.banipal.co.uk/book_reviews/104/that-smell-and-notes-from-prison/.

Allen Hibbard

Teaching Modern Arabic Literature in Translation in Middle Tennessee

I teach modern Arabic literature in translation at a regional institution, Middle Tennessee State University. Murfreesboro, Tennessee—where my university is located—has received considerable media attention since 2011 because of controversy surrounding the building of an Islamic center in the community. The title of a CNN special hosted by Soledad O'Brien gives a sense of some of the dynamics in Murfreesboro: "Unwelcome: Muslims Next Door." Debates about Islam have gone on inside the court-room as well in the public square. Local conversations of course inform the work done in the classroom. Like all teachers, I calibrate my teaching not only to the levels, abilities, backgrounds, and experiences of my students but also to my particular site.

Middle Tennessee State University recently established a modest Middle East center and a Middle East studies minor offering courses in Arabic, Hebrew, and Kurdish. The classes I have taught in the program are composed of diverse groups of students with varied interests. For example, my most recent Arabic literature in translation class included a United States soldier returning from Iraq, a middle-aged Kurdish man who had been a medical doctor before fleeing his homeland to resettle in Nashville, and a young Palestinian American who could understand spoken Arabic but could not read Arabic. There was also a handful of English majors and Middle East studies minors.

The Course: Arabic Literature in Translation

In order to complicate the simple us-them binary, I usually begin the course with maps, calling special attention to patterns of movement and migration. I focus on the Kurdish, Coptic, and Somali immigrant communities in Middle Tennessee and on United States military intervention in the Middle East, where many Americans, sometimes against their will, have spent time. I introduce students to excerpts of Edward Said's influential study *Orientalism*, summarizing its central arguments and urging them to approach the work critically, as many in literary and Middle East studies have done in the decades following its publication in 1978.

I propose that short of direct experience (or in addition to it), acquaintance with a region's literature provides one of the best ways to come to know a foreign culture. Reading narratives produced by people whose lives may seem quite radically different from ours provides a means for crossing lines imposed by historical distance, gender, race, age, and culture.

I built my class around the theoretical frame articulated by Martha Nussbaum in *Cultivating Humanity: A Classical Defense of Reform in Liberal Education*. Nussbaum claims that stories "cultivate in ourselves a capacity for sympathetic imagination that will enable us to comprehend the motives and choices of people different from ourselves, seeing them not as forbiddingly alien and other, but as sharing many problems and possibilities with us" (85). She notes that narratives, particularly fictional ones, are an extremely effective way to allow readers "to imagine what it's like to be in that person's place" (91).

A Focus on Poetry and Drama

Because students generally respond better to fiction than to other literary genres, I begin the class with short stories from the Middle East and end with the novel. More challenging to teach in translation than novels or short stories are poetry and drama, which demand of the teacher considerable flexibility, effort, and innovation, though they yield dividends that fiction can't. Both poetry and drama can open the door to Nussbaum's "sympathetic imagination," but careful analysis is needed, especially when one is teaching Arabic poetry in translation. Students must be introduced to its rich traditions in Arab culture as well as its conventions.

In my experience, students approach poetry—English as well as Arabic—with resistance and considerable trepidation, so I begin with Marianne Moore's famous lines on poetry: "I, too, dislike it. . . . / Reading it, however, with a perfect contempt for it, one discovers in / it after all, a place for the genuine" (36). I underscore how important poetry has been for Arabs over time. A good introduction for classroom preparation, which delves into the modern Arabic poetic tradition and its deep connections to the past, is Salma Khadra Jayyusi's *Trends and Movements in Modern Arabic Poetry*. I use anecdotes to impress on students the role in society played by poets. Cab drivers might be able to recite by memory lines from the classical Arab poet al-Mutanabbi. Even today, poets command more respect and enjoy more popularity than political leaders, as evidenced in the large audiences the poets attract. When Mahmoud Darwish, a Palestinian poet, went to Morocco to give a reading in 2000, for example, the event had to be relocated to a soccer stadium in order to accommodate the crowd of 24,000 (Jaggi).

It is also crucial to underline the continuities and ruptures—the conversations—between early (classical) poetry and modern (contemporary) poetry. Using strategies similar to those outlined by Rula Jurdi in her essay in this volume, I link this past and present for my students, insisting on the orality of poetry today, a feature that goes back to the seventh century, when public performances of poets were judged by quality of voice, cadence, gesture, and so forth (Stetkevych). A particularly useful resource in this regard is the *Princeton Online Arabic Poetry* site (www.princeton .edu/~arabic/poetry/index.html), which affords students a chance to hear Arabic poems read aloud or see the script and the form of the poem and read an English translation.

Because there is no one book available in English that covers the range and variety of modern Arabic poetry, I have cobbled together material from various sources. I use my own selections of poetry in order to discuss directly with students the vagaries of translation and publishing, some of which are addressed in Michelle Hartman's introduction to this volume. *Modern Arabic Poetry: An Anthology*, edited by Jayyusi, remains a key resource though published more than thirty years ago, but it does not foreground issues of translation as dramatically and visually as do bilingual editions of poetry. For such foregrounding, individual poetry collections and shorter anthologies can help the teacher prepare, even if they are not used in class as assigned reading material. I point, as examples, to the reflections on the translation of Darwish's poetry by his translators (Darwish, *In the Presence* and *Unfortunately*) and Shawkat M. Toorawa's comments on his translation of Adonis's *A Time between Ashes and Roses*.

In class, I emphasize the difficulties in replicating or conveying the meter, rhyme, sounds (assonance and alliteration), images, and meanings of the original in the target language. To do this, I use bilingual editions of poetry whenever I can. Two good collections are *Victims of a Map* (al-Udhari), which contains poems by Adonis, Darwish, and Samih al-Qasim, and *Arabian Love Poems*, by Nizar Kabbani.

Before we read and discuss poems in English translation, I present examples of the poets themselves reading their work in Arabic or of others reading it. I ask students simply to attend to the sounds, cadences, and gestures. On *YouTube* there are many examples of Darwish, al-Qasim, and Adonis reading their poetry. From this experience, students learn how poetry can be understood beyond its words, a process consistent with Nussbaum's perspective. The class comes to think—explicitly or implicitly, depending on the context—about what they do and do not understand and feel.

Another technique I use is to invite a native speaker of Arabic to come to class, read a poem or several poems aloud, and discuss its translation with us. A poem that I have used this way is "Travel Tickets" (تذاكر سفر ; Tadhakir safar), by al-Qasim:

وعندما أُقتلُ في يوم من الأيام
سَيَعثُرُ القاتل في جيبي
على تذاكرِ السفَر
واحدة إلى السلام
واحدة إلى الحقولِ والمطر
واحدة
إلى ضمائرِ البشر
أرجوكَ ألَّا تُهْمِل التذاكِر
يا قاتلي العزيز
أرجوكَ أن تسافر

(al-Udhari 58)

Abdullah al-Udhari's English translation appears on the opposite page:

On the day you kill me
You'll find in my pocket

Travel tickets
To peace,
To the fields and the rain,
To people's conscience.
Don't waste the tickets. (59)

In class, with our class visitor—in one case, a university doctoral student—we questioned some of the translator's choices. Then we worked together to create our own translation, though most students knew no Arabic. This process allowed them to experience firsthand the difficulty of capturing the meaning in English of a poem in a foreign language. We ultimately produced this translation:

One of those days when I'm killed
the killer will find in my pocket
travel tickets:
one to peace,
one to fields and rain,
one
to people's consciences.
(Please don't fail to use the tickets,
dear killer.
Please DO travel)

One does not have to know Arabic to see that our version attempts to preserve the line breaks and punctuation of the original poem. We also felt it was significant that the word واحدةٌ (wahidatun; "one") stands alone on the sixth line. Finally, and perhaps most important, we sought in our translation to emphasize the addressee in the poem—the killer.

To complement and provide contrasts with the poems in *Victims of a Map*, I have used *Arabian Love Poems*, by Kabbani, a popular Syrian poet. Kabbani wrote poems in response to political issues, such as the Palestinian struggle and the defeat of Arab countries in the Six-Day War in 1967, but all the poems in this collection dwell on the theme of love. Students have no trouble relating to them, and some are surprised at their frankness—for example:

I am the prophet of love,
Carrying surprises to women.
Had I not washed your breasts with wine,
They would have never blossomed.
My modest miracle
Made your nipples bloom. (45)

إني رسول الحبّ
أحملُ للنساء مفاجآتي
لو أنّني بالخمر لم أغسلهما
نهداكِ ... ما كانا على قيْد الحياة
فإذا استدارت حلمتاكِ
فتلك أصغَر مُعْجَزاتي.
(44)

Once again, as with the al-Qasim poem, we recognize the sparse style and
free verse form, in contrast with traditional Arabic poetry. We recognize as
well a sense of intimacy, both in theme and rhetorical posture.

Arabian Love Poems contains dozens of lyrical, modern love poems
written and translated in simple language, accessible to ordinary people.
Here is another favorite of mine I use in class:

> In the summer
> I stretch out on the shore
> And think of you
> Had I told the sea
> What I felt for you,
> It would have left its shores,
> Its shells,
> Its fish,
> And followed me. (109)

في أيّام الصيف
أتمدّد على رمال لشاطئ
وأمارس هواية التفكير به ..
لو أنّني أقول للبحر ما أشعر به نحوكِ
لترك شواطئَهُ ..
وأصدافَهُ..
وأسماكَهُ..
وتَبَعَني..
(108)

Compact and direct, the poem expresses profound feelings of love, a sort
of love letter meant for wooing, reminiscent of Shakespeare's sonnets.
And, like the sonnets, the poem presents a cluster of images, in this case
revolving around the sea (shore, shells, fish), all harnessed to display the
immensity and power of the speaker's love.

Though there is not a great deal of recent English-language criticism
on Kabbani, Mohja Kahf's article on his work as melding politics and erotics contextualizes his work broadly. When I teach modern Arabic poetry,

I frequently work comparatively, referring to Anglo-American traditions that many students are acquainted with. Kabbani's poems, in their form, style, and subject matter, call to mind the work of William Carlos Williams and H.D. in particular.

Kabbani's reputation of being the poet of women provides a good transition to discuss the long history of contributions of women poets to Arabic literature. To compensate for bias against them in the Arab literary tradition (too often reflected in anthologies), I highlight works by various well-known women poets from the second half of the twentieth century, including Nazik al-Mala'ika, an Iraqi. Al-Mala'ika's "Love Song for Words" (أغنية حبّ للكلمات) is particularly useful for class discussion. The final lines of the poem, as translated by Matthew Sorenson and Christopher Middleton, read:

> One day we will build a nest of dreams with words
> High up, a trellis for the ivies
> Fed with poetry
> Watered with words
> We will build a balcony for modest roses
> Its pillars made of words.
> (Jayyusi, *Modern Arabic Poetry* 336)

في غدٍ نبني لنا عشَّ رؤى من كلمات
سَامقًا يعترش اللبلاب في أحرفه
سنذيب الشعرَ في زخرفه
وسنروّي زهرَهُ بالكلمات
وسنبني شرفة للعطر والورد الخجول
ولها أعمدة من كلمات
(al-Mala'ika)

I stress al-Mala'ika's importance in the modernist movement, alongside the male poets, such as Adonis and Darwish; all of them broke with established poetic traditions and introduced new subject matter. "Love Song for Words" challenges Arab women poets to write their own experiences into the predominantly male poetic tradition. I ask my students who is meant by the poem's "we" and draw attention to the rich metaphors of building and making—with words and with natural material. I refer to al-Mala'ika's long collaboration with fellow Iraqi modernist poet Badr Shakir al-Sayyab, her reputation as a nationalist, and her role as founder of the free verse movement, despite the frequent exclusion of women from poetic and literary circles and criticism (Suleiman).

The collection *The Poetry of Arab Women* brings together a large group of contemporary Arab women poets located throughout the Arab world and outside it, writing in Arabic and other languages (Handal). The diverse voices found in this volume demonstrate that women poets discuss an enormous range of issues and from different perspectives. A poem from this volume that I teach is "A Country" (بلاد), by Fawziyya Abu-Khalid, from Saudi Arabia:

> Her hair is long, very, very long
> She wraps its ends around her feet as she stands
>
> Her fingers are long, very, very long
> She can pick the fruit from the lotus tree as she sits in her boudoir
>
> She bathes in rain gushing forth from her lap
> And she dreams. (Handal 71)

شعرها طويلٌ... طويلٌ... طويل.
تلفُّ طرفه على مشطِ رجلِها، وهي واقفةٌ أصابعُها
طويلةٌ
طويلةٌ
طويلة
تقطفُ نبقَ السِّدرةِ وهي جالسةٌ في خدرها
تستحمُ بمطرٍ يفورُ من حجرِها
وتحلم.

This powerful translation of Abu-Khalid's Arabic by Farouk Mustafa gives a sense of the dynamics of the original and could be retranslated in class to interesting effect, just as we retranslated al-Qasim's "Travel Tickets." The translator created a poem in a shape reminiscent of Williams's famous "Red Wheelbarrow." Unfortunately, because the original versions are not present, issues of translation are effaced in this volume and must be brought into the classroom by the teacher. But some works in the volume were originally written in English or French, and it can be interesting to work through the differences and similarities, to student ears, between the poems conveyed in translation from Arabic and the poems that are not. A listening exercise can be done that compares two short poems in class and asks students to guess which was originally written in which language. Such an exercise emphasizes the aural and oral nature of poetry.

Other collections of recent English translations of contemporary Arabic poetry can be brought into the classroom. *Angry Voices: An Anthology of the Off-Beat New Egyptian Poets*, compiled by Mohamed Metwalli and translated by Mohamed Enani, presents the work of nearly thirty Egyptian poets of the eighties and nineties who experiment with innovative themes, styles, and forms (Enani). *A Bit of Air*, by Walid Taher, an author and illustrator, and translated by Anita Husen, has enjoyed a good deal of popularity in Egypt. Influenced by the graphic novel tradition, the book features a series of short poems in handwritten Arabic on the left page, along with cartoon-like illustrations, faced with the English translation on the right. The poems are sardonic, biting, and often dark. Here is a sample:

> . . . . Drowning . . ?!
> So what if we continue to drown . . .
> It's a chance to live among the fish . . . tranquil . .
> Without problems . . . . .
> Without bickering . . .
> Without the pettiness of humans! (27)

> ...غرقانين..؟؟
> وإيه يعني نفضل غرقانين..
> حتى فرصة نعيش مع السمك... هاديين ...
> بلا مشاكل...
> بلا خناقات...
> بلا بواخة بني آدمين!
> (27)

Beneath the Arabic is an illustration: above the surface of a dark sea, a small white sail rises; beneath the surface, a simply shaped fish swims. Written and published before the January 2011 revolution in Egypt, these poems vividly display the energies and moods that lay behind that uprising.

Poetry is difficult to access in translation for many reasons, but the translation of Arabic dramatic literature presents its own challenges. Performance depends on the actors; on the lighting, staging, and costuming; and on the construction or adaptation of appropriate theatrical venues. It takes considerable cultural (and financial) resources to make theater viable; it takes community and audience participation. Dramatic works, because they are so public, often are subject to pressure to conform to social norms or political ideologies more than production in other genres, and that pressure can curb the range of the imagination. Yet another problem for Arab dramatists has been which language to write in. Formal Arabic, while understood throughout the Arab world, sounds stilted and artificial, particularly when spoken by actors onstage. On the other hand, the use of more realistic, everyday speech in local dialect tends to limit access to particular audiences and thus not produce a pan-Arab theater.

A good resource for thinking through the issues of translating plays is M. M. Badawi's classic *Early Arabic Drama,* which discusses the translations available, their quality, what will work best in the classroom, and how best to represent various styles, periods, and regions. M. Lynx Qualey has remarked that we "might see five plus novels and a half-dozen poetry collections [from Arabic] appearing in English translation, [but] it's a good year to find even one theatre production in print" (qtd. in Antoun). Thus, to teach these works, once again it is necessary to cobble together materials from diverse locations.

After independence and up to the Nasser period, the 1960s were seen by some as a golden age of Arab theater, particularly in Egypt. A key figure was Tawfiq al-Hakim, who produced more than eighty plays, many of which are suitable for teaching. Critical work on al-Hakim as a storywriter as well as a playwright is available in English, providing background information (Hutchins). His two-act play *The Tree Climber* (يا طالع الشجرة ; Ya tali' al-shajara), written in 1962 and translated by Denys Johnson-Davies, is lively, quick-paced, and accessible. Like many others of its time, the play was influenced by Western modern drama, particularly the absurdist plays of Eugène Ionesco. Luigi Pirandello and Bertolt Brecht also had a great influence on Arab playwrights in the 1960s as they experimented with the use of theater space, interactions with the audience, means of alienation (Brechtian *Verfremdungseffekt*), and political uses of theater.

Although Arab playwrights have often embraced and appropriated techniques employed by Western playwrights, they have also incorporated traditional, indigenous elements of performance. Many of their plays feature folkloric elements, such as the fool, Juha; *samir* ("evening entertainer"); and shadow theater along with such Western elements as breaking the fourth wall and the Pirandello-like intervention of the author into the action.

In teaching drama, I have extended my reach beyond Egypt to include Syrian and Moroccan plays, which represent traditions and styles not always covered in courses on Modern Arabic literature. Many of the works of Sa'dallah Wannous, a Syrian playwright, have been translated and are increasingly available. There is a large project of translating him by Marvin Carlson, Safi Mahfouz, Robert Myers, and Nada Saab. (Myers and Saab together wrote about his theater.) In my classes I have used his play *The King Is the King* (الملك هو الملك), which can be found in the volume *Modern Arabic Drama: An Anthology*, in a translation by Ghassan Maleh and Thomas G. Ezzy that works well in performance (Jayyusi and Allen 77–120; see Zahrawi).

Like other plays by Wannous, *The King Is the King* is a political allegory. Set against a *One Thousand and One Nights* backdrop, the lavish palace life of the king and vizier contrasts sharply with commoners' dreams of power and grandeur. The king gets bored with his role and decides to trade places with one of his subjects, Abu ʿIzza, who lords it over everyone in his family, drinking while his wife is working, enacting the fantasy that he is king. Once Abu ʿIzza assumes the role of king, he becomes more tyrannical than the real king ever was. Those who were the real king's mortal enemies (in particular, the shaykh and the merchant) become the new king's allies, collaborating with the state apparatus. The real king's personal servant doesn't recognize the king after this substitution, nor does the chief of police (whom the new king berates for lack of vigilance), nor does the executioner (for whose blade the new king develops a lust), nor does even the queen! When the new king's own wife and daughter come to visit him, the new king fails to recognize them. He orders a roundup of those suspected of plotting "along with anyone else who looks suspicious" (الذين تبدو عليهم، وجو ههم نوايا الشغف ولفوضى) and sets up "a security organization to watch over the Chief of Police's security organization" (سنشكل جهاز أمن يراقب مقدم الأمن وجهازه), prepared to shed blood with his own hands rather than rely on his executioner (*Four Plays* 118; Al-Aʿmal 569). As the new ruler tightens his grip, the lives of his subjects become more hopeless and desperate than ever. The play seems prescient in the light of political events in Syria today.

In teaching *The King Is the King*, I direct students' attention to the divisions of space—the palace, the street, and a typical Syrian home—that dramatize the relation between a repressive political regime and the perversion of personal lives. Abu ʿIzza's home is a domestic hell for everyone but especially for his wife and daughter. Patriarchal political structures are replicated, mirrored, in domestic spheres, a pattern emphasized when the master of the house becomes king. I also talk about the importance of stage directions and costumes in the play, as well as about Brechtian dramatic elements such as the use of placards bearing synopses of action—for example, "A STORY OF THE HISTORY OF THE MASQUERADE, AND THE SECRET OF THE HAPPY FAMILY" (97; حكاية عن تاريخ التنكر وسرّ الجماعة السعيدة) and "GIVE ME GOWN AND CROWN, AND A KING YOU WILL HAVE" (111; اعطني رداء ، وتاجاً، واعطك ملكاً).

Another short play by Wannous, *The King's Elephant* (الفيل يا ملك الزمان), found in Jayyusi's *Short Arabic Plays: An Anthology* (433–51), also works well in class. It deals with similar themes and dramatic techniques, though in a much more compressed space (roughly fifteen pages). The question posed by the play is what to do about the king's elephant, which once again has ravaged the village. Zakaria, the only named character in the play, proposes that the villagers take their grievance directly to the king. After a period of rehearsing their presentation, they go to the palace, where the contrast between the lives of these ordinary citizens and the life of their ruler becomes dramatically evident. In the presence of the king and all the trappings of his power, the petitioners freeze up and capitulate, telling him how much they love his elephant and requesting that it be given a mate. The king is pleased to have such devoted subjects, attentive to his needs. The short play feels like a horribly cruel extended joke.

A discussion of Wannous's plays naturally leads to questions of censorship and of how writers in the Arab world (and elsewhere) manage to launch strong political critiques despite tight restrictions (Zahrawi). As the character 'Ubayd says in *The King Is the King*, "The more they repress, the more we perfect our camouflage. That way, our movement will gain strength while the contradictions grow. We must strike at exactly the right moment—not a second too early or too late" (87; هم يمعنون في الإرهاب،، ونحن نمعن في التنكر. التناقضات تنمو، وحركتنا تشتد. ينبغي أن نتواقت مع اللحظة المواتية، لا نبكر ولا نتأخر [500–01]). Temporal displacement—setting the work in the time of the Abbasids rather than in the present—is one means of camouflage.

What makes both these plays by Wannous so powerful is how they dramatize the dynamics of the operation of repression and power, the distance between ruled and ruler, and the ways in which resistance is squelched by force or intimidation. They shed light on many of the conditions underlying the revolutionary forces that resulted in the so-called Arab Spring in places such as Tunisia, Egypt, Syria, and Bahrain. Readings and analyses of these plays with attention to the conditions under which they were conceived, written, and produced—during the rise of Ba'athist regimes in both Syria and Iraq—prompt discussion of the relation between authoritarian rule and the tragic scene in Syria today, where the Assad regime is still fighting to hang on to power.

To broaden the discussion, I pair *The King Is the King* with *Shakespeare Lane* (زنقة شكسبير), a recent play by Zoubeir ben Bouchta, a Moroccan playwright and an active, innovative figure on the contemporary cultural scene in Tangier. A favorite among students, this play contrasts quite sharply with Wannous's plays in tone, setting, and theme. The two together suggest the richness and diversity of Arabic drama today. Some scholarly work in English, particularly by Khalid Amine, has been done on this award-winning playwright, who is becoming increasingly renowned ("Performing Gender" and "Performing Postcoloniality"; see also Amine and Carlson).

In his preface to the English version, ben Bouchta characterizes the play as a hopeless love story in which characters spring "from the ashes of memory to shine on stage bearing the elegance of the past in the raiment of the present" (18). Central to the play is its geographic setting, the Moroccan city of Tangier. Beginning with the title and frequent references to Shakespeare in the opening scene and throughout, the city's long and legendary history of interactions with the West is felt in various ways (Hibbard).

We learn that Shakespeare Lane is the name of an actual street on the Marshan, the main location of the play's action. The play is laced with references to expatriate residents, such as Barbara Hutton, the Woolworth heiress who for some time had a house in the medina; David Herbert, son of an English lord, a flamboyant figure in Tangier's expatriate community; and Paul and Jane Bowles, American writers who lived in Tangier for decades in the second half of the twentieth century. We learn that Cabesota (a jester-like character whose name fuses the Spanish word for head, *cabeza*, with the name of a popular Moroccan card game, *sota*) had been in love with an Australian hippie in the 1970s, who gave him a guitar he still carried "slung over his shoulder like a gun" (25; معلق على كتفه كبندقية [9]):

> She's the one who taught me to play. . . . When I became proficient, she gave me this guitar. We'd sing all night. She'd sing Bob Dylan and I'd sing Nass Alghiwan, eventually she could sing Nass Alghiwan in English and I could sing Bob Dylan in Arabic. (46–47)

> هي اللي علمتني نَقَط. مللي تعلمت عطاتني هذ لكيطارة. كنا كانباتو نغنيوْ
> بزوج هي ي بوب ديلان و أنا ناس الغيوان. حتى تعلمت هي تغني ناس الغيوان
> باللينكليزية وتعلمت أنا نغني ي بوب ديلان بالعربية.
> (38–39)

The play seamlessly and naturally integrates local Tanjawi and Western elements, reflecting the history and character of the city (Khaloufi).

The conflict and action of the play call to mind the kind of obstacles and complications associated with love (with both comic effect and tragic outcomes) in plays such as *Romeo and Juliet*, *Othello*, and *Much Ado about Nothing*, a point of comparison that allows students, exploring the sameness and difference, to bridge the divide between self and other, West and East. We see from the start that things are off-key, not in harmony, not in their right places. Albarrani, the gardener (whose name—ironically, as it turns out—means "the stranger" in Moroccan dialect) is in love with

Marshana (a feminine form of Marshan), who is married to Elmehdi (or "the Messiah," again ironically named) and has a daughter with an incurable disease. The old plump nurse, Lady R'himu, is in love with Albarrani. And Bu Mwaret, the *f'qih* or legal representative, puts the moves on Lady R'himu. We learn that Albarrani and Marshana had a relationship in the past that was impossible to maintain because their families stood on opposite sides of disputes that took place a century ago, calling to mind the family feud in *Romeo and Juliet*.

Things swiftly come to a denouement in the final scene, which is titled "The Tower Has Collapsed" (طاحت الصومعة), as all the characters converge on the villa and truths are revealed. The letter that Lady R'himu summarizes and reads to Cabesota is from his distant Australian love interest; she announces the impossibility of continuing their relationship:

Marshana: Bin Laden's followers have messed with people's heads. In Australia everyone is anxious. Planes are no longer for travel but weapons. Blonds fear black hair. September 11th has confused her; her heart is torn. She loves you, yet she's afraid to live with you. Now, she doesn't know what to do. She says that you shouldn't write or call her anymore. . . . "We no longer fit together, please forget me. Our love story died when the towers collapsed; our love was buried under the wreckage of the Twin Towers. I'm left weeping." (92)

مرشانة:... صحاب بلادن عملو خبلاف عقول الناس. عندهم ف استراليا كلشي داخلو الوسواس. حتى من الطيابر كا يشوفوهم قرطاص. زعار الراس كا يسكنو لخوف مللي كاياقى ف طريقو كحل الراس. ١١ سبتمبر خلاها حايرة ف آش تعمل في بقلبها، وخِّ كا تبغيك، صبحت خايفة من لعيشة معاك. دابا هي حايرة ف أمرك وأمرها، قالت لك الله يخليك ما تبقاش لا تعيط عليها ف التيليفون ولا تكتب لها، وإذا جات على خاطرك نساها. هي ما تصلح لك وانت ما تصلح لها. للي بيناتكم مات نهار طاحو زوج الصومعات وحبكم انتم بزوج دفناتو تحت الردمة د توين سنطر وبكات.
(94)

The play's direct reference to 9/11, from a Moroccan perspective, tends to surprise students, provoking discussion in class about what that event meant for Americans as well as for Middle Easterners.

Because plays are written to be performed, I urge students to consider how these plays could be presented, both in their places of origin and in the United States. Writing assignments invite them to discuss how they would produce either the Wannous or ben Bouchta play for an audience in the United States. They are required to discuss what changes, if any, would be made if the play was produced in English translation.

I draw students' attention to the structure of *Shakespeare Lane*—a series of fourteen scenes or vignettes called "lightings" (الإضاءة), twelve of which take place in or around the garden of the villa. The other two are set on the coast, where Albarrani and Cabesota go off to fish. These discrete scenes, each having a clump of characters, allow a director to rehearse them separately before linking them together for the final performance. I have sometimes assigned scenes to students, asking them to rehearse outside class, then come back and present readings in front of their classmates.

When students read the play aloud, they are apt to pause or stumble over language and question whether some phrases would work for English-speaking audiences. These hesitations and doubts lead to a discussion about the singular challenges involved in the translation of drama. Students will sometimes rewrite lines to facilitate smooth delivery, continuing the process of translation! I ask them what a good or faithful translation is, one that is literal or one that adapts. Used in conjunction with similar exercises in poetry—such as translating the short poem by al-Qasim—students explore the challenges of translating different genres as well as different individual works.

The English edition of *Shakespeare Lane* includes introductory comments by the translator, Rajae Khaloufi; the editor, George Roberson; and the playwright. Khaloufi notes that translating the play was "a difficult task" and that one of the difficulties involved "the special intricacy of Moroccan dialectical Arabic" (12). The play was written and performed in a local dialect that would not be readily understood in most other Arabic-speaking countries. The translation project was a collaborative effort. Roberson notes that "to maintain and reflect the richness and polyphony of the city, some non-English words have been retained in the text" and that "local idioms sometimes were translated literally" (15). The example given, "[L]et me merge from my own eyelids," is a perfect place for students to begin the discussion.

In his "Between the Human and the Foreign: Translating Arabic Drama for the Stage," Mohammed Albakry addresses challenges faced by the translator of dramatic works from Arabic into English. Noting the often cited distinction between translations for the page and those for the stage, he argues for the production of translations that are accessible to audiences. "All translators," he writes, "have to consider how to make the text speak to an audience, but readers of a novel, for instance, could perhaps deal more easily with cultural *strangeness* in a translated book, whereas audiences at the theater do not have the luxury of rolling time back in a transitory performance" (507). Translations of dramatic works "need to be as self-contained as possible" and not depend on a lot of annotations and explanatory notes (509). Albakry's practice of translating Arabic drama, which avoids exotic and stereotypical portrayals in speech and costume, responds to Lawrence Venuti's call for preserving foreign elements in the translation against the impulse to domesticate translations to conform to norms, values, and linguistic patterns of the target culture. "I conceptualize this space as a place of encounter between the familiar and the foreign beyond the usual logics of assimilation and othering, where moments of genuine contact with the foreign could be played out, and cultural identity across differences could be negotiated," Albakry concludes (513).

In my course Arabic Literature in Translation, we attempt to take students from where they are when they enter the classroom to a broader, deeper, richer understanding of contemporary life and literature in the Arab world, to push them to a sympathetic but not simplistic exploration of the materials they are presented with, to have them identify with those materials on different levels. This process can be explicitly explained to them; it also works implicitly throughout the semester. Sometimes students find surprising and profound ways of engaging with poetry and drama, genres often considered more difficult to teach than fiction.

This approach can demand a good deal of effort from both teachers and students, but it can also be fun and exciting. I provide students with a sensory experience of being there that draws on the visual (*YouTube* performances), the auditory (recitation of poetry), and smells and tastes (an introduction to Arab cuisine). I have my students interact with guests from the region. This approach is multimodal, requiring teachers to continually look for new resources, to try things out and see what works. Students leave such classes with much more knowledge of Arab culture than what is afforded by stories reported in the media, and they are better prepared to think more critically about the works they encounter. They will therefore be better global citizens.

Note

I would like to thank the many friends and colleagues who responded to my pleas for assistance: Fadia Abdul-Qader Mereani, Mohammed Albakry, Mohammed Ghazi Alghamdi, Khalid Amine, Valerie Anishchenkova, Zoubeir ben Bouchta, Mohammad Dagman, Osama Esber, Ahmad Jeddeeni, Rajae Khaloufi, Kari Neely, George F. Roberson, and Stephen Sheehi.

Works Cited

Abu-Khalid, Fawziya. "بلاد" [Balad; A Country]. ماء السراب [Ma al-Sarab; Mirage]. Water Dar al-Jadid, 1995.

———. "A Country." Translated by Farouk Mustafa. *The Poetry of Arab Women: A Contemporary Anthology,* edited by Nathalie Handal, Interlink Publishing, 2001, p. 71.

Adonis. *A Time between Ashes and Roses.* Translated by Shawkat M. Toorawa, Syracuse UP, 2004. Bilingual edition, translation of وقت ما بين الرماد والورد [Waqt bayna al-ramad wal-ward].

Albakry, Mohammed. "Between the Human and the Foreign: Translating Arabic Drama for the Stage." *Educational Theory,* vol. 64, no. 5, October 2014, pp. 497–514.

Al-Hakim, Tawfiq. *The Essential Tawfiq Al-Hakim: Plays, Fiction, Autobiography.* Edited by Denys Johnson-Davies, American UP, 2013.

Al-Mala'ika, Nazik. أغنية حبّ للكلمات [Ughniyat hub lil-kalimat; Love Song for Words]. *Adab.com,* 9 Mar. 2016, www.adab.com/modules.php?name=Sh3er&doWhat=shqas&qid=422.

Al-Udhari, Abdullah, editor and translator. *Victims of a Map: A Bilingual Anthology of Arabic Poetry.* Saqi, 1984.

Amine, Khalid. "Performing Gender on the Tremulous Moroccan Body: Zoubeir Ben Bouchta's *Lalla J'mila.*" *TDR / The Drama Review,* vol. 51, no. 4, 2007, pp. 167–73.

———. "Performing Postcoloniality in the Moroccan Scene: Emerging Sites of Hybridity." *Contesting Performance.* Palgrave Macmillan, 2010, pp. 191–206.

Amine, Khalid, and Marvin A. Carlson. "Al-halqa in Arabic Theatre: An Emerging Site of Hybridity." *Theatre Journal,* vol. 60, no. 1, 2008, pp. 71–85.

Antoun, Naira. "Translating Theater to and from the Arab World." *Egypt Independent,* 17 Mar. 2013, www.egyptindependent.com/news/translating-theaterand-arab-world.

Badawi, M. M. *Early Arabic Drama.* Cambridge UP, 1988.

Ben Bouchta, Zoubeir. *Shakespeare Lane.* Translated from Arabic by Rajae Khaloufi, edited by George F. Roberson, preface by ben Bouchta. International Centre for Performance Studies, 2008.

———. زنقة شكسبير [Zanqat Shakespeare]. طنجيتانوس [Tanjitanus]. Wamda, 2011. Translated as *Shakespeare Lane.*

Darwish, Mahmoud. *In the Presence of Absence.* Translated by Sinan Antoon, Archipelago, 2011.

———. *Unfortunately It Was Paradise: Selected Poems.* Translated by Fady Joudah, U of California P, 2013.

Enani, Mohamed, translator. *Angry Voices: An Anthology of the Off-Beat New Egyptian Poets.* Introduction by Enani, compiled by Mohamed Metwalli. U of Arkansas P, 2003.

Handal, Nathalie, editor. *The Poetry of Arab Women.* Interlink Publishing, 2001.

Hibbard, Allen. "Tangier at the Crossroads: Cross-cultural Encounters and Literary Production." *Writing Tangier,* edited by Ralph M. Coury and R. Kevin Lacey, Peter Lang Publishing, 2009, pp. 1–12.

Hutchins, William Maynard. *Tawfiq al-Hakim: A Reader's Guide.* Reinner, 2003.

Jaggi, Maya. "Poet of the Arab World." *The Guardian*, 7 June 2002, www.the guardian.com/books/2002/jun/08/featuresreviews.guardianreview19.

Jayyusi, Salma Khadra, editor. *Modern Arabic Poetry: An Anthology.* Columbia UP, 1987.

———, editor. *Short Arabic Plays: An Anthology.* Interlink Publishing, 2003.

———. *Trends and Movements in Modern Arabic Poetry.* Brill, 1977.

Jayyusi, Salma Khadra, and Roger Allen, editors. *Modern Arabic Drama: An Anthology.* Indiana UP, 1995.

Johnson-Davies, Denys, editor and translator. *Egyptian One-Act Plays.* Heinemann, 1981.

Kabbani, Nizar. *Arabian Love Poems.* Translated by Bassam Frangieh and Clementina R. Brown, Three Continents Press, 1993.

Kahf, Mohja. "Politics and Erotics in Nizar Kabbani's Poetry: From the Sultan's Wife to the Lady Friend." *World Literature Today*, 2000, pp. 44–52.

Khaloufi, Rajae. Translator's preface. Ben Bouchta, *Shakespeare Lane*, pp. 11–12.

Myers, Robert, and Nada Saab. "Sufism and Shakespeare: The Poetics of Personal and Political Transformation in Saʿdallah Wannus's *Tuqus al-Isharat wa-l-Tahawwulat.*" *Theatre Research International*, vol. 38, no. 2, 2013, pp. 124–36.

Moore, Marianne. *The Complete Poems of Marianne Moore.* Macmillan, 1967.

Nussbaum, Martha C. *Cultivating Humanity: A Classical Defense of Reform in Liberal Education.* Harvard UP, 1997.

O'Brien, Soledad. "Unwelcome: Muslims Next Door." *CNN*, 2 Apr. 2011. *YouTube*, 28 Mar. 2011, www.youtube.com/watch?v=gRlqz3e9OrA.

Said, Edward W. *Orientalism.* Vintage Books, 1979.

Stetkevych, Suzanne. *The Mute Immortals Speak: Pre-Islamic Poetry and the Poetics of Ritual.* Cornell UP, 1993.

Suleiman, Yasir. "Nationalist Concerns in the Poetry of Nazik Al-malaʾika." *British Journal of Middle Eastern Studies*, vol. 22, nos.1–2, 1995, pp. 93–114.

Taher, Walid. *A Bit of Air.* Translated by Anita Husen, Center for Middle Eastern Studies, U of Texas, 2012.

Toorawa, Shawkat M. Translator's preface. Adonis, pp. xv–xvi.

Venuti, Lawrence. *The Scandals of Translation: Towards an Ethics of Difference.* Routledge, 2002.

Wannous, Saʿdallah. الأعمال الكاملة [Al-Aʿmal al-kamila; Complete Works]. Vol. 1, Al-Ahali, 1996.

———. *Four Plays from Syria by Saʾdallah Wannous.* Translated by Marvin Carlson et al., Martin E. Segal Theatre Center Publications, 2014.

Zahrawi, Samar. "Syrian Drama Escaping Censorship: Saʿdallah Wannous's *The King's Elephant* and *The King Is King.*" *Arab World English Journal*, vol. 6, no. 2, 2015, pp. 329–36.

Part III

Comparative Contexts, Youth Culture, New Media

Caroline Seymour-Jorn

Youth Culture in the Arab World: Explorations through Literature in Translation

Our role as critics and teachers and our relationship to the texts and authors we study at a particular historical moment should become objects of inquiry as much as the books themselves.

—Amal Amireh

Courses on global youth culture seem to have growing appeal among college students, perhaps because they have access to some aspects of global culture through the Internet. Certainly music, music videos, and sometimes translated lyrics are easily downloaded from the Web. American youth can see that there are new and divergent forms of music and art being produced globally and that some of it draws on musical and cultural forms they recognize. They are intrigued by, and want to know more about, the obviously changing and complex international contexts that are spawning new forms of popular culture. In the Middle East and North Africa, artists like Cheb Khaled and—more recently—music about the Arab Spring have captured a great deal of attention in the West (Gana). I believe that this curiosity provides teachers of Arabic literature and culture with a good opportunity to respond, by offering courses on Arabic literature by and about young people in the Middle East.

This essay discusses a popular undergraduate course that I have taught in recent years at the University of Wisconsin, Milwaukee. As a lower-level comparative literature offering, the course attracts students from across the disciplines. I use a set of five novels, of short to medium length, that explore the personal, family, social, work, and political experiences of youth in the contemporary Arab world. Four were written in Arabic and translated into English; one was written in English. They are *Girls of Riyadh* (بنات الرياض ; Banat al-Riyadh), by Rajaa Alsanea, who is from Saudi Arabia; *Being Abbas el Abd* (أن تكون عباس العبد ; An takun ʿAbbas al-ʿabd), by Ahmed Alaidy, who is from Egypt; *Always Coca-Cola* (دايما كوكا كولا ; Daʾiman coca-cola), by Alexandra Chreiteh, who is from Lebanon; *The Honey*, by Zeina Ghandour, who is from Lebanon and the United Kingdom; and *A Land without Jasmine* (بلاد بلا سماء ; Biladun bila samaʾ), by Wajdi al-Ahdal, who is from Yemen.

A stimulating course can be developed by underlining at the beginning that we are reading not ethnography but fiction by well-informed, sensitive, and creative native observers of their own cultures. Students should be challenged to reflect on the special perspective that a literary author may bring to social critique generally and to the treatment of youth specifically. I use novels that are written by both men and women and deal extensively with gender, allowing students to think about changing gender norms and roles. Because these novels are written about five countries or territories, each having a unique historical background, students can be asked to compare them with regard to how each work of fiction portrays its society in relation to other societies, including those of the West, some of which were former colonizers.

I emphasize two hermeneutic contexts of translated works. The first has to do with the complex process of using translation to understand the humanity of the other. I impress on the students that part of what we must do when we read literature in translation is to take on the responsibility of understanding the political, historical, and cultural contexts in which the text is produced (Appiah 399–400). We must try to gain insight into the humanity and conditions of people in very different places. It helps to understand what Pierre Bourdieu calls "the field of cultural production," so that we can understand some of the prevailing cultural aesthetic that produces the meaning and value of a piece of literature (30–73). In the Middle East, social or political critique often exists alongside literary innovation, and it is one of the qualities generally granted praise by a work's critics and readers.

The second context of interpretation has to do with the translations themselves. What does it mean to read a creative work from one linguistic and cultural environment in a version that has been designed for another audience? How do we know if a translation is good? Students are often aware that they are missing something when they are reading a translation. How can we deepen this awareness when most of them have little to no knowledge of Arabic? As always, we should also encourage students to think about the issue of representation. Why is a particular novel selected for translation? Who decides what gets translated? What types of texts will appeal to English-speaking audiences? And to what extent is a translation an original piece of literature? We may not be able to answer all these questions, but asking them generates new understandings of the Arab world and its position in a world of rapidly globalizing and youth-oriented markets, medias, and cultures.

Girls of Riyadh: **When Literary Experimentation Is Only Partly Reflected in Translation**

I have students read *Girls of Riyadh*, translated by Marilyn Booth, alongside her article in which she discusses what happened to her translation after she submitted it to Penguin Books ("Translator"). This pairing can initiate a discussion on the politics of the literary market, particularly with regard to gender, and on the potentially complicated relationship between translator and author. (Also see Booth, "'Muslim Woman,'" on the effect of market forces on the translation process.)

Although I ask the students to begin reading the translated texts right away, I usually spend the first few class sessions providing information about the geography and diverse cultural makeup of the Middle East and North Africa, since many lack this background. I provide social and political background each time we move to a new country.

American students are drawn to *Girls of Riyadh* because of its e-mail discussion list format and its readability. They quickly note, as have literary critics, its affinity to the British and North American genre of chick lit, the narrator offering light, chatty descriptions and reflections on her friends, their families, and their love lives (Al-Ghadeer 296). Yet, as Booth points out, Alsanea poses serious criticism of many aspects of Saudi life, including restrictive gender norms that ultimately disempower both men and women. She also effectively experiments with "(l)inguistic poly-exuberance, structural experimentation, and globalized and local pop culture references and texts" ("Translator" 200). Alsanea's electronic writing format is a good point of departure for discussing experimentalism in Arabic writing and a place to point out that generations of Arab authors, both male and female, have experimented with narrative forms to describe their changing societies.

Alsanea makes intertextual gestures when she uses poems of Nizar Qabbani, a Syrian, and lyrics from the popular Saudi singer Abdul Majeed Abdullah (3, 19). Slightly later, in chapter 9, she puts hadiths (sometimes with citations) and her interpretation of them into the prefaces of her e-mail messages concerning her friends Gamrah, Lamees, Michelle, and Sadeem. These hadiths support her progressive values, the importance of self-advocacy and action, and a man's consideration of his wife and family. Considerable richness can be added to the classroom discussion by incorporating criticism on the poetry of Qabbani, his advocacy of women's rights, the hadiths themselves, the nature of their codification, and the varying attitudes among Muslims toward them (on Qabbani, see Gabay 207–22; Kabbani; on the hadith, see Juynboll).

Booth relates that her original translation of *Girls*—in which she practiced a "maximum amount of 'literalist surrender'" in order to highlight Alsanea's language play, use of multiple vernaculars, and gender politics—was rejected by both Alsanea and Penguin. Alsanea made significant revisions to the translation, and what resulted, according to Booth, is a text that

> emphasizes immediate accessibility over "surrender to the text," similarity over difference, transparent "equivalence" over pitfalls of locality . . . it favors the "high readability" of chick lit over the punning satire, local embeddedness and intertextual play important to the power and novelty of this novel in Arabic. ("Translator" 201)

She provides examples of how the revised version erases the edginess and sly gender politics of the original Arabic and the way it plays with the terminology of the news and entertainment media. She points to the omission of Alsanea's use of أنساتي (anisati; "girls or young ladies") as an addition to the conventional "ladies and gentlemen"; *anisati* is one of the central categories of people that the narrator's e-mail messages address (202; Alsanea, *Banat* 9 and *Girls* 1). Booth argues that she opted for a translation that, if foreignizing in ways, nevertheless emphasizes the language experimentation that is so important to the quality of the Arabic prose and that addresses the globalized, heterogeneous quality of language in Saudi Arabia. The original prose also acknowledges the presence of a

Saudi bourgeois English, which Booth italicizes and spells phonetically to represent actual Saudi pronunciations (204–05; Alsanea, *Banat* 17 and *Girls* 7). This complex linguistic weave helps paint the girls of Riyadh as cosmopolitan actors, who, though they live with certain—and sometimes significant—restrictions, actively engage in a complex world both inside and outside Saudi society.

Booth concludes that Alsanea and Penguin opted for a bland translatese to appeal to the Western reader and feels that their erasure of the literary experimentation may have contributed to the poor reviews of the translation. She echoes Gayatri Spivak in emphasizing the importance of thinking about language as part of the process of understanding a translation. As Spivak points out, the way a woman writer inserts agency into her text may create a rhetoricity that distinguishes it and makes it effective for talking about women's worlds (179–80). Pairing *Girls of Riyadh* with Booth's detailed analysis of language play in the source text allows us to posit from the beginning that readers of translation should be willing to work a little harder to grasp not only the thematic context of translations, but also "*how* the text speaks to its first audience" ("Translator" 200).

Always Coca-Cola: Translating the Globalizing Body

Chreiteh's *Always Coca Cola*, translated by Michelle Hartman, has content similar to that of *Girls of Riyadh*—the lives and relationships of young women, but in Beirut—and a flowing, satirical style. But this novel has a very specific focus: the bourgeois west Beirut milieu of young women attending the Lebanese American University. The first-person narrator, Abeer Ward, comes from a conservative family. She is named after her father's flower shop (7), an instance of the text's persistent criticism of consumerism as it shapes both Beiruti lives and landscapes. Abeer's anxieties and preoccupations with her reputation will seem familiar to students just having read *Girls of Riyadh*. Yet Chreiteh's novel complicates students' assumptions about women's lives in the Middle East. Abeer's group of close friends is diverse, including Yana, a freewheeling Romanian woman who is separated from her husband and works as a model for the local Coca-Cola company, and Yasmine, a young woman of German and Lebanese parents who hails from the mountains, kickboxes for sport, and is generally viewed as lesbian.

Always Coca-Cola follows Abeer's efforts to get a trainee position at the Coca-Cola factory through Yana's new boyfriend, who is the manager.

Abeer is shocked when she learns that Yana is pregnant by this man. Abeer gets the job and is later raped at work by the boyfriend, who remains nameless throughout the novel. As part of the work's gender politics, most male characters are not named, referred to only in relation to the female characters. Chreiteh engages in what Hélène Cixous calls the "feminine practice of writing," as she generates new ways of expressing female experience and works against female self-disdain ("Laugh" 279–97 and "To Live" 83–92). Through Abeer's satirical voice, Chreiteh disrupts conventional standards about how women's experience is described. Abeer details her anxiety about using tampons for fear of puncturing her hymen. Chreiteh's prose subverts patriarchal notions about the female body: after her rape, Abeer notes that the pure blood of virginity, "the very reason for my entire existence," looks just like menstrual blood, which she always considered impure, odorous, and embarrassing (83).

I assign the translator's afterword as a follow-up reading, although it could also work as a prelude to the novel. Hartman observes that the novel represents intimate thoughts and discussion in Modern Standard Arabic instead of the vernacular (114–15). Chreiteh follows other Arab writers, like Salwa Bakr and Miral al-Tahawy, in opening up the world of women's feelings, frustrations, aspirations, and fears by expressing them with the standard language, which historically has been used primarily in formal, public, and male-dominated occasions and contexts. Chreiteh's ironic stance calls to mind Bakr's work in particular.

Abeer's rape and its aftermath are narrated in a curiously flat tone, which may be Chreiteh's attempt to convey the emotional detachment often associated with trauma, or it may be the relative inexperience of a first-time novelist. Abeer's minimal engagement with feelings of anger and violation and her focus on her loss of virginity nevertheless gets at the absurdity of a cultural obsession with a membrane to the neglect of the emotional life of girls and women. Through multiple references to the images of Yana's body on the Coca-Cola billboards through the (literal) windows of Abeer's world, Chreiteh cleverly combines her criticism of Lebanese patriarchal values with a trenchant condemnation of Western capitalism and commodification of the body.

Suneela Mubayi describes Abeer as a narrator with an apathetic response to the self-absorbed and consumer-oriented lifestyle of young university women in a city that was once "a laboratory for a progressive, vanguard culture" (540). This observation might lead to classroom discussion about the positions of young people in the region, many of whose lives have been shaped by a long history of sectarianism and political conflict and also by the rapid introduction of global consumer culture. Such a discussion can segue to the Egyptian novel translated by Humphrey Davies as *Being Abbas el Abd*.

Being Abbas el Abd: Translating Despair

If the overall tone of *Always Coca-Cola* is detachment, that of Alaidy's *Being Abbas el Abd* is confusion—of narrative voice, of temporalities, of the identity of primary characters, and of prose style: the computer, texting, and graffiti language has a disruptive effect. The narrator seems to be Abdallah, although we do not come upon his name until very late in the narrative. He is a depressed and disconnected young man who works in a video store where he dispenses films as though they were antidepressants, pushing the latest Michael Douglas film as a balm for the daily grind. The narrative jerkily shifts between first and third person. We learn about Abdallah's friend and roommate Abbas, an eccentric character who obsessively plays with his jacket zipper and lures Abdallah into strange social situations. Throughout, Abdallah spouts disjointed thoughts about his childhood and growing up, about being emotionally tortured by his psychiatrist uncle Awni, his psychotropic drug use, and his ideas about the failures of the older generation or generations, the abuse and commodification of women, and petropolitics.

Abbas arranges for Abdallah to have an entangled meeting with two women named Hind, one who appears to want a serious relationship and the other a prostitute. Abdallah's encounter with the latter provokes a sort of crisis. When she tells Abdallah that she was abused as a child, he comes to appreciate her as a human being rather than as "just a THING, a thing to be consumed and taken and thrown away" (91; حاجة)، (حاجة) ممكن تتاكل وتتاخد وممكن تترمي [An 14]). Eventually he finds himself in the apartment with both Hinds, who both believe that he is Abbas, because they know him only through cell phone conversations. The encounters with the Hinds push Abdallah toward psychosis. Relying on play with typeface and keyboard symbols, Alaidy navigates his readers through a scene in which Abdallah realizes that he is the same man as Abbas and as his Uncle Awni or Ab(Awni)bas—pushing the reader to suspect that the entire narrative is a complex, suicidal hallucination and that all three characters are voices emanating from one mind (88).

Because the narrative is so confusing, I remind students that one aspect of the novel is to raise questions about identity itself. What might an author accomplish by creating a primary character in such a liminal and elusive manner? Is Alaidy representing the shifting interpersonal, physical, hormonal experience of youth in general and specifically of youth relying on pharmaceuticals? Is he criticizing the failures of the older generation, Egyptian society, or the "Oriental Conscience" (23)? Of course, the novel also explores mental illness; we can read Abdallah as the schizophrenic product of childhood abuse. Other Arab authors have used the mad protagonist as a mode of social critique. Women authors such as Salwa Bakr in the *Golden Chariot* (العربة الذهبية لا تصعد إلى السماء ; Al-ʿaraba al-dhahabiyya la tasʿad ila al-samaʾ) have figured madness as a natural response for smart, creative women in a society that offers them little opportunity or respect. Is Alaidy figuring madness as a necessary outcome for a generation raised by disillusioned elders in the aftermath of Egypt's 1967 war with Israel and the social, economic, and political turbulence that characterized the final decades of the twentieth century? Hoda Elsadda's brief analysis of the book suggests that "the narrator suffers from his acute awareness of the gap that separates the national dream of progress and prosperity from the sordid political and social reality around him" (203). As Elsadda also notes, the novel is influenced by Chuck Palahniuk's *Fight Club*; like the American novel, it explores the crisis of masculinity in a hypercapitalist society. Students who have read Palahniuk's work or seen the 1999 movie based on it will undoubtedly have interesting comparisons to make between the two texts. A discussion could revolve around the question of what types of masculinity are represented by Abdallah and Abbas.

One way to help students work through this confusing and dense narrative is to have them do dramatic readings of interchanges between Abbas and Abdallah and to talk about the issues, cultural references, and angry diatribes that each brings forward (e.g., 30–37). They should come prepared for these readings by doing research on the many social and political references with which the text is peppered. Tarek El-Ariss offers an insightful treatment of *Being Abbas el Abd* in his *Trials of Arab Modernity*, which can offer additional ideas for how to think about the novel.

The Honey: Representations of Gender and Political Oppression

The issue of gender roles is prominent in Ghandour's short novel *The Honey*, which is set in the Israeli-occupied West Bank. The only English-language work considered in the class, it represents an important trend in literary writing in the Arab world, that of poetic prose. Authors writing in this style in Arabic include Etidal Osman (Booth, *My Grandmother's Cac-*

tus 67–90) and Ebtihal Salem (Booth, *Children*), two Egyptians whose short stories have been translated into English.

The Honey is a highly elliptical treatment of a young person's spirituality, of rebellion against gender norms and political oppression, and of the contradictions inherent in any society. It resists the attempt to read it as sociological commentary, which helps us dismantle Western assumptions about the Arab—and particularly the Palestinian—other. It is a polyphonic narrative in the Bakhtinian sense—six narrators tell the story of Ruhiya, the daughter of the Palestinian village muezzin, and Yehya, who is about to commit a suicide bombing in Jerusalem. A complex symbolism permeates the text as color, sound, and a generational dualism raise a multitude of questions about traditionalism and sexism in Palestinian society, rapacious colonialism and militarism in Israeli society, and the fate of Abrahamic peoples who are fatally engulfed in political and wartime rhetoric and revenge.

Any treatment of literature on Palestine and Israel requires a sensitive presentation of the historical events and tragedies surrounding the creation of the state of Israel and the plight of the Palestinians inside the 1948 borders and the occupied territories during the succeeding decades. Without a sense of Palestinian geographies of displacement, containment, and exile, the setting and references in the text will not make sense to many students. Joel Beinin and Lisa Hajjar provide a good outline of the history of the conflict. Rawan Damen and Dima Damen offer an accessible discussion of some basic realities of Palestinian teens in the West Bank and Gaza Strip. Additionally, it may be useful to screen parts of the feature-length film *Slingshot Hip Hop*, to give students a sense of other creative productions coming out of Palestine.

Because of the mythic and sometimes dreamlike quality of *The Honey*, I approach the novel from a thematic perspective, and two of the most striking themes are female aspiration and desire and the transgression of gender and religious norms. On Ruhiya's entry into the world, her mother takes great pleasure in her birth, gently rebuffs the village women's traditional condolences on not having produced a male child, and adores her baby: "Neither did their condolences dim the brilliance of the love she immediately felt for the baby" (19). Ghandour evokes the Sufi language of spiritual yearning to describe Ruhiya's wish to use her voice to speak the Qur'anic verses that her dying father has taught her. Although she has been taught that a woman's voice is *'awra*, or a source of shame, and should not be raised in public, she determines to make the call to prayer that her father cannot. As he lies dying, she climbs to the top of the minaret to make the call to prayer and thinks, "I am bloated right now with the love God has shown me. But nothing has changed; I just am where I should be, holding my breath for an intrepid amount of time and asking the morning if she will be mine . . ." (26).

The narrative describes the village's ambivalent response to Ruhiya's call as something both beautiful and shameful. But in the end it is her voice—her transgressive call from the minaret—that mysteriously reaches Yehya and turns him away from his act of bombing. Generational dualism appears in the oblique suggestion that Ruhiya and Yehya are both actually the product of Hurra's rape by Farhan, a villager known as "the Honeyman." The fifth narrator, a girl named Asrar, calls Ruhiya and Yehya "the siblings of Farhan's split seed" (84). Yehya, who appears to have been tortured by the Israelis, seeks violence and revenge, but Ruhiya, also a subject of political oppression, has an abiding spirituality that serves to quench that violence. Other dualities in the text are Arab-Jew, occupied-occupier, Western observer–traditional villager, but none of these roles is construed in essentialist terms. The novel promotes instead a positive feminine principle, like the honey that flows throughout the narrative: it may or may not be enough to facilitate healing. Ghandour, drawing on the time-honored tradition that honey has healing properties, refers to the Qur'anic *surat al-nahl* ("The Bees"), which describes bees as a gift of God that provide a substance that is curative for humankind (Al-Qur'an 16.68–69).

A Land without Jasmine: **An Arabic Detective Novel**

Al-Ahdal's *Land without Jasmine*, translated by William Maynard Hutchins, is a detective story set in a Yemeni city. In my experience, American university students find it compelling. The novel is a complex, polyphonic narrative that relates the disappearance of Jasmine Nashir al-Niʿam, a first-year university student in the Faculty of Science, and the subsequent sighting of a mysterious man by the pomegranate tree where her bag and clothes are found. There are six narrators: Jasmine herself; Abdurrabbih, the police inspector; Nasir, the proprietor of the university canteen; Ali, an adolescent neighbor; Deputy Inspector Mutiʿ; and Jasmine's mother, Wahiba.

The novel bears a strong resemblance to مقام عطية (Maqam ʿAtiyya; "The Shrine of Atiyya"), by Bakr, an Egyptian, which was translated into English (Bakr, *Wiles* 126–78). Bakr's novella tells the story of the life of Lady Atia and the strange events surrounding her funeral and shrine at the Greater Cemetery in Cairo. The journalist assigned to investigate the case solicits testimonies from people who knew Atia, but he fails to obtain a consistent portrait of her: some people describe her as saintlike, others as vulgar and slovenly. Similarly in al-Ahdal's novel, the narrators who tell the story of Jasmine describe her as a legendary beauty and paragon of virtue, as a loose girl who only pretends to be virtuous, and as a genius with vast knowledge of ancient Yemeni civilizations. Members of her family threaten to kill her if she is found to have lost her virginity, and they do kill Ali, on the suspicion that he kidnapped her.

Both al-Ahdal's and Bakr's texts raise questions about how women are viewed in society, emphasizing the fact that small clues about a woman are often used to discredit her moral fiber, and her being discredited can profoundly affect her life and that of her family. Both Bakr's and al-Ahdal's texts often refer to history (of Egypt and Yemen, respectively) and link the disappeared woman with that history to suggest that in the ancient civilizations women were more respected. In al-Ahdal's novel, Jasmine is compared with Bilqis, legendary queen of Yemen, known in the west as the Queen of Sheba. Al-Ahdal's literary experimentation diverges from Bakr's, however, in that the accounts given by Ali, who is smitten with Jasmine, and the entries Jasmine's mother finds in her diary contain sexually explicit passages, the thoughts, feelings, and fantasies of pubescent youth. Because of these passages, and because of his other, earlier controversial work, al-Ahdal was censored and sent into exile for a while in 2002. The narrative suggests that Jasmine disappears after she reaches puberty and has a sexual dream, but her disappearance can also serve as a metaphor for the veiling and relative seclusion that many Yemeni women face in adolescence.

Teaching this text to Western students can be challenging because of references to popular Muslim beliefs and to the Muslim supernatural, so it is worth spending a little time explaining the ideas, both religious and secular, about the jinn or afreets. The sometimes mystical tone of the narrative can be related to that of *The Honey*, and students can be prompted to think about the efficacy of this style for the treatment of gender and political issues. *A Land without Jasmine* presents a damning criticism of Yemeni social attitudes toward women and female sexuality and thus might reinforce Western stereotypes about the absolute nature of patriarchy and sexism in Middle Eastern societies. For this reason students should be encouraged to consider the polyvocality of the narrative, because the author explores the complexity of human perception and the way in which it affects relationships. Al-Ahdal's characters form opinions about Jasmine on the basis of their limited experience with her and their beliefs and desires, their ideas about the opposite sex, and their conflicts concerning sexuality. It is this exploration of human subjectivity and what it means to understand another person that I find most interesting about the novel, and, of course, such an exploration transcends cultural boundaries.

The Arabic-language novels and the one English-language novel discussed in this essay are only a tiny part of the literature being written in the Middle East and North Africa. So we may ask, Why were these works in particular published and selected for translation? Why are we teaching them and not other works? That they are about young people in globalizing contexts and about sexuality, political violence, and "honor killing" is undoubtedly a reason that they interest Western students. Do they then perpetuate orientalist-essentialist notions of a highly sexualized and violent Middle East? Are we missing other experimental novels that don't have as much of this type of content? Perhaps. Yet each of these novels contains two elements singled out by important literary critics, like Ferial Ghazoul and Richard Jacquemond: the combination of literary innovation and prominent social or political engagement is often regarded by them as ideal. This is significant, because Egyptian critics and critical perspectives are influential in the pan-Arab literary sphere. In *Girls of Riyadh*, *Being Abbas el Abd* and *Always Coca-Cola*, the aesthetic innovation that garnered attention involved the different levels of Arabic, including emerging slangs and forms of Arab-English. In *The Honey*, the experimentation involves the use of English to generate a poetic prose that describes both intimate female experience and gender and political oppression in the West Bank. In *A Land without Jasmine*, the author explores adolescent sexuality in a polyvocal text. Fruitful discussion can be had with students about what these literary products of dynamic and creative imaginations can teach us when we read across languages and cultures.

Works Cited

Al-Ahdal, Wajdi. بلاد بلا سماء [Biladun bila sama'; A Land without a Sky]. Markaz ibadi lil-dirasat wa-l-nashr, 2008. Translated as *A Land without Jasmine*.

———. *A Land without Jasmine*. Garnet Publishing, 2012.

Alaidy, Ahmed. أن تكون عباس العبد. [An takun 'Abbas al-'abd]. Dar Merit, 2003. Translated as *Being Abbas el Abd*.

———. *Being Abbas el Abd*. Translated by Humphrey Davies, American U in Cairo P, 2009.

Al-Ghadeer, Moneera. "Girls of Riyadh: A New Technology Writing or Chick Lit Defiance." *Journal of Arabic Literature*, vol. 37, no. 2, 2006, pp. 296–302.

Alsanea, Rajaa. بنات الرياض [Banat al-Riyad]. Dar al-Saqi, 2007. Translated as *Girls of Riyadh*.

———. *Girls of Riyadh*. Translated by Rajaa Alsanea and Marilyn Booth, Penguin, 2007.

Appiah, Anthony. "Thick Translation." *The Translation Studies Reader*, edited by Lawrence Venuti, 2nd ed., Routledge, 2004, pp. 389–401.

Bakr, Salwa. العربية الذهبية لا تصعد إلى السماء [Al-ʿaraba al-dhahabiyya la tasʿad ila al-samaʾ; The Golden Chariot Does Not Ascend into the Heavens]. Dar sina li-l-nashr, 1991.

———. *The Golden Chariot*. Translated by Dinah Manisty, Garnet Publishing, 1995.

———. مقام عطية [Maqam ʿAtiyya; The Shrine of Atiyya]. Dar al-fikr li-l-dirasat wa-l-nashr wa-l-tawziʿ, 1986.

———. *"The Wiles of Men" and Other Stories*. Translated by Denys Johnson-Davies, Quartet Books, 1992.

Beinin, Joel, and Lisa Hajjar. "Palestine, Israel, and the Arab-Israeli Conflict: A Primer." *Middle East Research and Information Project*, Feb. 2014, www.merip.org/primer-palestine-israel-arab-israeli-conflict-new.

Booth, Marilyn, translator. *Children of the Waters*. By Ibtihal Salem, Center for Middle East Studies at the U of Texas, 2002.

———, ed. *My Grandmother's Cactus: Stories by Egyptian Women*. Quartet Books, 1991.

———. "'The Muslim Woman' as Celebrity Author and the Politics of Translating Arabic: *Girls of Riyadh* Go on the Road." *Journal of Middle East Women's Studies*, vol. 6, no. 3, 2010, pp. 149–82.

———. "Translator v. Author (2007): *Girls of Riyadh* Go to New York." *Translation Studies*, vol. 1, no. 2, 2008, pp. 197–211.

Bourdieu, Pierre. *The Field of Cultural Production*. Columbia UP, 1993.

Chreiteh, Alexandra. *Always Coca-Cola*. Translated by Michelle Hartman. Interlink Publishing, 2012.

———. دايما كوكا كولا [Daʾiman Coca-Cola]. Arabic Scientific Publishers, 2009. Translated as *Always Coca-Cola*.

Cixous, Hélène. "The Laugh of the Medusa." Translated by Keith Cohen and Paula Cohen. *The Signs Reader*, edited by Elizabeth Abel and Emily K. Abel, U of Chicago P, 1983, pp. 279–97.

———. "To Live the Orange." *The Hélène Cixous Reader*, edited by Susan Sellers, Routledge, 1994, pp. 83–92.

Damen, Rawan, and Dima Damen. "Palestinian Territories." *Teen Life in the Middle East*, edited by Ali Akbar Mahdi, Greenwood Press, 2003, pp. 149–64.

El-Ariss, Tarek. *Trials of Arab Modernity: Literary Affects and the New Political*. Fordham UP, 2013.

Elsadda, Hoda. *Gender, Nation, and the Arabic Novel*. Syracuse UP, 2012.

Gabay, Z. "Nizar Qabbani, the Poet and His Poetry." *Middle Eastern Studies*, vol. 9, no. 2, 1973, pp. 207–22.

Gana, Nouri. "Rap and Revolt in the Arab World." *Social Text*, vol. 30, no. 4, 2012, pp. 25–53.

Ghandour, Zeina. *The Honey.* 1999. Interlink Publishing, 2008.

Ghazoul, Ferial. "Mohammad Afifi Matar." *Belles étrangères Egypte*, Ministère de la Culture et de la Francophonie, 1994.

Jacquemond, Richard. *Conscience of the Nation.* American U in Cairo P, 2008.

Juynboll, G. H. A. *Encyclopedia of Canonical Hadith.* Brill, 2007.

Kabbani, Nizar. *Arabian Love Poems: Full Arabic and English Texts.* Translated by Bassam K. Frangieh and Clementina R. Brown, Three Continents Press, 1999.

Mubayi, Suneela. Review of *Always Coca-Cola. Journal of Arabic Literature*, vol. 43, 2012, pp. 540–42.

Palahniuk, Chuck. *Fight Club.* 1996. W.W. Norton, 2005.

Spivak, Gayatri Chakravorty. "The Politics of Translation." *Outside in the Teaching Machine*, Routledge, 1993, pp. 179–200.

Tahawy, Miral al-. الخباء [Al-khiba']. Dar al-adab li-l-nashr wa-l-tawziʿ, 1999. Translated as *The Tent.*

———. *The Tent.* Translated by Anthony Calderbank, American U in Cairo P, 2003.

Mara Naaman

Teaching New Egyptian Writing: Experimental Style in Arabic and the Undergraduate Reader

Teaching Arabic Literature after the Arab Spring

Every year that I taught my course on modern Arabic literature in translation, I handed out a brief survey at the end of the semester to gauge student response to the material, asking which works the students would choose if they were constructing a syllabus for the course. According to these surveys, they choose novels on the basis of two criteria (out of six options given): novels should "help us understand the issues in the Middle East" and be of "literary value." When asked what novel they might recommend to a friend, the favorite by far was Mohamed Choukri's *For Bread Alone* (الخبز الحافي ; Al-Khubz al-hafi), followed by Tayeb Salih's *Season of Migration to the North* (موسم الهجرة إلى الشمال ; Mawsim al-hijra ila al-shamal) and Naguib Mahfouz's *Miramar* (ميرامار). A few students said that Abdelrahman Munif's *Cities of Salt* (مدن الملح ; Mudun al-milh) was their favorite work, despite its length. I am always surprised (and admittedly relieved) to find that although students value the political or social content of a work, they also value a work that has a challenging or innovative style.

When students indicate a preference for texts written by the younger generation of Arab writers, I am especially pleased. In general these are texts that are not written in a conventional, realist style (thus making them a challenge to teach) and that have been translated from an idiomatic Arabic that borrows heavily from the language of youth culture and digital technology. The Arabic classics are timeless, in that the human universals they express are relevant to any generation, but teachers of Arabic literature, world literature, or comparative literature should also include the voices of new writers—writers who bear witness to a social and political reality radically different from that of the early to mid twentieth century, who have helped catalyze and energize many of the protests of the Arab Spring, and who continue to write in the belief that their creative work is a political and artistic imperative in the face of the chaos, loss, entrenched poverty, and unpredictable cycles of violence that have plagued the countries of this region.

For many of the American students who attend Arabic or Middle Eastern studies courses, literature is a point of entry for making sense of the ongoing conflicts in the Middle East and of the issues and faces that fill the media. Students have seen Arabs as militants enraged at a protest or as refugees grieving after an attack or a death. Young people like themselves, in photographs and live coverage, played central roles in the demonstrations and violent confrontations that came to be called the Arab Spring. Yet few students in my 200-level course ever read in high school a book translated from Arabic—except selections from the stories of *One Thousand and One Nights*. Finding a way to connect these generations and cultures at this particular historical moment is, I believe, central to our job as teachers of Arabic literature in translation.

Contextualizing the Writing of the 1990s Generation

I highly recommend to professors who would like to integrate young Arab voices into their English-language curriculum two novels: Ahmed Alaidy's *Being Abbas El-Abd* (أن تكون عباس العبد ; An takun ʿAbbas al-ʿAbd), translated by Humphrey Davies (2006), and Hamdi Abu Golayyel's *Thieves in Retirement* (لصوص متقاعدون ; Lusus mutaqaʿidun), translated by Marilyn Booth (2006). The teaching of both requires a fair amount of context, discussion of translation issues, and patience with students' biases and literary tastes. Students often feel alienated by what are for them obscure references, youth jargon, and sheer zaniness. I've heard them say that these works are "trying to be deep," "pseudo," or "an inside joke that we don't get." But including these criticisms or grievances in class lectures and discussions can be a catalyst that makes the teaching of these works rewarding and productive.

The novels of Alaidy and of Abu Golayyel belong to what is often called the 1990s generation of new writing. This group of mostly Egyptian writers declared themselves an emergent literary movement in Cairo intent on publishing works that were a departure from the writing of the 1960s generation. Wanting to reflect their social realities, they tended to come from the nonelite classes and maintained in their works a youth-dominated, iconoclastic worldview.

In *Conscience of the Nation*, Richard Jacquemond discusses, in the contemporary Egyptian literary scene, generational cycles of innovation and the controversial issue of periodization. He notes that there are limitations to attempts by scholars to understand writing collectives in generational terms. Classification by generation can be as legitimate—or as arbitrary—as classifcation by theme or genre (social realist, modernist, fabulist, etc). Many of the claims that the 1990s generation writers made as to what differentiates them from their predecessors are similar to those made by the 1960s generation of Egyptian writers (171): both groups defined themselves in opposition to the writers who came before them, and both said that they were expanding the definition of the Arabic novel. Jacquemond observes that another similarity between the two groups is that all the writers were at the beginning of their writing careers (170–71). But generational grouping has a use-value: the self-naming, he points out, drawing on Pierre Bourdieu, is "part of a collective strategy for access to resources and the conquest of symbolic power, within a strongly hierarchical field" (172). Belonging to a broad literary movement, in other words, gives weight to a young writer's work in a literary scene that is highly competitive and dominated by older writers.

In "Aesthetics of the New Novel: Epistemological Rupture and Literary Space" (جماليات الرواية الجديدة القطيعة المعرفية والنزعة المضادة الغنائية), Sabry Hafez reads the late-twentieth-century, early millennial "new novel" in Egypt as a product of the changing geography of the city, and of the social and economic changes that have taken place in Cairo since the 1970s. Dividing the city into three parts, he writes that the new authors are "children of the third city," which is the urban periphery, and that their novels reflect this peripheral and increasingly diffuse space: their relatively short length; their episodic quality; the dwelling on the physical, corporeal, and geographic; and the unpredictability of their narration, in which links between events are not necessarily causal. Although these works clearly have a structure, they are organized as something of a "textual maze," echoing the winding quality of many of the informal housing communities of the third city (186–97).

Both Jacquemond and Hafez trace the contours of this new literary movement, which is marked by the increasing popularity of self-publishing and by the rise of the independent book publisher Merit, established in 1998 and run by Mohammed Hashem.

It is Hashem's support and promotion of the works of this generation (along with the publishing house Dar al-Sharouk) that has helped liberalize and expand the literary landscape in Cairo (Obank 63). The young writers, before the demonstrations of the Arab Spring, claimed downtown Cairo (وسط البلد ; wust al-balad), with its iconic status and palpable sense of revolutionary history, as a new bohemia, a public sphere inherited by their generation. For all Egyptians, the downtown has always been a locus of literary and political activity, but these writers made it their intellectual home.

Their edgy, politically provocative works, although initially dismissed by the Egyptian intelligentsia, have now gained acceptance and popularity. Major academic and commercial literary publications—*Akhbar al-Adab* (أخبار الأدب), *al-Qahira* (القاهرة), and *Fusul* (فصول)—published reviews of these novels and poetry collections. Major Arabic literary prizes—the Naguib Mahfouz Medal for Literature, the Sawiris Cultural Award, the International Prize for Arabic Fiction (IPAF or the Arabic Booker)—have recognized these writers. Many of their novels have been translated into English and published by the American University in Cairo Press as well as by Bloomsbury Qatar Foundation Publishing.

Among the themes of these texts are the 1990s and millennial youth culture as a quirky, self-referential world unto itself, a culture often marked by cynicism, black humor, and candid sex; criticism of the Islamification of Egypt—that is, displays of Muslim identity and religiously justified forms of social policing; the mining of ethnic or religious minority communities for stories; the claiming of class-specific spaces (informal communities, lower-middle-class neighborhoods) as sites having unique cultural and social value; and satire on the bankruptcy of political movements leading up to and after the Arab Spring. In many of these works of fiction an identification with the lower classes seeks to shock not only the elite Egyptian reader but also the Westerner reading a translation. The state as a monolithic agent of oppression, a commonplace in the fiction of the 1960s generation, is virtually nonexistent, as is the desire to represent familiar or knowable worlds (as in the tradition of social realist or contemporary realist narratives). The world of youth is depicted with abundant vernacular and insider references. In short, these novels explore the literary-minded culture of new Egyptian artists finding their way in a chaotic political and material landscape.

Strategies for Teaching *Being Abbas El-Abd*

While there are many works by newer Egyptian writers recently translated into English that are equally provocative and innovative in their style, I teach Alaidy's novel because it garnered a fair amount of critical attention (which is useful for students interested in researching the text further) and soon after its publication came to be considered (however controversially) the manifesto of this generation of writers (Baheyya). I emphasize three ideas when working through this text with students: first, its effort to articulate the voice of late 1990s–early millennial reality; second, its incorporation into Egyptian colloquial language of youth jargon and a tech-inflected idiom; third, its use of a split personality as a vehicle for offering a social critique of contemporary Egypt.

One of the first things students mention when responding to this text is how it seems to imitate Chuck Palahniuk's 1996 novel *Fight Club*. In interviews, Alaidy openly discussed his admiration of and indebtedness to Palahniuk's work and in fact mentions Palahniuk in the book's dedication. Students familiar with *Fight Club* (the novel or the 1999 film version) will recognize similarities in the motifs, literary strategies, and general tone of the two works. Some of my students went so far as to call Alaidy's novel a poor Egyptian knockoff of *Fight Club*. I find this accusation of derivativeness an ideal opportunity to discuss the issue of literary influence, cross-linguistic and cross-cultural literary borrowings or theft, and the global circulation of American culture and its resonances in other cultures.

Palahniuk's narrator embodies a generational voice—a manic, culturally and psychopharmaceutically anesthetized narrator whose split personality epitomizes the divide between passive social conformity in one narrative persona (his unnamed self) and the ego-driven, powerful, and physically predatory Tyler Durden character in another. Alaidy, playing with the split personality device in a similar way, uses an unreliable narrator as the voice of his generation of Cairene youth. Of this generation he writes:

> Tell yourself what you tell others but don't believe it.
> Egypt had its Generation of Defeat.
> We're the generation that came after it. The 'I've-got-nothing-left-to-lose generation.'
> We're the autistic generation, living under the same roof with strangers who have names similar to ours. (*Being* 36)

قل لنفسك ما تقوله للآخرين، لكن لا تصدقها.

في مصر كان هناك جيل "النكسة".

نحن الجيل الذي يليه. جيل "معنديش حاجة أخسرها".

نحن جيل من المتوحدين نحيا تحت السقف نفسه، مع غرباء لهم أسماء تُشبهنا.

(An takun 41)

Alaidy mocks the conformity of the Egyptian middle class (everyone is named Muhammad) and points to a generational divide, implicitly contrasting the bankruptcy of the politics of the old guard, particularly the post-1967 writers, with the youth of the millennial era (see Davies's translator's note [*Being* 127]). He further uses autism (توحّد; tawahhud) as a metaphor for alienated youth or, as Tarek El-Ariss puts it, a way to show satirically that Egyptian young people are connected to one another virtually but unable to communicate with one another socially—a generation entirely "disconnected from family and state" ("Hacking" 537).

Alaidy pledges to "challenge the reader to engage with the psychotic mind" (4–5) by using first- and third-person narrative shifts between Awni and Abbas, who may be read as a voice fabricated by Awni, as an alter ego, or simply as another character. Determining the exact relationship among Awni, Abbas, and, later, Abdullah is impossible, but my students routinely come up with many inventive ideas about that relationship. Alaidy disorients the reader by rendering in a literary way the psychotic mind (as Palahniuk and others have done), in which reality is not stable. This instability becomes a metaphor for the lives of youth inside the absurd political and social world of contemporary Egypt.

Several students, having spent a great deal of time trying to figure out how these different voices are threaded together in the novel, felt disappointed that there was not one correct reading of the ending or one prevailing interpretation of what happens to Awni. It is important to stress repeatedly that this frustration is part of Alaidy's game. Our disorientation and displeasure—with ambivalent endings, with impenetrable language—

are part of what makes postmodern works difficult to teach. The narrator says, "If this were a novel it would now be time for you to stop and have a sandwich. / Unfortunately, however, it isn't. / This is not a novel" (*Being* 51; لو كانت هذه رواية، فينبغي عليك الآن التوقف وإعداد شطيرة. ولكن للأسف [An takun 54]. ليست كذلك. هذه ليست رواية.). Through this lovely metafictional gesture he calls into question the very writing of novels. If this is not a novel, what is it? Finding an answer is part of the fun of teaching the work, especially when students contemplate their own means of expression, both digitally and otherwise. Alaidy's novel should be read with levity—it is a romp, a postmodern trip through the mind of a middle-class Egyptian twenty-something as he attempts to flush out his thoughts onto the page.

Consider too El-Ariss's notion that Alaidy's project is a form of hacking, read as an infiltration or "act of sabotage." The author is figuratively hacking the novel by "cutting it down" and offering to readers, in the form of this work, the fragments that remain ("Hacking" 543). Alaidy's mimicry of his generation's voice is an interpretation of how technology has influenced the way we represent ourselves and the fluidity and mediated quality of our contemporary reality. His language play ranges from using English words to imitating his peers' agile and often humorous use of colloquialisms to literally writing words as they sound when spoken in certain contexts. For example, Alaidy spells out in Arabic الرانديفو "rendez-fou" (using the *f* for the *v* in Arabic) for the French word *rendez-vous* (An takun 27). In Arabic, *v* can be written using *f*, so this importing of the French phrase into Arabic might seem correct, but "rendez-fou" simultaneously plays on the idea of replacing "a meeting" with the phrase "to make mad (*fou*)" in French. It is difficult to capture the layers of linguistic play here in English, which has only a Latin alphabet; Davies renders the play by keeping the *f* intact instead of replacing it with a *v*, preserving the juxtaposition of *rendez-vous* and *rendez-fou* (*Being* 22).

When Alaidy mocks the French inflections of Arabic by Egyptians of a certain class with the word سمبتيك ("sympathique"), Davies accentuates the French pronunciation with "zympathigue" instead of translating with "sympathetic" (29; 24). The Egyptian class subtext may not be conveyed, but the zany or somewhat affected pronunciation of the word will be understood by the English reader. The colloquial is sometimes translated in an obvious way, such as "cool" for ماشي (maashi) or "sonny" for the ephithet يا ابني (ya ibni) (31; 26, 27), yet on other occasions Davies makes subtle choices to capture the laid-back tone of the text and the hyperbole in the dialogue. For example, the phrase ‏ها ايه نظامك؟‏ (ha eh nizaa-mak; literally, "So what's your program?") is translated as "Sowassup?" (31; 26). The phrase ‏منتئة وسخة‏ (manti'a wiskha; literally, "dirty or bad area"), a transcription of colloquial spelling, is translated as "the Baaad Part of Town"(32; 28). If there are Arabic speakers in the class, one might have them read a sentence or two of the original text to demonstrate how Alaidy uses the colloquial to capture the musicality of the Egyptian vernacular instead of using Modern Standard Arabic.

One might also show students the printed Arabic original and point to Alaidy's putting the occasional English word in both dialogue and narration, his creative punctuation (e.g., multiple exclamation marks), and his use of different fonts, Web site addresses (29), and tech phrases like "upgrade" and "update" (42). When Alaidy uses English written in Latin letters in his text, Davies has to convey this code-switching. For example, the word ‏هراء‏ (hura'; "bullshit" or "nonsense") is written out in Arabic, but then the word "pull-shit" appears in parentheses next to it (42; 36). Davies includes "pull-shit" exactly as it is in the Arabic text but not indicating in any way that the English is written as English. Part of the humor is the way the *b* and *p* sounds get muddled when certain English words are spoken by Arabs. Alaidy is satirizing contemporary Egyptian vernacular, which is filled with English, sometimes French, and Arabic words pronounced in a manner unique to Egypt and to this young generation.

When Alaidy includes an English phrase with the word ‏ترجمة‏ (tarjama; "translation") and then the translation written in Arabic next to it (parodying the easy code-switching of his generation), Davies gives the English reader the sense of two languages in play. In the original, for example, "I forgive u" is accompanied by ‏ترجمة : سامحتك‏ ("translation: saamahtak"), and Davies writes, "I forgive u," then "she says, dubbing herself in English" (45; 41).

In a talk at the American University in Cairo shortly after the publication of the translation, Davies discussed (alongside Alaidy) his uncertainty with his translation choices, which he expressed in his translator's note. He worked line by line with a native Egyptian speaker to ensure that no nuances were being missed. He debated whether to use British or American slang and considered how to visually show the integration of English phrases in the original Arabic, whether by changing the font or adding words to point to a certain phrase. Davies keeps a consistently playful tone in his translation but does not domesticate the text for the English reader. By preserving the deeply local and often inscrutable references in the work, he replicates the alienation an Egyptian reader might experience, particularly one unfamiliar with the English-inflected youth vernacular and the subculture of Cairo's young bohemian set.

By allowing the text to remain foreign in translation and by embracing certain postmodern techniques, the English rendering captures the difficulty of reading this text in Arabic, even if it is somewhat jarring or frustrating for the student reader in English. Having students read the translator's note helps catalyze discussions about the role of the translator, the degree of collaboration between translator and author, and the extent to which translated texts like this are creative works in their own right.

Strategies for Teaching *Thieves in Retirement*

Abu Golayyel's *Thieves in Retirement* is the first of two novels published by this Bedouin Egyptian. Abu Golayyel also published two volumes of short stories. His second novel, الفاعل (2008; al-Fa'il), translated by Robin Moger as *A Dog with No Tail* (2009), received the Naguib Mahfouz Medal for Literature, which is awarded annually by the American University in Cairo. The novel, an excellent example of Cairo's new literature of the urban periphery, fits well into units on the city and on the cultural production of informal communities. It is also a contemporary interpretation of Arabic outlaw literature. In teaching this work, I stress three themes: first, the setting of the novel in a dystopian track of government housing on Cairo's urban fringe, where an informal economy and tribal justice system prevail; second, the work as an expression of minority consciousness and especially of the plight of the Bedouin in modern Egypt; third, the way the narrator functions as an antihero (a modern *su'luk* [صعلوك]), where thievery and the tempting of death echo themes in pre-Islamic *su'luk* poetry. Others may want to include a discussion of Sayf, the queer, cross-dressing character, and how queer identity is represented in this lower-class milieu. El-Ariss offers ideas about how to reflect on this character (*Trials* 114–44).

The novel revolves around a building in a district near Manshiyat, an industrial outpost of Helwan in Cairo erected in the 1960s as part of Nasser's strategy to provide housing for the working classes. The narrator, a young Egyptian Bedouin who seeks to make it as a construction contractor, is in need of an affordable place to live that will enable him to commute to the center of the city. The owner of the building, Abu Gamal, a retired factory worker, spends his time policing the building, watching the comings and goings of the people in the neighborhood. Though the narrator is an outsider to the district, Abu Gamal rents him a room in an apartment in the building that he shares with his family and two other tenants.

We meet Sayf, Abu Gamal's homosexual son, whose singing and cross-dressing have become an embarrassment to the family; Gamal, the oldest son, a storyteller and aspiring poet who attempts to save the family's honor by having Sayf institutionalized; and Amer, the youngest son, who supports his drug addiction by stealing. The narrative shifts among the lives of the brothers, offering often humorous portrayals of their antics and surprisingly ruthless strategies for survival and entertainment. These scenes are interrupted by the narrator's musings on Bedouin identity and flashbacks to his own family. The novel captures the lawlessness and violence of the informal economy in this no-man's-land on Cairo's urban periphery, where most of the residents are deeply attached to their rural origins yet proud to live in Nasser's government housing instead of in the shantytowns nearby. Of this industrial area, called Newtown, Abu Golayyel writes:

> It's a mongrel place, part village and part unplanned city fringe, des-
> tination of squatters and incomers, although, thanks to the wave of
> Gamal Abd al-Nasir's hand, it has a definite class identity. And perhaps
> by virtue of that very same gesture, the Manshiyat's residents are well
> placed to look down their noses at the populace of adjacent neighbor-
> hoods. Although they have rebelled against the tin shacks they threw
> up immediately after the historic hand flick—rebelled and moved into
> real houses—they remain loyal to their villages, those faraway farming
> villages that they never, ever visit, yet the memories of which give them
> a sense of security and protect them from the betrayals of time and the
> bosses at the factory. (*Thieves* 78)

المنشية حالة هجين بين القرية والحي العشوائي. وبفضل إشارة عبد الناصر
حُددت طبقة سكانها. وربما بفضلها أيضا يحظون باحتقار سكان المناطق
المجاورة، ورغم أنهم تمردوا على أكواخ الصفيح التي بنوها على عجل
بعد الإشارة التاريخية وسكنوا في البيوت إلا أنهم ما زالوا أوفياء لقراهم
.. قراهم البعيدة التي لا يزورونها مطلقا، إلا أن ذكرياتهم تشعرهم بالأمان
وتقيهم غدر الأيام ورؤساء المصانع.

(Lusus 80)

Just as the district's residents are loyal to their villages of origin, the narrator negotiates between his identity as a second- or third-generation

Bedouin and his new home on the margins of Cairo. In this respect, the work is the story of a migrant's passage. Unlike in Miral al-Tahawy's portrait of an insular Bedouin community in the desert, dominated by women, in *The Tent* (الخباء ; Al-khiba'), here the margins become a surrogate community for a range of quasi-minority figures (Saidis, Bedouin, Nubians, Copts). The novel thus offers a counter-history of the Bedouin migrant experience: their journey from the desert to settlements and finally to the periphery of the city. Being an outsider vis-à-vis the family in the district of Manshiet Nasser creates a fear that the narrator cannot shake. He responds to it by reflecting on the stories of his family, their traditions and nomadic life, and the Bedouin ethos that privileges tribal honor and courage in the face of harsh conditions and danger.

Critics have focused on the social dimensions of this new Egyptian writing, Abu Golayyel's work included, because its subject matter provides information about the liminal zones on Cairo's periphery and the youth demographic that is literally writing itself out of the margins. In her introduction to the English translation of Abu Golayyel's work, Booth carefully discusses how the novel bears witness to Cairo's changing urban landscape (*Thieves* xii–xiv). Dina Heshmat's work on the novel and the city draws on Abu Golayyel's novel as an example of a new literature that explores the "ruralization of the city" (ترييف المدينة ; taryif al-madina) and the rural migrant's "ghetto" (64).

But part of the charm of the work, and part of what makes it a great novel to teach in translation, is in its literary crafting and the way its motifs echo themes in both classical Arabic poetry and contemporary popular culture. It struggles to reconcile two narrative registers: first, that of the modern Bedouin—the ethnic identity that the narrator unearths through digressions and flashbacks; second, his self-reflexive and satirical metacommentary on the pose of the artist and the idea that life imitates art. All the characters want to be artists of one sort or another (poets, professors, writers, singers, master thieves). On a very basic level, this text is about transcendence through storytelling and the extent to which we imagine our own lives as fiction. The novel opens with the lines:

> Suppose that the life you think is your own, the life you are living at this very moment, is really the life of a character in some novel. . . . Here is a fellow who can't seem to fill the tedium of his days but by making up characters, even though they always come out flabby and exaggerated. (*Thieves* 1)

افرض – مثلاً – أنك تعيش حياتك كشخصية في رواية ما،... ولا يجد ما
يستعين به على وقته الممل سوى صنع شخصيات رغم هلاميتها
ومبالغتها،

(Lusus 7)

Abu Golayyel blurs the line between fiction and reality here. He mocks
the pose of the writer as autonomous and in control and points to the
constructed quality of writing.

The tone of the narrator is unstable throughout: he shifts to a confessional mode, then back to his satirical voice. For example, he is rattled by
witnessing an explosive fight in the stairwell of his new residence between
Abu Gamal and Gamal, because the violence reminds him of his own lack
of control:

> Until recently I believed that a person's life unfolds along a line that
> shoots straight away from his past. The farther time carries you, I
> thought, the surer you can be that this past will not repeat itself. . . .
> The past is for *back there*, for forgetting; and the present is given to the
> past, which swallows it. Our life's meaning is its end, marked out from
> the start. But the repetition of the fights in this house has made me
> doubt all of that. Indeed those fights have convinced me from up close
> that the past may well return. I can see now that anyone's life is noth-
> ing but an assemblage of repeated scenes. (*Thieves* 8–9)

إلى فترة قريبة كنت أظن أن حياة الواحد تسير على خط معاكس لماضيه،
و كلما تقدم به الزمن تأكد من استحالة عودة هذا الماضي مرة أخرى،
وكنت أتخيل هذه المسألة على النحو التالي... الماضي للخلف و للنسيان،
والحاضر للماضي، و حياتنا إلى نهايتها المحتومة، و لكن تكرار معارك هذا
البيت جعلني أشك في ذلك، بل و أتأكد عن قرب من إمكانية عودة الماضي،
و من أن حياة الواحد ما هي إلا مجموعة من المشاهد المكررة.

(Lusus 14)

The events that unfold in the remainder of the novel make sense only in
the content of this passage.

The journey in the work is a journey backward for the narrator. He
recognizes the danger that Abu Gamal's family poses for him, that for
them he is a form of prey. Therefore he must summon something of his
Bedouin self, a self from which he thought he was moving away. He writes,
"Death is the endpoint of every danger, and at the same time it's the exemplary way to make peace with all those dangers out there" (*Thieves* 17;
الموت هو غاية كل خطر، و هو في نفس الوقت الوسيلة المثلى للتصالح مع الأخطار
[Lusus 22]). As he explains in a few earnest passages to his reader, the
Bedouin lives with a constant sense of how the desert, with its many un-

knowns, can assail the traveler. The only recourse the traveler has is to embrace this fear, to move, like the heroic poet, toward death.

Yet this is not a novel written in the heroic mode. If anything, our narrator is an antihero, like the outlaw poet of early Arabic poetry—the *su'luk*. The *Encyclopedia of Islam* defines the *su'luk* as a "brigand-poet and mercenary in time of need," on the basis of poems from the early Islamic and Umayyad periods ("Ṣuʿlūk"). He skulks, mocks, and broods. He notices in Amer the skill of a seasoned thief, though the purpose of the thieving is to sustain a hashish addiction. As Amer finds ever more novel ways to steal from his family, he stirs a desire lodged deep in the narrator, who confesses:

> I always think I could have been a professional thief, a seasoned, smooth thief who stages stunning victories. I'm not talking about those low-down, pathetic burglars who fall back on elementary and undemanding gambits (thuggery plain and simple). Those folks aren't thieves, they're lunatics, and their natural habitat is the asylum, not prison. The thief I had in mind would be a conceptual thinker, a true intellectual, indeed a genius of a thief whose only motive is the pure pleasure of setting in motion and seeing through his shrewd schemes which require efforts far beyond the value of whatever it is he is bent on thieving. (*Thieves* 75–76)

> دائما أفكر بأنني كان يمكن أن أكون لصا محترفا، لص ماهر يحقق نجاحات باهرة، أص ليس من هؤلاء اللصوص المساكين الذين يلجؤون إلى حيل ساذجة وسهلة كالبلطجية، فهؤلاء ليسوا لصوصا، إنهم معتوهون. مكانهم الطبيعي مستشفى المجانين وليس السجن. اللص الذي توقعته لص مفكر، لص عبقري لا يسرق سوى للاستمتاع بتنفيذ خططه الذكية التي أنفق فيها جهدا يفوق قيمة ما يسعى لسرقته، فغايته ليست تلك الأشياء التي يسرقها، ولكن فعل السرقة نفسه. أن تحس ذلك الإحساس الممتع بأنك مهم، بأنك مطارد، بأنك لعبت على الآخرين.. نومتهم مغناطيسيا وحصلت على ما تريد مع الحفاظ على تقديرهم البالغ لك.
> (Lusus 78)

The novel plays on this notion of thievery as an art, as a modern move-ment toward danger, a way of tempting death. When the narrator catches Amer stealing from the narrator's room, something breaks in him, and the novel marches toward its inevitable end. He writes, "[W]hen I am among our historic and mortal enemies, the settled farmer population, I exude the image of a poor wretch just going about my business meekly. Among my own people though, I am a Bedouin whose eyes give off sparks" (*Thieves* 55; فأنا بين أعدائنا الفلاحين مسكين وفي حالي، وبين أهلي بدوي يتطاير الشرر من عينيه [Lusus 57]). This firmly rooted sense of pride gives him no choice but to restore his honor and avenge the crime. Echoing the earlier scenes on the ethos of the nomad in the face of danger, he fashions the perfect trap for Amer, moves boldly against fear and toward death, and his life comes full circle: he is the Bedouin he always was, courageous in the face of what he knows will be the end:

> I didn't feel at all malicious toward him. Sometimes I had frightened myself with the hunch that the electric current I had engineered with my own hand would strike him. But I thought he deserved the work of making a fitting ending to this novel, which would also put limits on my fear. *Sometimes a foolhardy rush toward the place where danger lurks is the best way to dispel your fear.* That's what Gamal wrote. I was somewhat like a hunter: usually he doesn't hate his prey, but he's eager all the same for it to fall into his trap. It's true that at various miserable points I had felt like letting go, but I always gained the upper hand over my antagonist by imagining that I had really killed him. I imposed a future on myself in which, as with the past, there was no turning back, no way to change one's mind. (*Thieves* 124–25)

> لم أكن أحس بالضغينة تجاهه، وأحياناً كنت أرتعب من هاجس أن يصعقه التيار الكهربائي الذي نصبته بيدي، ولكن اعتبرته جديراً بصنع نهاية مناسبة لهذه الرواية، ووضع حد لخوفي، "أحياناً يكون الاندفاع الأهوج إلى مكامن الخطر هو الطريقة المناسبة للخلاص من الخوف" هذا ما كتبه جمال.. كنت بشكل ما أشبه الصياد فهو عادة لا يكره فريسته ولكنه يتلهف دائماً لسقوطها في شركه، صحيح أنني على فترات متباعدة وكئيبة، كنت أحس بالتخاذل. ولكني دائماً كنت أقوّي عزيمتي بتخيل أني قتلته فعلاً، كنت أفرض على نفسي مستقبلاً، كالماضي لا رجعة فيه.
> (Lusus 126–27)

Echoing the passage at the beginning of the novel, the narrator reads his fate as the inevitable consequence of his need to defend his honor. In essence he allows himself to revert to an intuitive self—an instinctual mode of being. There is a symmetry in this reversion. In his reflections on the Bedouin and the hazards of an environment in which space dictates one's actions, one's identity, he concludes that in the space of Manshiet Nasser, Newtown, he has become the hunted. Accepting that fate, he hunts in kind, as thief, as *su'luk*, and as the heir to his Bedouin past.

Ultimately Abu Golayyel manages to blend the playfulness of a self-referential, postmodern narrative with elemental themes on the cyclical nature of time and the coming into self-knowledge. By locating his novel in the liminal space of an industrial transit community, he offers a biting social commentary on these urban outposts and the way of life they engender for a generation of Egyptian youth.

For American students, understanding the Arab Spring, which began in December 2010 in Tunisia and spread throughout the Arab world, requires a grasp of the social and cultural contexts that gave rise to such an outpouring of dissent. The novels by Egypt's new writers help provide some of these contexts by representing the diverse realities of the lower and middle classes and refracting them through the worldview of the young adult writer. These novels strive to find a sense of identity, purpose, or use and to navigate their social place in the world. Their unconventional structures, inside references, use of the vernacular, et cetera can make them seem impenetrable at first. But when enough context is provided and there is discussion of translation as a creative give-and-take process, these novels can serve as fresh, important additions to any course on Arabic literature or world literature that includes Arabic works.

Mustafa Zikri, an Egyptian writer, writes that the generation of the 1990s "abandoned the big issues that occupied the older generation" (82). In some respects this charge is true. Many of the new novels take place in very local worlds and seem to speak only to an audience of insiders belonging to marginal spaces. There are no overt indictments of the Egyptian state (during or after the ousting of Hosni Mubarak), though there are asides about the bleak political situation and satires on Egyptian bureaucracy. There are no damning criticisms of United States intervention in the region, of the hypocrisy of the Egyptian intellectual, of the proliferating regional wars, of the refugee crisis, and so on. Instead there is description in vivid detail—and with a sense of detachment and humor—of self-contained, stylized worlds in various corners of Cairo.

On a formal level, *Being Abbas el Abd* and *Thieves in Retirement* share a direct, unmediated approach to writing. Hashem notes that Alaidy and Abu Golayyel have both cast off the decorative elements (المحاسن البديعية ; al-muhasin al-bida'iyya) of their earlier writing to create fictional environments that are closer to lived experience and specific social worlds. The incorporation of colloquial or journalistic Arabic is part of this direct approach. There is an overwhelming desire to dispense with pretense and artifice, to unmask and satirize political, religious, and social posturing in all its forms.

Finally, these writers share an acute sense of class consciousness, whether it is articulated through an exploration of ethnic or minority identities or through a description of the reality of space-specific oppression. Coming from the lower and middle classes, most of these writers were not educated at elite institutions (such as the American University in Cairo or at universities abroad), nor have many of them devoted themselves to political activity, as writers of past generations did—with the exception of participation in small activist groups, like Kifayah (كفاية), and in protests during and after 25 January 2011. Instead, their works chronicle the humorous ways by which people learn to get by and claim authority in the face of their lack of agency and economic mobility in an increasingly diffuse and chaotic city. There is humor in the face of despair, frankness as an answer to artifice, class identity as depoliticized (or subtly politicized), and fiction as a form of life writing, a way of marking ground and bearing witness to a present that seems to have no logic. It is in these texts that a modern Egyptian subjectivity, however inchoate, is inscribed.

Note

The English translation of an Arabic title or text is mine, unless otherwise indicated.

Works Cited

Abu Golayyel, Hamdi. الفاعل [al-Faʿil; Actor]. 3rd ed., Dar Merit, 2009. Translated as *A Dog with No Tail*.

———. *A Dog with No Tail*. Translated by Robin Moger, American U in Cairo P, 2009.

———. لصوص متقاعدون. [Lusus Mutaqaʿidun]. Dar Merit, 2003. Translated as *Thieves in Retirement*.

———. *Thieves in Retirement*. Translated by Marilyn Booth, Syracuse UP, 2006.

Alaidy, Ahmed. أن تكون عباس العبد [An takun ʿAbbas al-ʿAbd]. Dar Merit, 2003. Translated as *Being Abbas el Abd*.

———. *Being Abbas el Abd*. Translated by Humphrey Davies, American U in Cairo P, 2006.

Baheyya. "Generational Angst?" *Baheyya: Egypt Analysis and Whimsy*, 22 June 2005, baheyya.blogspot.com/2005/06/generational-angst.html.

Choukri, Mohamed. الخبز الحافي [Al-khubz al-hafi]. Al-Saqi, 2009. Translated as *For Bread Alone*.

———. *For Bread Alone*. Translated by Paul Bowles, 2nd ed., Telegram Books, 2007.

El-Ariss, Tarek. "Hacking the Modern: Arabic Writing in the Virtual Age." *Arabic Literature Now: Between Area Studies and the New Comparatism*, edited by Amal Amireh and Waïl S. Hassan, special issue of *Comparative Literature Studies*, vol. 47, no. 4, 2010, pp. 533–48.

———. *Trials of Arab Modernity: Literary Affects and the New Political*. Fordham UP, 2013.

Hafez, Sabry. جماليات الرواية الجديدة: القطيعة المعرفية والنزعة المضادة للغنائية [Jamaliyat al-riwayah al-jadidah: al-qatiʾa al-maʿrifiya wa-l-nazʿa al-mudadda li-l-ghinaʾiyah; Aesthetics of the New Novel: Epistemological Rupture and Literary Space]. *Alif*, vol. 21, 2001, pp. 184–246.

Hashem, Mohammed. Interview by the author. 5 May 2007.

Heshmat, Dina. "De la ville vertige à la megapole fragmentée." *Lettre d'information de l'Observatorie Urbain du Caire Contemporain (CEDEJ)*, vols. 6–7, Spring 2005, pp. 60–66.

Jacquemond, Richard. *Conscience of the Nation: Writers, State, and Society in Modern Egypt*. Translated by David Tresilian. American U in Cairo P, 2008.

Mahfouz, Naguib. ميرامار [Miramar]. Faggala, 1968.

———. *Miramar*. Translated by Fatma Moussa Mahmoud, Anchor Books, 1993.

Munif, Abdelrahman. *Cities of Salt*. Translated by Peter Theroux, Vintage Books, 1989.

———. مدن الملح [Mudun al-milh]. Al-mu'assasah al-'arabiya, 1984. Translated as *Cities of Salt*.

Obank, Margaret, editor. "Egyptian Publisher Merit Wins International Award." *Banipal: Magazine of Modern Arab Literature*, vol. 25, Spring 2006, p. 63.

Palahniuk, Chuck. *Fight Club*. W. W. Norton, 1996.

Salih, Tayeb. موسم الهجرة إلى الشمال [Mawsim al-hijra ila al-shamal]. Dar al-'Awda, 1969. Translated as *Season of Migration to the North*.

———. *Season of Migration to the North*. Translated by Denys Johnson-Davies, New York Review of Books Classics, 2009.

"Su'luk." *Encyclopedia of Islam*, 2nd ed., *BrillOnline Reference Works*, reference works.brillonline.com/entries/encyclopaedia-of-islam-2/suluk-COM_1120.

Tahawy, Miral al-. الخباء [Al-khiba']. Maktabat al-Usra, 2001. Translated as *The Tent*.

———. *The Tent*. Translated by Anthony Calderbank, American U in Cairo P, 1998.

Zikri, Mustafa. "No More Big Issues." *Banipal: Magazine of Modern Arab Literature*, vol. 25, Spring 2006, p. 82.

Anne-Marie McManus

Syrian Literature after 2000: Publics, Mobilities, Revolt

Students today arrive at works of Syrian literature and art with precon-
ceptions shaped by media representations of dictatorship and the Assad
regime; popular revolt and the uprising that began in March 2011; Islamic
"terrorism," figured most notoriously in a group called the Islamic State;
and a civil war that is frequently explained in terms of resurgent sectarian
identities. But if Syrian literature for our students is to be anything other
than a transparent window onto a conflict, we must develop reading methods that engage with these works as translated, aesthetic objects, produced
in a particular historical moment but not directly reducible to historical or
political discourse.

Syrian literary production today is no longer confined to novels, short
stories, and poetry, nor is it reliant on institutionalized publication methods. The shift toward Internet-based circulation has opened up literary
and cultural fields to include *Facebook* statuses, protest banners, *YouTube*
videos, and documentary shorts. These materials are often translated into
many languages at their point of origin and attest to the rapid temporalities that structure contemporary networks of production and movement.
They also offer rich opportunities for the study of mediation and translation. Many Syrians writers today live in diaspora, with intellectual and

artistic centers in France, Lebanon, Turkey, and the United Kingdom. The activists and writers who operate in translation are often fluent in the vocabularies of literary and political theory that form a global currency in the anglophone academic world and often frame their interventions through research produced by North American and European scholars. They do so in order to elucidate their claims on Syrian politics and social worlds. More than ever, the borders among the publics that these global literary works address are blurred.

This essay applies models from circulation and translation studies to ongoing transformations in local and international circulation networks and considers their implications for teaching contemporary Syrian and Arabic literatures. Circulation studies draw attention to the modes and networks by which works move within and across reading publics as well as to the ways this movement generates new meanings and reading practices (Edwards). This approach permits us to understand translation both as a material act, bound by finite institutional, legal, and market structures, and as a rerendering of language and meaning that requires careful attention to textual aesthetics and signification. Studying circulation invites reflection on the changing dynamics of regional and international markets for Arabic literature and its translation; of institutional supports and prizes; and of our own consumption patterns for literature inside and outside the classroom.

These sociological concerns do not sideline questions of language, style, and representation but inform them. Microchoices that translators make in rendering texts legible or exotic and translational commentaries (e.g., afterwords, forewords, footnotes) can also call on us to read literature through paradigms of protest and revolution, sectarian identity, or regional politics. By introducing these concerns in the classroom, we can help our students develop critical reading practices that are in step with the changing contours of Arabic literatures after the uprisings of 2011.

Rebecca Walkowitz's notion of born-translated literature underscores the importance of reading for multiple, overlapping publics in post-2011 poetry, film, and protest art. I use the frictions implicit in translation to emphasize an emerging but understudied thematic: the translatabilities and untranslatabilities between Arabic and a newly visible Kurdish language in today's Syrian cultural production. The works I discuss in this essay also challenge the existence of a temporal delay in translation that, as Walkowitz has noted, shapes canonical theories of translation in North American academia (e.g., Walter Benjamin's "The Task of the Translator"). Working with contemporary literatures, she asks how scholars might engage with works that are produced in translation. Such born-translated works do not begin in "unique geographies, writers, and idiolects . . . [they] begin comparatively and collaboratively, in multiple language editions and in several geographies at once or nearly at once" ("Close Reading" 171).

The relevance of Syria's born-translated, post-2011 works in poetry and film comes into focus when they are read against the predominant form of the preceding decade: the novel. After 2000, the Syrian novel housed the development of a major literary and social dynamic, which I define as the literature of the Events. I use circulational readings to trace the local publics these novels called into being against the backdrop of a twenty-first-century social and political movement, the Damascus Spring or movement for civil society (Lesch 83–92; Kawakabi; Ziyada). I use Khaled Khalifa's novel *In Praise of Hatred* (مديح الكراهية [2006]) to suggest that this subset of Syrian novels can be understood as part of a broader effort to institute new modes of speech, circulation, and sociability—that is, new publics—before 2011 (on publics, see Warner).

The Literature of the Events

Khalifa's *In Praise of Hatred,* translated into English in 2012 by Leri Price, stands out among translated Syrian novels for its literary ambition as well as for the uniqueness of its narrative voice. It can be described as a stream-of-consciousness work insofar as it circles through chains of associations based on image, memory, and scent. The primary speaker is a young woman who joins an Islamist organization in Aleppo, and much of the novel winds through the maze of her thoughts and sensations. This narrative style relies on the translational genealogy of William Faulkner's *The Sound and the Fury* in Arabic, which Khalifa has adopted to represent the dying days of a formerly aristocratic family who resides in Aleppo. This spatial focus, overlaid onto the feminized, domestic space that the narrator inhabits, is punctuated by transnational flights that follow jihadists and spies to Yemen and modern-day Uzbekistan. The novel thus presents ample opportunities for discussions of translation, world literature, and narrative voice. Not least of these opportunities is the novel's arrival in English with its final chapter, seventy pages, expunged.

Despite occasional digressions, *In Praise of Hatred* follows a chronological path, with references to events that took place in Syria between

1979 and 1982. The book was originally published in 2006, but its reception in English has been heavily influenced by media interest in the post-2011 conflict in Syria and by Khalifa's public embrace of the revolution. I have argued elsewhere that novels produced before 2011 in Syria must be read with attention to historical context rather than as a representation of latent revolutionary spirit. Nowhere is this caution more important than in the reading and teaching of the literature of the Events (الأحداث ; al-ahdath), a subgenre that comprises novels, prison memoirs, and short stories.

Until 2011, the euphemism "the Events" was used in ordinary speech in Syria to refer to a period of state-civil conflict, mass detention, urban warfare, and intense social turmoil between 1979 and 1982 (Batatu 260–79; Pierret 64–72; Seale 316–38). The major landmarks of the political history of this time are the attempted assassination of Hafez al-Assad in 1980; the state's massacre, in retaliation, of political prisoners in Tadmur Prison; and the shelling of Hama in 1982, in which an estimated 30,000 people were killed. Today, as control over speech has loosened, the Events are often invoked through Hama, which represents the catastrophe of this period. The literature of the Events seeks to reinstate this history in the semipublic domain of novelistic discourse and to inscribe individual lives and experiences into the official, censored history. Indeed, these works often take up history and its narrative construction as a theme for literary consideration (e.g., Hassan; Yazbek).

In Praise of Hatred takes the unusual step of narrating from the perspective of a Muslim woman who comes to support political Islam against the state instead of from the perspective, for example, of a secular intellectual. It remains far from the site of Hama's tragedy but weaves it into a local narrative that is framed by the siege of Aleppo and by the imprisonment of the narrator's aunt in her own house because of her transgressive love affair with a regime officer. As the tension builds, news filters in of what has befallen Hama:

> In February news came from Hama that the rebellion had begun to sow fear that the small town would be destroyed and its inhabitants brutally murdered. The battle approached its end. . . . The bodies of victims were lined up in the streets of Hama but no one could be found to bury them. . . . Future generations would narrate the madness which could have been avoided, thus granting the chance of a life to the children who had loved jumping into the Orontes River from the wooden waterwheels. (*In Praise* 151)

الأخبار القادمة من حماة حول العصيان الذي بدأ يثير الخوف من قسوة
القتل وتدمير المدينة الصغيرة. اقتربت المعركة من نهايتها ...وصُفَّت جثث
قتلى في الشوارع لا تجد من يدفنها ...سيروي الأجيال القادمة أن ما حدث
جنون كان من الممكن تجنّبه لتمنح فرصة الحياة لأطفال يعشقون القفز إلى
نهر العاصي من فوق النواعير الخَشبيّة...

(Madih 156)

Although this passage is delivered in the narrator's voice, it digresses into metahistorical awareness in the gesture toward future narratives and in the metonymic representation of the tragedy through the landmarks of the river and the waterwheels.

It is widely assumed that, in daring to deal with the Events, Khalifa's novel pits memory against censorship, rendering his novel a form of resistance to the state. An afterword by Robin Yassin-Kassab, a Syrian novelist, drives this point home, casting Khalifa as an iconoclast who broke a regime taboo (300). Yassin-Kassab is not alone in this reading. Hassan Abbas, a Syrian critic, situated the novel in what he termed, in 2009, "storytelling against forgetting," which encompassed prison memoirs, novelistic representations of the Events, and sociopolitical activism.

Yet the language of Khalifa's text presents a paradox. On one hand, the novel reinserts censored history into public discourse. On the other hand, this push against the deletion of the past is not expressed overtly in the Arabic text. Rather, we find that paratexts around the translation of the novel interpret the text as representing the Events. For example, the "atheist party" is the Ba'ath Party (Yassin-Kassab 300); the Islamist group that the narrator and her relatives join, "our organization," is the Muslim Brotherhood (*In Praise* 151). The "commander of the death squad" is Rifaat al-Assad, who is the brother of Hafez al-Assad and who oversaw the razing of Hama in 1982. "Death squad" is Price's perfectly reasonable translation for Khalifa's "Battalions" or "Companies of Death" (225). But the Arabic expression was an unmissable reference for Syrian readers: Rifaat al-Assad commanded the elite Defense Battalions (Batatu 232–36). Yassin-Kassab concurs, describing such euphemisms as "unmistakable" references. Yet readers of the novel in translation must of course rely on explanatory paratexts to grasp the the historical backdrop that the novel invokes and presumes (300).

A parallel example of this allusive language is Alice Guthrie's translator's note to Zaher Omareen's "A Bedtime Story for Eid" (أم عَمرة ; Umm 'Amra), a short story published in English in 2014. The Arabic version is not yet published. The note highlights what appears to be a unique quality of this work in the description of the Events in Hama after 1982:

> There is much that is not spelled out [in this story] as it might be if
> it [were] directed at the foreign reader: the words "massacre," "arbi-
> trary detention," or "torture" don't appear here, but are signaled by
> euphemisms such as "the Events," "serving a sentence," or "having
> medical needs." There are several other references that readers unfa-
> miliar with Syria may be confused by: Tadmor and the Palestine Branch
> are both prisons notorious for extreme torture; the "Tadmor Events,"
> as they're known in Syria, refers to a massacre of at least a thousand
> inmates inside the prison in 1980. (Omareen)

A young author writing in the diaspora, Omareen is in fact perpetuating a
defining technique of the literature of the Events that has become established over the past decade and a half: euphemism. The persistence of this
mode into the present day and into the diaspora confirms that the device is
now a literary convention, not simply a pragmatic hedge against censorship.

As teachers, we should draw our students' attention to the decisions
translators make about how much to explain, in text or paratext, and how
much allusion to preserve. In the classroom, the clarification of Syrian history is an indispensable accompaniment to reading the literature of the
Events, but it should not promote the notion that this history is a stable,
graspable object around which the literary work is merely circling. Such a
reading marginalizes the aesthetics of allusion, reducing it to a covert, politicized expression that is the result of the threat of censorship. By reducing
the literary language of the Events to the fear of punishment, we not only
fail to account for the use of allusion in the diaspora but also, more importantly, overlook a concern that permeates representations of the past and engagements with the present in Syrian literature: violence in its myriad forms,
personal and political, silenced and anticipated, recalled and repressed.

One example of this aesthetic in *In Praise of Hatred* is the narrator's
outright rejection of language. Her affirmation of silence, articulated in
the narrative, is a repeated trope that draws attention to her claustropho-
bic inner life and marks her slow conversion to hatred and the celebration
of violence, which is frequently directed against women. At first, the narrator's interior life is spacious, with ecstatic, Sufi-inflected religious visions.
With time, however, her silence is linked to an increasingly stern piety,
framed in the novel as a rejection of eroticism and desire, and an accompanying impulse to withdraw from the world:

> I began to guard myself against this rebellion named "body"; I obdu-
> rately hated my incipient breasts. . . . When I saw uninhibited girls un-
> doing their bras and showing their cleavage to the breeze and the sun

in the small square, or for the titillation of the young men crowding around the entrances of the girls' schools, I felt rage at their filth. . . . I would sit on the comfortable chair [in my room], lost in thought for hours at a time. . . . My room opened directly onto the courtyard and from the window I could see the radiant silver moonlight on the surface of the pool as I felt a chill seize me. I was powerfully drawn to this scene, and clung to its every detail; it became my little world. I decorated the walls with the paintings I made during my period of silence, which continued until I lost any desire to speak at all. (16–18)

بدأت أقي نفسي من هذه المعصية المسماة جسداً، كرهت نهديَّ المتفتحين بصلابة، تبرعمت حلمتاهما السمراوان بشكل كامل... حين أرى طالبات صفي يرخين سوتياناتهن معرضات أثداءَهن للهواء و الشمس في الباحة، أو لإغراء الشباب المتقاطرين على دروب مدارس البنات أشعر بغضب من دنسهن...أجلس على الكرسي المريح، أشرد ساعات...غرفتي تنفتح مباشرة على أرض الحوش، من نافذتها أرى ضوء القمر الساطع بفضته على البحرة فيشدّني المشهد وأحسّ ببرودة تداهمني، تعلّقت بتفاصيلها، أصبحت عالمي الصغير، زيّنت جدرانها بلوحات رسمتها أثناء فترة صمتي الذي امتدّ، بدأت أفقد شهيتي للكلام.
(Madih 22–23)

This withdrawal is associated with the narrator's growing sense of hostility toward the world; she does not even speak to the people she purportedly trusts. Her words are replaced by drawings, and she interprets doodles in the margins of her estranged brother's books as "a letter Hossam had written to me, replacing the years of silence and estrangement with confidences as between friends" (*In Praise* 99; ما كتبه حسام كان رسالة إليَّ تعويضاً عن صمتنا سنوات طويلة وعدم البوح بأسرارنا كأي صديقين [Madih 104]).

She begins to code her violent dreams into a system of images that has the express purpose of precluding legibility:

I tried to capture whatever I could remember, and having decided to write it down, I bought a pink notebook and coloured pens. The writing changed into drawings. I found the pictures to be a way of confessing that no one could unravel, even when the notebook fell into my aunt's hands. The most beautiful of these dreams I had drawn as a tree with a squirrel standing on one of its branches, laughing as it looked at the clouds. It was a dream that a man ripped off Fatima's bra and was raping her in the school courtyard. . . . (56–57)

حاولت تثبيت ما أستطيع تذكّره، قرّرت كتابتها، اشتريت دفتراً زهريّاً و أقلاماً ملوّنة، تحوّلت الكتابة إلى رسوم أحببت غرابة أشكالها، وجدتها وسيلة للبوح لا يستطيع أحد كشفها متى وقع الدفتر بين أيدي خالاتي، أجمل تلك الأحلام رسمتها كشجرة يقف على أحد أغصانها سنجاب يضحك وهو

ينظر إلى الغيوم، كان حلماً عن رجل يمزّق "ستيان" فاطمة و يغتصبها في باحة المدرسة...

(61–62)

The imagined rape of Fatima, the narrator's classmate who describes the content of porn films, is a positive event for the narrator, in that it imaginatively polices the conspicuous sexuality of female bodies that plagues her and arouses her desire throughout much of the novel. Her implication in this symbolism for sexual violence is apparent in the passage that follows her drawing of the dream, where she considers how to draw "the man's member" (عضو الرجل). The threat of heterosexual desire is evident when she recoils from this act of drawing: "[I was] afraid that desire might possess me and destroy my dignity, blowing me away like grains of sand from the steps of an ancient house" (57; خوفاً من حالة شهوة قد تدمّر وقاري وتذروني كحبّات رمل على درج بيت عتيق [62]). Her wish to avoid comprehension is thus connected to her withdrawal into the codes of hatred as a structuring relation between the self and the outside world. The grounding potential of hatred can be felt in reference to this disavowal of language and of writing in particular: it is embraced as a substitute for shared signification. "Silence [is] best when face to face with our enemies" (242; الصمت أفضل ما نفعله حين نكون وجهاً لوجه مع أعدائنا [254]), she declares; the novel suggests that there are few people, even in her family, whom she does not perceive as an enemy.

After students have worked through these early sections, they will be primed to address the narrator's sudden conversion away from hatred in the final section of the novel, the third in the original, which is devoted to the narrator's imprisonment by the state. Her newfound sociability is marked by a lightening of Khalifa's prose. Turning from inner digression and toward others, the narrator begins to rewrite her past, orally, in collaboration with another woman: Sulafa, who has been imprisoned for Marxist activities. "Now our conversation was unceasing: we each reshaped our past so that the memories were no longer the preserve of an individual, but could belong to both of us together" (246; بدت أحاديثنا المتواصلة لا نهاية لها، رسمنا سوية خطّ أقدارنا من جديد، تنازلنا طوعاً عن كل ما عشناه لنعيد ترتيب كل شيء... [258]). The discursive construction of a history that overcomes political and sectarian difference takes the narrator to other spaces in Syria, notably the city of Latakia, and through experiences that the reader understands are fictions, such as swimming naked in the sea. The malleability of memory and its implication in the creation of new bonds, whether social or familial, are central to the prison section. The triumph of sociability is combined with the triumph of heteronormativity, expressed in figures of female reproduction and in the bond between the two women in prison. The narrator's fear of desire as self-obliteration is replaced by statements of a heterosexual and self-affirming desire, coded as a natural resurgence: "[W]e felt reassured that our deprived bodies were still capable of dreaming, like the bodies of any normal woman, with predatory lust" (282; ونطمئن إلى أن أجسادنا المحرومة مازالت تحلم كأجساد أية نساء [302]).

How might these analyses inform a classroom discussion of how the novel relates to the world outside the text? Teaching with circulational methods, we can draw together Khalifa's thematization of code and his use of allusion as markers of shared signification. This use (or rejection) of common signifiers presumes a present-tense understanding with readers or a public, "the kind of public that comes into being only in relation to texts and their circulation" (Warner 66). In this approach, texts are not the single-handed creators of their publics but rather participants in an ongoing conversation, one whose terms, scope, and stakes may be shifting but that nevertheless retain a sense of intelligibility between participants. When Michael Warner states that a public "exists *by virtue of being addressed*," it is to underscore this tension between the preexisting intelligibility of language, style, and genre, on one hand, and the open-ended quality of the future reader, the future public, on the other (67).

Such insights help contextualize for students Khalifa's novel, which was published the year after the final knell sounded over the Damascus Spring. In 2000, Hafez al-Assad, who had ruled Syria since 1970, died, and his son Bashar inherited the presidency. Beginning that year, hopes for change led to a series of publications and associations that aimed to institute new models of speech and sociability inside Syria. In May, the Committees for the Revival of Civil Society in Syria convened, bringing together writers, intellectuals, professors, filmmakers, and artists. Several months later, the Manifesto of 99 appeared in Lebanon's *al-Hayat* newspaper. Its ninety-nine signatories called for the end of the emergency law; the release of political prisoners; freedom of assembly, the press, and expression; and the protection of civil society from the forces of law and surveillance ("Statement"). It was followed in January 2001 by the bolder Manifesto of the 1000, which called for the right to form political parties—previously a power held only by the Ba'ath.

This reform movement circulated ideas through transnational, Arabic-language print culture but also through salons, conferences, and lectures that were held on history, culture, and ideas in public venues and in people's homes across Syria. The few testimonials recorded from participants suggest an agonistic mode of debate: "People voice their views, others disagree; and when the forum ends, people go home without ever resolving the argument" (Pace and Landis 123).

In readings of allusive speech in the novel, students might be invited to consider that *In Praise of Hatred* is about a woman overcoming sectarian hatred but that the novel does not name sects. Alawites, for example, are described as people who "descended from the mountains" (118; انحدروا من الجبال [123]). This allusion codes sectarian identity through a historical moment well-known among Syrians: the rise of the Baʿath to power in the 1960s and the upheaval in class and power dynamics that occurred when some Alawites left their traditional rural areas to rise in state institutions and public life (Batatu 144–75). This shift displaced the long-standing Sunni elite, represented in the novel by the narrator's nostalgic family. In a novel framed by sectarian hatred, this historically inflected gesture toward sect through class and geography suggests that a great deal may be lost when we translate a local signifier for sect into historically disembodied identities. While it is important to decode Khalifa's references, which are left unexplained in Price's translation, in classroom readings of the novel we should pay attention, first, to this allusive use of language as a literary device and, second, to the ways such readings disrupt North American concepts of sect as a permanent, ahistorical construct.

Khalifa's novel is not reducible to the goals of the Damascus Spring. Nevertheless, his transgressive yet allusive speech practices, developed in a novel that indexes sectarian intolerance to the narrator's desire to be illegible, participate in broader debates in which the very representation of the Events was staked to the project of building a new kind of civil society. Hovering between existence and aspiration, the new public of a Syrian civil society haunts the novel's pages: the complicit comprehension of that public and its recollection of trauma are invoked through allusion.

The novel is truncated in the translation, ending on an artificially triumphant note because of the deletion of the narrator's return to society after her imprisonment, a return that, despite her newfound tolerance, is not completely successful (McManus). In the classroom, students may be invited to reflect on a novel in which character development and plot are brought to an abrupt end. The English text relies on the prison term for narrative closure, diverting a plot based on the narrator's inner world to the external fact of her prison sentence. The original novel, by complicating her trajectory of reform after prison, conveyed a pessimism that is removed in translation, a pessimism that attests to the urgency of calling a future public into being through the transgressive act of representing the Events in print culture.

After 2011: Revolutionary Mobilities

The practices of speech and representation associated with the early years of the Syrian revolution (2011–13) broke away from the themes and conventions of the literature of the Events. The explosive shift toward multivalent sites of production and new media that began in 2011 has imposed new aesthetic and documentary codes, particularly in film (Boex); new rhythms of production; and new modes of transmission (e.g., circulation by e-mail and *Facebook*). Reading Syrian works today requires attention to *Facebook* pages, *YouTube* publication details, numbers of likes, comment feeds, and more. This change in the modes of production has also broken down traditional hierarchies for Syrian authors: young writers can upload their works without requiring the intermediary of a publishing house, though publication remains the gold standard of legitimation for many.

When we consider this shift against the backdrop of the movement for civil society in the previous decade, it becomes apparent that the circle of individuals and groups who can weigh in on representation and speech and, more importantly, who can be heard has widened dramatically. In the newly democratic field of representation that opened with the uprising, cultural production is no longer restricted to elite salons or institutions. A now-famous example of unknown voices entering the cultural field is the village of Kafranbel, whose witty protest banners and videos gained fame in Syria and abroad through an online and social media presence (see *Occupied Liberated Kafranbel*; Matar). For many, this plurality is to be celebrated as a revolutionary act in itself: an expression of the diverse, underrepresented voices who populate Syria.

A comparative classroom reading of post-2011 works with the literature of the Events will bring to light the ceding of allusion to overt languages of protest, particularly in new media forms associated with film, image, and song. Instructors might assign Lisa Wedeen's study of political humor and protest under Hafez al-Assad, *Ambiguities of Domination*, as a resource to draw out the importance of the change. Wedeen, a political theorist, used materials ranging from jokes and comedy shows to film and political posters in 1980s and 1990s Syria to argue that the power of the state lay in its ability "to make people say and do what they otherwise would not" (83–84). In the politics of "as if," she argued, what mattered was reproducing regime fictions externally—not believing internally (69).

A famous example of the protest art that, in 2011, exploded this political norm in public is *Syrian Revolutionary Dabke*, a video of a protest in Hama that was dubbed and subtitled by a group called the Creative Syrian Revolution. In the video, a crowd fills a blurry screen. It is nighttime, and they surge in rhythmic unison as a man on a stage leads them in a song of call and response. The collective voice of the song is a unified "we" that denigrates Assad and regime associates by name. The protest is its own public, founded in a language that revels in its iconoclasm. In these speech acts, blared in public squares, we find the linguistic parallel to the physical toppling of the statues of Hafez al-Assad and the ripping of posters of Bashar in cities and villages.

However, through cell phones and *YouTube*, a spontaneous protest became "Revolutionary Dabke," its afterlife stretching far beyond its original moment and public. The viral popularity of the song was initially believed to have caused the death of Ibrahim Qashoush, a young man reportedly found with his vocal cords cut out. Although ties between him and the song have now been disproved, he was subsequently honored as the Nightingale among Syrian activists (Wedeen, "On Uncertainty"). His death was commemorated in *YouTube* retrospectives and a work by Khalil Younes, a young Syrian painter, called *About a Young Man Called Kashoosh* (Souria Archives; Younes).

Students might trace the ways Syrian cultural actors took up contemporary events to narrativize and produce revolutionary history across media. A push to canonization often attempted to stabilize the multiplicity of new modes of speech, but this process was not without tension. Younes's painting depicts the purported author of the Hama song in an image that renders the violence of his murder with quasi-scientific precision. The painting maps his muscular and skeletal anatomy, and, as Qashoush gazes upward, the blood drains from a clean cut across his throat. Yet the artist cautions, "I don't want people to idolize Qashoush . . . he is ultimately just one of thousands of people who have died during the uprising" (17). Those who were on the alert against new idols and slogans argued that the sanctification of figures and causes was itself a product of the regime's political culture—a culture that would require more than insults and satire to dislodge (e.g., Younes; Omareen, "Symbol").

The afterlife of "Revolutionary Dabke" stretches farther, to North American classrooms, where we watch it remastered and subtitled in English. Students might be asked to acknowledge themselves as consumers of works of art that bear political claims beyond Syrian publics. The lyrics to "Revolutionary Debke" are reprinted in the collection *Syria Speaks*, the editors framing the song through Mikhail Bakhtin's carnival (Halasa et al. 210–12; Bakhtin 4–15). The introductory text explains that the song's rhythm and structure echo the Syrian wedding tradition of the *arada* (عراضة), which aligns well with Bakhtin's treatment of popular art (210). Wedeen's *Ambiguities of Domination* also appears as a theoretical lens in *Syria Speaks*: Omareen invokes Wedeen's work to explain the need for a "new grammar of dissent" in Syrian art ("Symbol" 101).

What are we as instructors to make of Syrian cultural actors who invoke Bakhtin, a well-worn touchstone in anglophone Arabic literary studies, or Wedeen's scholarship to translate the contours of protest art in Syria? My concern is not to assess the validity of this move but to linger over the ways in which classroom discussions may naturalize these acts of framing. In so doing, we discount ongoing (untranslated) debates about the ability of Syria's elite cultural actors to access—to say nothing of conceptually translate—the popular art of 2011–13 (Wannous). We also gloss over how editors and translators of anthologies use theoretical paradigms to translate for us—an interpellated, purportedly global anglophone public—the stakes of literary and cultural production today.

Yet this them/us conceptualization leaves something to be desired. It perpetuates the notion that Syrian cultural actors belong to a bounded, intellectual space that is primary (in terms of a work's time line, the work preceding its translation), monolingually Arabic, and Syrian and that our classrooms are intellectually separate, chronologically secondary spaces of consumption. The movement of Syrian intellectual and cultural actors into the diaspora and their engagements with theory produced in European and North American spaces, in and across multiple languages, suggest the need for new reading methods, as do the prominence of born-translated works and the sheer speed of cultural production today. In response to these challenges, contemporary scholarship in world literature may offer some suggestions.

Syrian Literature, Born Translated

Born-translated literatures require scholars to revisit the notion that reading literature is a seamless "encounter between literary history and political theory" that will locate a work's origin in a national collective with a unified national language (Walkowitz, "Comparison Literature" 243). Instead of seeking to determine, finally, the community to which a work belongs, Walkowitz suggests, scholars should develop reading methods that attend to thematics and acts of translation in the work itself (248).

The born-translated works produced in the Syrian diaspora and circulated online use strategies of juxtaposition that attest to the necessity of addressing multiple publics at once—an act that foregrounds the irreducible frictions and excesses of translation. An original text, typically in Arabic, is marked as original but not necessarily privileged; it appears alongside its translations into English, French, and other languages. Such juxtapositions can shift the focus of reading from a question of locating a work's national origins to that of tracing the overlapping, multilingual publics it interpellates.

Abounaddara, a documentary film collective, includes juxtaposed translations in its online archive: films subtitled in English or French appear next to their originals. In a nod to weekly protests that began in 2011, they have uploaded a film each Friday, temporally aligning their cinematic production with early revolutionary practice. Their shorts are usually less than five minutes long. The collective, diasporic since its beginnings, is based in France. Its films (to date) have been set in Syria, Lebanon, Turkey, and various European countries.

The collective's defining cinematic aesthetic is a single screen shot, reminiscent of a confessional space, in which an unnamed person recounts an experience. In *The Sniper*, for example, a sniper measures his grief for his wife's miscarriage against his apathy for the men he shoots (Abounaddara Collective). In *The Exodus*, a small child tells us about a frightening, unrelatable dream that prevented him from crossing the sea to Europe. Although the viewer understands that these shots are part of a larger conversation, there is usually a sense of narrative closure: a story comes to an end, marked by words (e.g., "and that's it"), a long silence, or a sigh. By removing the films from the conversations that produced them, the collective preserves a sense of seamless entry into a conversation that is only rarely disrupted by reminders that the viewer is not, in fact, the person behind the camera.

In this confessional mode, the films evoke the possibility of, or even demand, a future reconciliation in Syria. As Gayatri Spivak has argued (181–82), a politics of reconciliation relies on ethical listening, which is "predicated on the listener's willingness to enter into" an encounter with another's experience (Bennett 105). As Jill Bennett underscores, the listener inhabits the space between her experience and the speaker's instead of rendering it foreign or domesticating it into comfortable compassion. Ethical listening is preserved in cinematic encounters where the viewers may struggle to locate themselves—linguistically, ethically, and politically—vis-à-vis the intimate confessions emerging from an uprising that has become a war.

A simple point of departure to introduce these concerns with students is to ask, To whom are the films directed? Students might understandably assume that the collective addresses a Syrian, Arabic-speaking public first and an international public, spectators to a distant conflict, second. Yet the collective's films frequently address non-Syrians and distant spectators directly, as in *Media Kill*, with its tagline "Stop watching! We are dying." Moreover, their born-translated films perturb the notions that their primary public conforms to a monolingual national community with clearly delineated responsibilities and that international publics, addressed through translation, are absolved from the call to enact ethical listening.

For example, one of Abounaddara's films thematizes incomprehension and diaspora through selective absences of translation. In *Aïcha*, two languages, Kurdish and Turkish, are spoken on a major street lined by international clothing retailers, which some may recognize as Istanbul's Istiklal Street. Only select portions of the dialogue are translated into English; so far, no other version of the film exists. In other words, the born-translated version of the film is not a supplementary copy of an Arabic original.

The little girl for whom the film receives its title loiters at night near a group of street musicians, and, as the crowds disperse, one of the musicians asks, in Kurdish, subtitled, for her name. She answers, "Aïcha!," but otherwise she communicates only through gesture. We understand that she is from Syria because a Turkish-speaking man, who intervenes in the conversation, tells us as much. She is clearly alone and vulnerable. The rest of the Turkish spoken around her is not translated, and she is gradually pushed out of the group. The film ends on her rediscovery of the camera. She is perched on the threshold of a closed storefront; a bright, intelligent smile spreads across her face, and she holds the camera's gaze as the shot fades. The smile is as inscrutable and the action to which it calls the viewer is as unnamable as the image is insistent. The film will be variously comprehensible to speakers of English, Turkish, and Kurdish—but not to speakers of Arabic, who might, like the child, grasp only proper names: Suriye, Aïcha.

The homogeneity and monolingualism of a Syrian nation are similarly disrupted in Abounaddara's *I Have a Friend from Kurdistan–Syrian Kurdistan* (لي صديق من كردستان / Kurdistana Sûriya). In the film, we stumble, as though we were travelers, on two men sitting by a rural road; they point us in the direction of Kurdistan and call us in Arabic to drink tea with them. One of the men describes in Arabic his military service in the Golan Heights while his companion pours tea and tells the camera, again in Arabic, "Welcome." But they switch abruptly into Kurdish, gazing away from the camera toward the surrounding countryside and sharing a short conversation that is not subtitled for the Arabic-speaking viewer.

This film invokes two nationalisms: one through the mention of the Golan Heights, the cause célèbre of Syria's pan-Arab state, and the other through Kurdistan. These nationalisms are juxtaposed without resolution, much as the two titles for the film suggest appositional but untranslatable readings of national space. The Arabic figures Kurdistan as an elsewhere, whence friends are remembered, while the Kurdish title renders Kurdistan as here and Syrian. The absence of translation functions as a guardian of that overlapping incommensurability in a film that is permeated by tokens of friendship and hospitality. Yet it is also an invitation for speakers of Arabic, whether Syrian or not, to encounter their incomprehension of a language that was banned by the Baʿath from educational institutions. The film thus serves as a bilingual reminder of the "difficulty of registering . . . the history of violence suppressed by fluency and monolingualism" (Walkowitz, "Comparison Literature" 240).

For Golan Haji, a poet, the perpetual translation in the monolingualism imposed on Syrian Kurds provokes broader considerations about poetic language. A translator between English and Arabic, Haji seizes on the process of translation in speech as a metaphor for the act of writing:

> I think that every writing is a translation. For me as a Kurd, I talk in Kurdish but I write in Arabic. But it's not as simple as that. . . . Something is lost, and the writing is always incomplete. When you try to find the right word or the right image, and it's not always possible, the poem takes its beauty from this process of imperfection. It's always imperfect, and that's why the writing never ends. Just as the idea of identity ends in death, when one is dead, that's his final identity. One is always looking for others in other places and languages. ("Every Writing")

Haji is reflecting here on the imperfection of translation as being the generative aporia of language, the motor of supplementarity that drives the poem. Translation, as an act rather than a metaphor, is in turn figured as tracing "the movement of the shadow of meanings," a process that for the poet relies on understanding and remaining aware that "your roots are everywhere, in all continents" ("Every Writing"). These comments on translation and Kurdish-Arabic bilingualism may provide a frame through which to approach his texts in the classroom.

There is currently no centralized online archive for Haji's poetry: his translations are scattered across Web sites dedicated to Arabic and world literatures, poetry, and regional affairs. Written against the backdrop of contemporary violence, the poetry provides another representional frame through which to view contemporary Syrian literature, one that does not conform to expectations of political discourse or even to newly established codes of representation for revolutionary art. Instead, Haji's translational poetics limns a perpetual search for a resting place in diaspora and exile. An example of his poetry appeared on the *Words without Borders* blog under the title "Autumn Here Is Magical and Vast," and the site gives readers the choice to view the Arabic poem and its English translation, performed by Stephen Watts, side by side or separately. The immersion in poetic language, in "Autumn," generates a text rife with unstable signification and images of instability. The poem ends on a note of overt indeterminacy:

> if you opened any door
> to reassure yourself or to leave
> you would open perplexity
> the mirror would come closer, higher.
> Like two old enemies
> your eyes gaze into your eyes.

وإذا فتحتَ أيِّ باب،
لَتطمئنّ أو تغادر،
فتحتَ الحيرة.
ستدنو المرآة وتعلو،
كعدوّين قديمين
ستحدّق عيناك في عينيك.

Like the smile that ends *Aïcha*, Haji's poem impels the reader forward in search of a resting place, a certainty that is withheld. This withholding of narrative closure, political clarity, and empathic resolution can provoke exciting and challenging conversations in the classroom. For, if we can imagine Syrian readers in shifting, multilingual configurations of publics, we might in turn come to see ourselves as interpellated into transnational publics that cannot be divorced from—yet also cannot be reduced to—the contemporary politics of American intervention in the region.

In Abounaddara's *The Unknown Soldier*, a four-part interview with a Free Syrian Army fighter, we hear the struggle of a man to make sense of the fact that he has taken up arms and killed—most troublingly, that he has slit another man's throat. His face is obscured in shadow, though light occasionally touches one side of his face. In part 1, his assertions of certainty and necessity tiptoe between abysses of doubt: "It's my right [to kill]. It's not wrong. Even if it's wrong, it's my right. We don't have a choice." This monologue soon gives way, in part 3, to expressions of dissociation and grief: "My soul left my body and wept." Students in Europe and the United States might be reminded, in viewing this series, of debates over their governments' military and financial support for Syrian opposition groups, whose individual voices and personal reflections are utterly occluded in contemporary representations of the war on terror. Faced with the complexity of this man's testimony, we might well ask, How are we to engage this film? respond to this transnational politics? The ethics of listening to Syrian voices in this case becomes a necessary practice for the North American classroom, a practice bound up in notions of locality and politics even as it inhabits, uncomfortably, the distance between spectator and other, a Syrian soldier's splitting self and intimate grief.

The imaginative, horizontal, and even rhizomatic quality of publics should not obscure the materially uneven quality of networks for the production, translation, and publication of Arabic literature in translation. Certainly, the legacy of orientalism continues to loom large. Yet this term underdescribes the reading practices of American students who have grown up with wars in Iraq and Afghanistan as an interminable condition of the present and who have been shaped by their belonging in various publics of American class, race, gender, and politics. The hunger for translated literature and art of the "Arab Spring" has been a striking characteristic of popular and academic cultures in the United States since 2011, but we might ask what the circulation and consumption of this revolutionary art brings to our understanding of more local notions of revolution and street politics

This essay has attempted to shift a dominant model of reading, which we might term "resistance literature," following Barbara Harlow's influential formulation, from a vertical model of authorial protest against a state (or occupying power) to a horizontal analysis. This shift is not to deny that some Syrian literatures, particularly post-2011 texts that have been translated into English, protest the state (or the regime), its institutions, and its policies. But reading literary texts solely for what they are "really saying" about politics risks flattening out aesthetic complexity and modes of signification in order to produce a neatly packaged political sense. Moreover, translating all Syrian literature into a paradigm of resistance to the Assad regime makes a range of other engagements with collective world-making drop out of view. In turn, we may fail to grasp the silences and anxieties that pervade contemporary Syrian literature about the very possibility of creating new social, intimate, and political worlds under the weight of dictatorship and war. These anxieties have never been more pressing than they are in the context of today's violence and social fragmentation.

Note

English translations of Arabic are mine, unless otherwise indicated.

Works Cited

Abbas, Hassan. حكايات ضد النسيان: قراءة في بعض النتاج الروائيّ المعاصر في سورية. [Hikayat didd al-nisyan: qira'a fi ba'd al-nitaj al-riwa'i al-mu'asir fi suriya; Stories against Forgetting: A Reading of Several Contemporary Syrian Novels]. *Al-Adab*, vol. 57, nos. 9–10, 2009. PDF file, www.adabmag.com/node/234, 24 May 2014.

Abounaddara Collective. *Aïcha. Vimeo*, 3 Oct. 2014, vimeo.com/107948804.

———. *The Exodus. Vimeo*, 29 Nov. 2013, vimeo.com/80600876.

———. *Media Kill. Vimeo*, 7 Aug. 2012, vimeo.com/47100634.

———. *The Sniper. Vimeo*, 18 Apr. 2014, vimeo.com/92318306.

———. *The Unknown Soldier, Part 1. Vimeo*, 14 Dec. 2012, vimeo.com/54135942.

———. *The Unknown Soldier, Part 3. Vimeo*, 7 Dec. 2012, vimeo.com/55082448.

Alsarraj, Manhal. "As the River Must: Excerpt." Translated by Ghenwa Hayek, *Banipal*, www.banipal.co.uk/selections/79/231/manhal-alsarraj-sarraj/.

Bakhtin, Mikhail. *Rabelais and His World*. Indiana UP, 2009.

Batatu, Hanna. *Syria's Peasantry, the Descendants of Its Lesser Rural Notables, and Their Politics*. Princeton UP, 1999.

Benjamin, Walter. "The Task of the Translator." *Walter Benjamin: Selected Writings, Volume 1: 1913–1926*, edited by Marcus Bullock and Michael W. Jennings, Belknap Press, 1996, pp. 253–63.

Bennett, Jill. *Empathic Vision: Affect, Trauma, and Contemporary Art*. Stanford UP, 2005.

Boex, Cecile. "La vidéo comme outil de l'action collective et de la lutte armée." *Pas de printemps pour la Syrie*, edited by François Burget and Bruno Paoli, La Découverte, 2013, pp. 174–83.

Edwards, Brian T. "Logics and Contexts of Circulation." *A Companion to Comparative Literature*, edited by Ali Behdad and Dominic Thomas, Wiley-Blackwell, 2011, pp. 454–72.

Haji, Golan. "Autumn Here Is Magical and Vast." Translated by Stephen Watts, *Words without Borders*, Mar. 2013, www.wordswithoutborders.org/article/autumn-here-is-magical-and-vast.

——— "Every Writing Is a Translation." *Prairie Schooner*, 16 May 2013, prairieschooner.unl.edu/blog/golan-haji-every-writing-translation.

Halasa, Malu, et al., editors. *Syria Speaks: Art and Culture from the Frontline*. Saqi Books, 2014.

Harlow, Barbara. *Resistance Literature*. Methuen, 1987.

Hassan, Rosa Yassine. حرّاس الهواء [Hurras al-hawa'; Guardians of the Air]. Al-Kawkab Books, 2009.

Kawakabi, Salam. أصوات سورية من زمن ما قبل الثورة [Aswat suriya min zaman ma qabla al-thawra; Syrian Voices from before the Revolution). Bayt al-Muwatin, 2013.

Khalifa, Khaled. *In Praise of Hatred*. Translated by Leri Price, St. Martins Press, 2014.

———. مديح الكراهية [Madih al-karahiya]. 2nd. ed., Dar al-Adab, 2008. Translated as *In Praise of Hatred*.

Lesch, David. *The New Lion of Damascus: Bashar al-Assad and Modern Syria*. Yale UP, 2005.

Matar, Mezar. "Cartoons by Kafranbel." Halasa et al., pp. 102–03.

McManus, Anne-Marie. "The Contemporary Syrian Novel in Translation." *Arab Studies Journal*, vol. 12, no. 1, 2014, pp. 322–33.

Occupied Liberated Kafranbel: The Little Syrian Town That Could. 30 Oct. 2014.

Omareen, Zaher. "A Bedtime Story for Eid." Translated by Alice Guthrie. *Words without Borders*, Oct. 2014, www.wordswithoutborders.org/article/a-bedtime -story-for-eid.

——— "The Symbol and Counter-Symbols." Halasa et al., pp. 84–101.

Pace, Joe, and Joshua Landis. "The Syrian Opposition: The Struggle for Unity and Relevance, 2003–2008." *Demystifying Syria*, edited by Fred H. Lawson, Saqi Books, 2009, pp. 120–43.

Pierret, Thomas. *Religion and State in Syria*. Cambridge UP, 2013.

Seale, Patrick. *Asad: The Struggle for the Middle East*. U of California P, 1990.

Shadid, Anthony. "Lyrical Message for Syrian Leader: Come On Bashar, Leave." *The New York Times*, 21 July 2011, www.nytimes.com/2011/07/22/world/ middleeast/22poet.html?_r=0.

Souria Archives. "Syria: Never Forget Ibrahim Qashoush." *YouTube*, 27 June 2012, .

Spivak, Gayatri. "The Politics of Translation." *Outside in the Teaching Machine*, Routledge, 1993, pp. 179–200.

"Statement by Ninety-Nine Syrian Intellectuals." Translated by Suha Mawlawi Kayal. *Middle East Intelligence Bulletin*, 5 Oct. 2000, www.meforum.org/ meib/articles/0010_sdoc0927.htm.

Syrian Revolutionary Dabke. Music and translation by Creative Syrian Revolution, *YouTube*, 2 July 2011, www.youtube.com/watch?v=xCS8SsFOBAI.

Walkowitz, Rebecca L. "Close Reading in an Age of Global Writing." *Modern Language Quarterly*, vol. 74, no. 2, 2013, pp. 171–95.

———. "Comparison Literature." *Comparison: Theories, Approaches, Uses*, edited by Rita Felski and Susan Stanford Friedman, Johns Hopkins UP, 2013, pp. 235–52.

Wannous, Dima. سوريا تتحدّث: لغة ما قبل الثورة [Suriya tatahaddath: Lughat ma qabla al-thawra; Syria Speaks: A Language from before the Revolution]. *Almo-dononline*, 7 Sept. 2014, www.almodon.com/culture/2014/9/7/.

Warner, Michael. *Publics and Counter-Publics*. Zone Books, 2005.

Wedeen, Lisa. *Ambiguities of Domination: Politics, Rhetoric, and Symbols in Contemporary Syria*. U of Chicago P, 1999.

———. "On Uncertainty." 8 Oct. 2016, typescript.

Yassin-Kassab, Robin. Afterword. K. Khalifa, *In Praise*, pp. 297–302.

Yazbek, Samar. صلصال [Silsaal; Clay]. Dar al-Adab, 2011.

Younes, Khalil. "Painting the Revolution." *Culture in Defiance: Continuing Traditions of Satire, Art, and the Struggle for Freedom in Syria*, edited by Malu Halasa, Prince Claus Fund for Culture and Development, 2012, pp. 16–19.

Ziyada, Radwan, editor. ربيع دمشق [Rabiʻ Dimashq; Damascus Spring]. Markaz al-Qahira li-dirasat Huquq al-Insan, 2007.

M. Lynx Qualey

Teaching Arabic Literature in Open Spaces

Open-space teaching initiatives, particularly massive online open courses (MOOCs) but to a lesser extent blogs, have been popping up in great numbers in the last three years. There have been several Arabic-literature-themed blogs, yet in the well-funded MOOC enterprise it seems there has not yet been one to focus on Arabic literature in translation. In May 2014, Jordan announced the first Arabic-language MOOC site, in cooperation with one of the major MOOC manufacturers, edX. The new Jordanian site, Edraak, promises to offer not just Arabic-language classes but also a series of English-language MOOCs targeted at a non-Arab audience. "These MOOCs will allow Arabs to tell their story with their own narrative," a *Wamda* report said. The Web site quoted Nafez Dakkak, the manager of Edraak, as saying that the Edraak courses would provide an alternative to "the Arab story with a Western narrative, which is so often heard" (Pirkle). It's possible, even likely, that these English-language MOOCs will soon offer an Arabic literature component.

Despite its associations with government and venture capital, and despite Thomas Friedman's incessant cheerleading ("Professors' Big Stage" and "Revolution"), this new form of open online education has interesting pedagogical possibilities. Arabic literature will likely find its way into

MOOCs, for better and for worse. Certainly, teaching Arabic literature in open spaces runs into obstacles that don't face the teaching of English literature MOOCs. But it also creates greater opportunities for interesting educational disruption.

The MOOC Student of Arabic Literature in English

How will apparently global open-course learners approach works of Arabic literature in translation? While popular-media tropes about Arabs and Muslims have been well explored, no large-scale surveys suggest how these tropes will affect an ordinary English-language reader's reception of Arabic literature. Questions from readers, as well as reviews by nonspecialists, offer some insight into the challenges we face in teaching a literature seen primarily if not exclusively as of ethnographic interest.

John Updike, a seasoned novelist when he picked up Abdelrahman Munif's *Cities of Salt* (مدن الملح ; Mudun al-milh), saw the book through a political and ethnographic lens. In his 1988 review in the *New Yorker*, published three days after Naguib Mahfouz's Nobel Prize was announced, Updike wrote, "The most fabulous geological event since the explosion of Krakatoa surely was the discovery of oceans of petroleum beneath the stark and backward Muslim realms of the Persian Gulf" (117). Here, his ideas of what Arabs are—historically and anthropologically—seem to have overshadowed his idea of what Munif's book is. If reviewing is a form of translation, Updike has rewritten large swaths of the book to fit his understanding of "Muslim realms." Further, he judges the book entirely as a mimicry of Western forms, unaware that Arabic literature has a history pre-*nahda*, before the early-twentieth-century renaissance in Arabic letters.

Twenty-six years later, most mainstream book reviews no longer explicitly refer to "stark and backward Muslim realms," although such depictions are widely available elsewhere. The reception of Arabic literature in English changed dramatically after the events of September 2001 and the conflicts that have grown out of them. As Humphrey Davies, leading translator, has noted, "There probably was a little time lag—telephones weren't ringing on the 12th of September" (Lynx Qualey, "Humphrey Davies Interview"). These events spurred not just a momentary interest in Arab lives but also a greater investment from defense and military sources in Arabic-language learning. The effect on Arabic literature in translation, and on teaching it, is yet to be fully felt.

In the short term, the number of Arabic books translated annually into English has jumped considerably since 2001. The international literary blog *Three Percent*, affiliated with Open Letter Books and the University of Rochester, put Arabic, in mid-2014, as the fourth-most translated language for the year, following only French, Spanish, and German (Post). This new crop of books has also attracted wider literary interest. In the last decade, several Arabic novels and poetry collections have won or been shortlisted for important awards and accolades, such as the Independent Foreign Fiction Prize (IFFP), the Best Translated Book Award, the *Publishers Weekly* annual top ten, and *The New York Times* notable book of the year. However, the language used by critics and givers of awards often still uses the ethnographic lens. The IFFP news release announcing *The Iraqi Christ*'s win of that prize praises the book by noting, "*The Iraqi Christ* offers an unforgettable and often harrowing insight into life in contemporary Iraq" (*Independent Foreign Fiction Prize Winner*).

The language with which Arabic books are reviewed may have changed since Updike's essay on *Cities of Salt*, but popular-press reviewers still tend to focus on what a book will teach readers about the Middle East. The book is, on its own, supposed to provide educational material about Arab history and politics. An April 2014 review on NPR by Alan Cheuse is gentler than Updike's but, like Updike's, focuses on a magical ethnographicism, telling readers and listeners that *In Praise of Hatred* (مديح الكراهية ; Madih al-karahiya), by Khaled Khalifa, a Syrian novelist, "will teach you some important things about this still mysterious time and place."

Adam Talib, a translator and Arabic literature professor, made a stab at addressing this issue in his American University in Cairo lecture "Translating for Bigots." He had in mind the ordinary reader, who comes to a work of Arabic literature in translation weighted down with received cultural knowledge about Arabs. Talib suggested that there is often "a hostility in the reader's mind" to characters and situations that don't fit the images that the reader has developed about countries in which most of the people are Arabs (Lynx Qualey).

Talib spoke particularly about the images of Arab and Muslim women. This popular cultural knowledge, he observed, is manifested in the dust jackets of many Arabic-language works in English. The jackets often feature a woman clad all in black with nothing but her kohl-rimmed eyes showing, offering a conscious or unconscious echo of the jackets used by popular "saving Muslim women" narratives that have been popular since the 1980s and 1990s, with blockbuster titles like Betty Mahmoody and

William Hoffer's *Not without My Daughter* (1982), which became a popular film of the same name in 1991; *I Am Nujood, Age Ten and Divorced* (2010); and Jean Sassoon's best sellers throughout the last fifteen years. It is impossible to guess how this and other popular cultural knowledge will influence an individual reader, but we must acknowledge that an influence exists in different forms for different open-space students from different nations.

New readers, in any case, will probably see the Arabic novel not as part of a blended tradition of thousands of years but—like Updike—as a form borrowed wholly from the West.

Who's in Charge? Who Sets the Tone?

In a closed classroom environment, an instructor might start by addressing the hows and whys of reading literature or with the long and multivocal traditions of creative writing in Arabic. But in an open classroom, the learner can easily skip past or fail to notice such introductions. In the streamlined MOOCs, learning is both asynchronous and cafeteria-style, because students can enter at any moment, select which pieces interest them, and ignore those that don't.

True, there are learners who begin at the beginning, check off every lesson, take all the quizzes, and qualify for a completion certificate. If MOOCs are to replace introductory coursework, as some would have it, this approach could become the way a significant number of students access courses. But currently only about five to ten percent of MOOC learners follow through with an entire course.

Even if students complete a course from beginning to end, there is still the issue of authority. In open spaces, students turn not to an instructor but to TAs, technological helpers, and fellow commenters on discussion boards. It is also much easier, in an open online space, to ignore ideas that contradict our own. As Art Markman, a professor of psychology at the University of Texas, Austin, noted in an interview with *Scientific American*, because comment section discourses don't happen in real time, commenters can write lengthy monologues. This practice tends not to leave them open to other ideas; monologuing entrenches them in their viewpoints (Wolchover).

Indeed, in my experience as the editor of the blog *Arabic Literature (in English)*, comments occasionally respond to one another but most are monologues that deliver opinions and can be sharp, attacking another commenter or me. Give-and-take, where two or more respondents change their mind, is rare. A closed classroom thus has an important advantage in helping students understand the context in which they are reading Arabic literature and in helping them talk through their ideas.

Until better open online education forms come along, MOOC proponents argue that closed classrooms are great but very few students will ever take a closed-classroom course on Arabic literature in translation. Are MOOCs an opportunity to bring a large community to the rich world of Arabic literature in translation? Is mass education a way to bring education to the masses?

Education for the Unserved and Underserved?

In early 2013, my eldest son, who was then in fourth grade in a United States public school, was told that he must use *Achieve3000*, a Web-based mass instruction portal, to prepare for his end-of-grade exams (www .achieve3000.com). On the site, a new topic appeared for him every few days. My son would take a survey about this topic, read an article, answer a series of comprehension questions, and perhaps type in a few comments. At the end, he would retake the survey.

One of these *Achieve3000* articles was about the United States–based One Laptop per Child (OLPC) initiative. In simple, positive language, the article outlined how OLPC had dropped off tablet computers with preloaded programs in two remote Ethiopian villages, where children didn't have access to formal schooling (Talbot). It went on to say that a few of the children taught themselves how to read—in English—without any assistance or support, and it profiled one of them. The article implied that this program could fundamentally change a poor child's future: being literate could give the child access to better information, a better job, and better health. The implication lay heavily on the page that, with the help of a single iPad and a little work, the world was a poor child's oyster.

The article's message is hard to miss. If a fourth-grader does miss the message, a survey is there to drive it home: before and after the article, the children are asked, Can people, if they set their mind to it and work hard, accomplish anything? Each time my son and I accessed *Achieve3000* together in 2012–13, the children knew how to respond to the site's survey questions. I never saw one who had less than ninety percent correct answers, even before reading the article. In the article and comprehension questions and survey about the article, the message to students is strong:

Location, class, history, and even access to teachers don't matter for educational attainment.

This conviction is also at the center of much of the excitement around MOOCs. When *The New York Times* declared 2012 the "Year of the MOOC," they noted, "The shimmery hope is that free courses can bring the best education in the world to the most remote corners of the planet, help people in their careers, and expand intellectual and personal networks" (Pappano, "Year"). Friedman, a *New York Times* columnist, later declared, "Nothing has more potential to lift more people out of poverty" ("Revolution"). In this nod toward a world underclass, MOOCs share a superficial similarity with radical public education initiatives: they are ostensibly free and open to all, and they redefine whom education benefits.

Although this "shimmery hope" sits at the center of the MOOC story, it rests uncomfortably next to the significant venture capital that has gone into supporting MOOC platforms, which create the expectation that MOOCs will turn a profit. Thus far, MOOCs have not balanced their books. In the summer of 2003, Coursera announced that it had raised an additional $43 million in venture capital from its startup base of $22 million, while its only significant revenue, $800,000, came from selling completion certificates. This imbalance creates a situation where a platform's founders have had to look for new ways to monetize education. They say they aren't worried: "Our VCs keep telling us that if you build a website that is changing the lives of millions of people, then the money will follow," Daphne Koller, a Coursera cofounder, said in 2012 (Young).

The money hasn't followed yet. Product pathways must be created, new consumer habits established, and new social expectations fostered. One monetizing suggestion has been to change introductory university courses to a MOOC format, which could be franchised by high-prestige universities. Why have a thousand introduction to Arabic literature in translation courses, the reasoning goes, when you could have just one? Critics rightly counter that this change could spawn a whole new set of inequalities.

Meanwhile, the story the MOOC cheerleaders tell remains that of an equalized playing field. As Jeffrey R. Young writes in his introduction to *Beyond the MOOC Hype: A Guide to Higher Education's High-Tech Disruption*, "Imagine the implications: a kid in Mongolia could learn advanced mathematics using a village computer and become a great scientist; a single parent in a rural town could finish college and start a career; a professor could teach people around the world with little need for college at all." The "kid in Mongolia" is a real person, although he was hardly "using a village computer." As *The New York Times* reported, the efforts of Battushig, who was fifteen years old, were strongly supported by his high school principal, who brought in an instructor from MIT, Tony Kim, to do lab work with the students and teach alongside the MOOC (Pappano, "Boy Genius").

The MOOCs say they are radically open to all who read and write in English worldwide. Yet the data in the recently published *HarvardX and MITx: The First Year of Open Online Courses, Fall 2012–Summer 2013* suggest that the "kid in Mongolia" is hardly the typical student. One of a series of white papers published by joint Harvard and MIT teams, it indicates, unsurprisingly, that the existing streamlined MOOCs serve those who are already educationally and economically privileged (Ho et al. 2). The same can be said of blogs and other forms of online open education.

Who Are Open Education's Students? Who Might Take an Arabic Literature MOOC?

HarvardX and MITx, which both run courses on the same edX platform, found that in their first year "[t]he most typical course registrant is a male with a bachelor's degree who is 26 or older." For certain courses, the paper reported, educational attainment was higher. In the course Health in Numbers: Quantitative Methods in Clinical and Public Health Research, for instance, the typical student had a master's degree, and more than ten percent of registrants had PhDs. In part, the predominance of students with degrees might have been a product of the project's newness and of the way it was marketed.

The study authors were quick to note that not all their registrants were male, twenty-six or older, and college-educated. A total of 213,672 (29%) reported their gender as female; 234,463 (33%) reported a high school education or lower; 20,745 (2.7%) "have IP or mailing addresses from countries on the United Nations list of Least Developed Countries."

Educational attainment correlated not only with students' enrolling in the course but also with their staying in the course, which is important, since as many as a third of those who register for MOOCs do nothing more than that: they never access even one piece of the course material. Those who registered, viewed the material, and followed the course to the end, achieving certified status, "generally had a higher average educational level than noncertified students" (Ho et al. 2). Scott Carlson and Goldie

Blumenstyk, reporters for *The Chronicle of Higher Education*, argue that MOOCs generally serve wealthier students, who have a greater familiarity with the mechanisms of higher education: "The students from the bottom tier are often the ones who need face-to-face instruction most of all."

To what extent MOOCs or other forms of online open education work and for whom are still unanswered questions. Although HarvardX and MITx have gathered a large amount of data about the MOOC users and their behavior, "approximately 20 GB of data per course," this study is largely statistical and not descriptive (Haber; Reich). Its authors said that in the future they hope to collect information about learners' prior knowledge and motivations as well as externally validated assessments of student learning (Ho et al. 35). Thus far, none of the data that have been collected indicate how a student's life and thinking might be influenced by these courses.

Koller and her coauthors argue that learner motivation is the key to success of open online education. But learner motivation is also a tricky thing. Alice Guthrie and Alexandra Buchler's research for *Literature across Frontiers* suggests that, when readers approach Arabic literature, they often are seeking ethnographic information. Although this goal is not unreasonable, a literature course may not be the best place to meet it. A common complaint of Arab authors who have had their work translated for Western audiences is that everything is viewed through a political prism, whereas American or Swedish works are not. In a Skype interview, Ghayath al-Madhoun, a Syrian Palestinian poet, said that a Swedish poet had written of his work, "This is how political poetry should be if we want to take it seriously." But, al-Madhoun added, "I didn't agree with her. This is not political poetry. If this is political poetry, then her poetry should be political."

A student's motivation might also be informed by the "weaponization" of Arabic-language instruction that Christopher Stone describes. Since 2001, Stone writes, support for Arabic courses has surged. By 2009, Arabic was already the eighth-most studied language in the United States, according to an MLA survey report ("New MLA Survey Report"). It's not unreasonable to think that many of these students might be studying Arabic to prepare for a military- or intelligence-oriented career. But Stone notes that there are a number of explicit links between language and culture learning and preparation for war:

A 2012 article in the University of Texas at Austin's *Life & Letters* entitled "Humanities and the Military" describes a collaboration between

Flagship students there and Texas Army National Guard soldiers in a "weekend-long language and culture workshop conducted by the College of Liberal Arts' Department of Middle Eastern Studies and Center for Middle Eastern Studies for soldiers who will soon be deployed to Afghanistan." One of the coordinators of the program is quoted as saying "All of the participants seemed intent on learning as much as they could about Afghani culture because they knew that this information might help them accomplish their mission more effectively."

This kind of motivation, both personal and national, places Arabic, including the study of Arabic literature, in a larger web of meanings and raises questions about the utility of literary study.

There is no indication right now that large numbers of intelligence-oriented learners are also interested in Arabic literature. So who would be interested in taking an Arabic literature MOOC? Among them would be the people who visit and subscribe to the blog I founded and edit, *Arabic Literature (in English)*, because they are also motivated to seek out open online knowledge.

Who Are the Users of *Arabic Literature (in English)*?

When I began *Arabic Literature (in English)*, I imagined, somewhat like wide-eyed MOOC supporters, that I would be reaching out to a largely new audience, to readers who had little or no familiarity with Arabic literature. I imagined attracting readers who would be much like students in an introductory literature course at a university, with little or no background in language or literature.

Indeed, some of my readers fit this profile. But they are in the minority, at least among those who subscribe, e-mail, and comment. The users of the blog tend to skew Arab—approximately thirty percent of subscribers identify themselves with recognizably Arab names. Many of the others have an interest in Arabic literature, and a large number of subscribers are editors, educators, and translators or master's and PhD students in Arabic literature.

One of the most difficult things about managing a space like *Arabic Literature (in English)* is that the readers come from markedly different backgrounds. In most closed courses, there are admissions requirements and some degree of leveling that bunches introductory learners with introductory learners and advanced learners with advanced learners. Teaching an open course, however, brings together a people with no previous knowledge and award-winning professionals in the field. In Harvard's Health in Numbers course, for example, just over ten percent of registrants had PhDs, while fifteen percent had a high-school degree or no degree at all.

Open courses reach people not only with disparate backgrounds and scholarly experience but also from different countries, who are approaching the subject through very different associations and lenses. In the report from HarvardX and MITx, 28% of learners came from the United States, followed by India, the United Kingdom, Brazil, Canada, and Spain. The user breakdown will probably be different for different courses. The WordPress platform on which *Arabic Literature (in English)* runs began tracking countries from which the site was accessed on 25 February 2012. From that point through the morning of 11 July 2014, the top users were also the United States (28% of use, or 291,370 views), then the United Kingdom (104,635), Egypt (87,185), Canada (35,317), Italy (34,247), United Arab Emirates (32,727), Germany (25,172), France (23,977), Lebanon (23,608), Saudi Arabia (21,614), India (20,946), Jordan (19,980), Morocco (16,877), Philippines (16,789), Australia (16,739), Spain (12,991), Netherlands (12,642), Sweden (12,616), Turkey (12,213), and Tunisia (11,800).

None of these data give any information about learner motivations, but we can expect that an introductory learner in Canada and a scholar based in Jordan will be looking for different things.

Also, as with any open space, there is the possibility that some users will sign up primarily in order to air their views. At a 2012 talk I gave at the American University in Cairo (AUC), Ferial Ghazoul, an AUC professor, asked how the Web site managed to deflect hate speech from its discussion boards. I answered, as I would now, that this has never been a problem ("Blog"). The sort of reader who is attracted to a literature blog is different from one who might be found on a political or advocacy blog. Blogs form interest communities, and most readers stay in their interest communities. Although there are stray comments here and there—mostly when Palestine is involved—the human-generated comments are by and large on-topic.

In short, although there are widely varied audiences interested in learning more about Arabic literature in open environments, most of their members are readers or learners who are already attuned to the field in some way.

Non-MOOC Teaching in Open Spaces: Blogs

A blog can be thought of as an open online learning project, even though MOOCs overshadow almost all such initiatives. The blog format is in many ways similar to that of the connectivist MOOC pioneered at the University of Manitoba. A literature-oriented blog can provide background information, scholars' and translators' views, suggested reading lists, discussion questions, analysis, and access to reading material, among other things. Blog posts also can easily be copied onto other blogs, with commentary added. They can be suggested as extra reading material for students, as *Arabic Literature (in English)* is at a number of university courses in the United States and Canada and *Editoriaraba* is in Italy (editoriaraba.com).

Blogs typically don't predict where they are going next, and they are not organized by a syllabus. Instead, posts are released regularly, with sometimes little to connect one day's material with the next. Other blogs that work in the space of mine are *Editoriaraba*, by Chiara Comito, an Italian graduate student and activist, and *Arab Hyphen* (arabhyphen.com), by Tasnim Qutait, a graduate student. Elias Muhanna's *Qifa Nabki* (www.qifanabki.com) also sometimes strays into this territory. All these blogs have an asynchronous, disconnected character. Some, like *Nabki*, respond to the news; others, like Qutait's, respond to her personal research and interests.

As in the typical streamlined MOOC, some readers access material every day or on most days and others access only a small portion of the material. Material is not viewed in any order or according to any schedule. As Andrew Dean Ho and his coauthors point out, "Asynchronicity is a defining feature of open online learning," and this is as true for blogs as it is for MOOCs. Those who register for a blog might have joined for a single feature and might not read anything again after that. Or they might return irregularly, whenever a headline strikes them or they are researching a particular topic.

Interest in Arabic literature is often pegged to the news cycle. Viewers will look at articles about Palestinian literature, for example, on the heels of an invasion or bombardment of Gaza; interest in Egyptian literature will increase during a big protest in Cairo. At the end of July 2014, during Operation Protective Edge in Gaza, four of the top five pages being read at my blog were about Gaza and literature; one of these was from nearly two years earlier, November 2012.

Asynchronicity means that some things must be repeated continually. Although blog material builds on past discussions and although some readers have been around for many years, other readers show up for the first time on any given day. For this reason, the discussion about the relation between the use of Modern Standard Arabic (MSA) and dialects in Arabic literature has been repeated both on *Qifa Nabki* and on *Arabic Literature (in English)*.

Discussion boards have a large impact on blog use and on learning through blogs, particularly when many of the readers or learners are experts in the field. The blog editor, like the instructor, generates the content and sits at the head of the experience. But the online platform flattens and extends the classroom space. When one attends a lecture by Muhanna, the possibilities for response are circumscribed by the classroom context and by Muhanna's authority as a professor. But online, *Qifa Nabki*'s readers can easily respond, can cut apart and remix his essay, and can position themselves as his equal or superior. Online, authority shifts from being centered on the instructor to being shared, if not equally, by everyone in the learning community. The lack of formal assessment, such as a grade, also works to shift authority.

This shift of authority has positive aspects. Comments posted to a discussion board tend to be more monologues than part of a genuine discussion, but some of them, often criticisms of a post, are insightful. A bright community of readers or learners can bring a great deal to the discussion, particularly when multiple bloggers discuss an issue together. When Muhanna wrote about translating the children's movie *Frozen* into Arabic, and about the attendant issues of using MSA or colloquial Arabic, the *Arabic Literature (in English)* blog ran several responses, and the Jordanian *7iber* blog translated these into Arabic (7iber.com). Muhanna also returned to the *Arabic Literature (in English)* blog several times in order to weigh in there. Thus blog readers, some of whom will be more knowledgeable than the blogger of the initial post, are part of the teaching process, and teaching can cross from one space into another.

But sometimes the authority of the lecturer is key, as it allows for a real-time moment of confrontation and correction. When I was teaching Introduction to Third World Literature at the University of Minnesota in 2006–07, I had each of the students bring in a short literary text to one of the class meetings and present on it. Students were meant to read the text, give context, and lead a brief discussion. Although this was ostensibly a decentered exercise, I was still standing at the front of the classroom.

One student brought in Dunya Mikhail's poem "The War Works Hard" (الحرب تعمل بجد ; Al-Harb taʿmal bi-jidd), from the collection with the same title. The poem opens: "How magnificent the war is! / How eager / and efficient!" (كم هي مجدّة الحرب / ونشاطة / وبارعة). With very clear irony, the poem continues:

> It contributes to the industry
> of artificial limbs,
> provides food for flies,
> adds pages to the history books,
> achieves equality
> between killer and killed,
> teaches lovers to write letters,
> accustoms young women to waiting,
> fills the newspapers
> with articles and pictures,
> builds new houses
> for the orphans,
> invigorates the coffin makers,
> gives grave diggers
> a pat on the back
> and paints a smile on the leader's face. (6)

تساهم في صناعة الأطراف الاصطناعية
توفّر طعاما للذباب
تضيف صفحات إلى كتاب التاريخ
تحقّق المساواة بين القاتل والقتيل
تعلّم العشاق كتابة الرسائل
تدرّب الفتيات على الانتظار
تملأ الجرائد بالمواضيع والصور
تشيّد دورا جديدا لليتامى
تنشّط صانعي التوابيت
تربت على أكتاف حفاري القبور ترسم ابتسامة على وجه القائد
(25–27)

The student, a strong supporter of the United States military, reading the poem as a straightforward ethnographic text, urged her fellow students to see how war could be a boon to a community. Inside a closed classroom, we were able to turn this moment into an opportunity to discuss the characteristics of literary irony, its uses, its literary relatives, and its limitations. Although the presenting student was not convinced, the confrontation was beneficial to all the others in the classroom, who became more aware of how irony is crafted when seeing it through the eyes of a student who saw none.

In an open space, learners and readers make use of one another's experiences but are much more on their own. In a discussion of Updike's review of Munif's *Cities of Salt,* for instance, one commenter, a young instructor at Oxford, disagreed with my criticism of Updike and asserted, at the end, "But thanks for the link to Updike's review. I shall recommend it to my students in the fall." Another commenter responded, asking rhetorically, "We should judge Tennyson by how closely he matches Abu Nuwas?" He also urged the Oxford instructor, "Do recommend the Updike to your students, but please, as a case study in blinkered, uninformed, provincialism" ("On an Eighty-First Birthday").

There is no evidence that the Oxford instructor even returned to look at the follow-up comment. In an online space, there is no real-time relation that holds learners or users immediately accountable for their speech.

Other Ways of Teaching in Open Spaces: Samia Mehrez's Course Translating Revolution

In February 2011, Samia Mehrez, an Egyptian professor, announced that she would be shifting her spring seminar from a class about modern Arabic literature to one titled Translating Revolution. She set up a blog for the class (translatingrev.wordpress.com), where the students could post their translated works and commentary on the translation process. Although many other courses have set up student blogs, this one offered translations of texts about which English-language readers were particularly curious during a time of heightened interest in the events in Egypt. A number of articles were written about her project in places like *Asymptote, Open Democracy,* and *Arabic Literature (in English).*

Although not all the blog comments were on-topic, the site clearly had an audience beyond the classroom. Thus, while Mehrez was teaching the students and they were teaching one another, they were also opening what they had learned to a wider audience.

It did not end there: the class led to a May 2011 symposium open to the general public and held at the American University in Cairo's downtown campus. Many of the talks, given by the students, drew full rooms of thirty or more attendees, many from outside the university. The students also put together a book, edited by Mehrez, *Translating Egypt's Revolution: The Language of Tahrir.* The book was not open, as it was published in hardcover by AUC Press and had a price ($29.95). But the students came to a public forum a second time to present about the book. Interest in this presentation was so high that there were chairs and a screen set up outside the AUC's Oriental Hall so that those who didn't fit inside could still experience the talk.

It's clear that students in the small seminar benefited greatly from the course. For some it was a life-changing experience. It's difficult to know what the wider audience got from the course, but I found their presentations instructive. Through them, I was able to think through issues of translating humor as well as how the Tahrir moment, gathering in unexpected mass protest against an established regime, was translated into other cities around the world.

A Future of Hybrids

It's easy to dismiss MOOCs as nonsense, seeing them so fervently championed by Friedman and by venture capitalists. And it is very possible that MOOCs, despite large investments from universities and private sources, will go the way of eight-track tapes. But whether they persist or something else comes to replace them, they signal a strong desire for change in higher education and a particular appetite to see it happen in shared spaces online. At the moment, the "shimmery hope" of magically lifting the whole world "out of poverty" has obscured the obstacles to teaching open online courses across geographic boundaries.

Teaching an Arabic literature in a MOOC—that is, asynchronously, to a widely varied group of learners, without a way to assess their learning, with decentered authority—will take careful planning. Any MOOC, like any blog, is very time-consuming. Louis Bloomfield, a physics professor at the University of Virginia, told Jeffrey Young that it took him a thousand hours to produce his first MOOC, which meant working more than eighty-hour weeks, to the point where "[m]y family held an intervention."

As Young points out, MOOC production and support can be costly. There's no reason to think that teaching an Arabic literature MOOC will take less time than to teach a physics MOOC. Even my *Arabic Literature (in English)* blog takes on average twenty hours a week to edit and produce.

But there are ways to bring the teaching of Arabic literature into open spaces without turning the effort into a second job. Mehrez's blog, which had its roots firmly in her classroom, was considerably less time-intensive than a blog like *Editoriaraba* or *Arabic Literature (in English)*, which must create their own learning communities. There is certainly room for more hybrid models: indoor-outdoor blogs that benefit both the students in a classroom and reach out to a larger community, or ways for outdoor blogs to be used inside classrooms. Indeed, instead of focusing on entirely online models, the most interesting work may be in creating learning projects that can make bridges from the classroom to outside and back again.

Works Cited

Al-Madhoun, Ghayath. Interview by the author. 1 May 2014.

Carlson, Scott, and Goldie Blumenstyk. "For Whom Is College Being Reinvented?" *The Chronicle of Higher Education*, 17 Dec. 2012, www.chronicle .com/article/The-False-Promise-of-the/136305.

Cheuse, Alan. Review of *In Praise Of Hatred*. *NPR*, 22 Apr. 2014, www.npr .org/2014/04/22/305960115/book-review-in-praise-of-hatred.

Friedman, Thomas. "The Professors' Big Stage." *The New York Times*, 5 Mar. 2013, www.nytimes.com/2013/03/06/opinion/friedman-the-professors-big -stage.html?_r=0.

———. "Revolution Hits the Universities." *The New York Times*, 26 Jan. 2013, www.nytimes.com/2013/01/27/opinion/sunday/friedman-revolution-hits -the-universities.html.

Guthrie, Alice, and Alexandra Buchler. "Literary Translation from Arabic into English in the United Kingdom and Ireland, 1990–2010." *Literature across Frontiers*, 29 July 2014, www.lit-across-frontiers.org/wp-content/up loads/2013/03/Literary-Translation-from-Arabic-into-English-in-the -United-Kingdom-and-Ireland-1990-2010-final.pdf.

Haber, Jonathan. "Just Lectures? A Review of the edX Justice MOOC." *MOOC News and Reviews*, 29 July 2014, moocnewsandreviews.com/just -lectures-review-of-edx-justice-mooc/.

Ho, Andrew Dean, et al. *HarvardX and MITx: The First Year of Open Online Courses, Fall 2012–Summer 2013*. *Social Science Research Network*, 22 Jan. 2014, ssrn.com/abstract=2381263.

Independent Foreign Fiction Prize Winner Announced. BookTrust, 22 May 2014, www.booktrust.org.uk/d/news-and-blogs/news/291.

Koller, Daphne, et al. "Retention and Intention in Massive Open Online Courses: In Depth." *Educause Review*, 29 July 2014, www.educause.edu/ero/article/ retention-and-intention-massive-open-online-courses-depth-0.

Lynx Qualey, Marcia. "The Blog as a Cross-Cultural Salon." *YouTube*, 19 Apr. 2012, www.youtube.com/watch?v=5nnfsRUxLTA. American U in Cairo, 26 Mar. 2012.

———. "The Humphrey Davies Interview." *Quarterly Conversation*, 7 Dec. 2009, quarterlyconversation.com/the-humphrey-davies-interview.

———. "Translating for Bigots." *Arabic Literature in English*, 4 Nov. 2013, arablit.wordpress.com/2013/11/04/translating-for-bigots/.

Mehrez, Samia, editor. *Translating Egypt's Revolution: The Language of Tahrir*. American U in Cairo P, 2012.

Mikhail, Dunya. الحرب تعمل بجد [Al-harb ta'mal bi-jidd]. Damascus: Dar al-mada, 2000. Translated as *The War Works Hard.*

———. *The War Works Hard.* Translated by Elizabeth Winslow, New Directions Publishing, 2005.

"New MLA Survey Report Finds That the Study of Languages Other Than English Is Growing and Diversifying at US Colleges and Universities." *Modern Languages Association*, 8 Dec. 2010, www.mla.org/pdf/2009_enrollment_survey _pr.pdf.

"On an Eighty-First Birthday: Why Does Abdelrahman Munif Not Make the 'World Literature' Canon?" *Arabic Literature (in English)*, 29 May 2014, arablit.org/2014/05/29/on-an-81st-birthday-why-does-abdelrahman-munif -not-make-the-world-literature-canon/.

Pappano, Laura. "The Boy Genius of Ulan Bator." *The New York Times*, 14 Sept. 2013, www.nytimes.com/2013/09/15/magazine/the-boy-genius-of-ulan -bator.html?pagewanted=all.

———. "The Year of the MOOC." *The New York Times*, 3 Nov. 2012, www .nytimes.com/2012/11/04/education/edlife/massive-open-online-courses -are-multiplying-at-a-rapid-pace.html.

Pirkle, Hayden. "Arabic MOOC Platform Edraak Launches to Bring Quality Education." *Wamda*, 15 June 2014, www.wamda.com/2014/06/first-arabic -mooc-platform-launches-quality-education.

Post, Chad. "Translation Database Update, Including 442 Titles Coming in 2014." *Three Percent*, 20 May 2014, www.rochester.edu/College/translation/ threepercent/index.php?id=11222.

Reich, Justin. "The First Year of edX: Research Findings to Inform Online Learning." *Education Week*, 21 Jan. 2014, blogs.edweek.org/edweek/edtechre searcher/2014/01/the_first_year_of_edx_research_findings_to_inform_on line_learning.html.

Stone, Christopher. "Teaching Arabic in the US after 9/11." *Jadaliyya*, 11 Apr. 2014, www.jadaliyya.com/pages/index/17286/teaching-arabic-in-the-us-after -9-11.

Talbot, David. "Given Tablets but No Teachers, Ethiopian Children Teach Themselves." *MIT Technology Review*, 29 Oct. 2012, www.technologyreview.com/ news/506466/given-tablets-but-no-teachers-ethiopian-children-teach-them selves/.

Updike, John. "Satan's Work and Silted Cisterns." *The New Yorker*, 17 Oct. 1988, pp. 117–19.

Wolchover, Natalie. "Why Is Everyone on the Internet So Angry?" *Scientific American*, 5 July 2012, www.scientificamerican.com/article/why-is-everyone -on-the-internet-so-angry/.

Young, Jeffrey. *Beyond the MOOC Hype: A Guide to Higher Education's High-Tech Disruption.* The Chronicle of Higher Education, Kindle ed., 2013.

Selected Arabic Literary Works in English

This is a list of the Arabic works discussed in this volume that have been translated into English.

Abu Golayyel, Hamdi. *A Dog with No Tail*. Translated by Roger Moger, American U in Cairo P, 2009.

———. *Thieves in Retirement*. Translated by Marilyn Booth, Syracuse UP, 2006.

Al-Ahdal, Wajdi. *A Land without Jasmine*. Translated by William Maynard Hutchins, Garnet Publishing, 2012.

Alaidy, Ahmed. *Being Abbas El-Abd*. Translated by Humphrey Davies, American U in Cairo P, 2006.

Al-Aswany, Alaa. *The Yacoubian Building*. Translated by Humphrey Davies, HarperCollins Publishers, 2006.

Al-Daif, Rachid. *Learning English*. Translated by Adnan Haydar and Paula Haydar, Interlink Publishing, 2007.

Al-Daif, Rachid, and Joachim Helfer. *What Makes a Man? Sex Talk in Beirut and Berlin*. Translated by Ken Seigneurie and Gary Schmidt, Center for Middle Eastern Studies at the U of Texas, 2015.

Al-Hakim, Tawfiq. *The Essential Tawfiq Al-Hakim: Plays, Fiction, Autobiography*. Edited by Denys Johnson-Davies, American U in Cairo P, 2013.

Al-Koni, Ibrahim. *Gold Dust*. Translated by Elliott Colla, Arabia Books, 2008.

———. *The Puppet*. Translated by William M. Hutchins, Center for Middle Eastern Studies, U of Texas, 2010.

Al-Mala'ika, Nazik. "Revolt against the Sun." Translated by Emily Drumsta, *Jadaliyya*, 28 Feb. 2013, www.jadaliyya.com/pages/index/10391/revolt-against-the-sun-by-nazik-al-malaika.

Alsanea, Rajaa. *Girls of Riyadh*. Translated by Marilyn Booth, Penguin Books, 2007.

Al-Shaykh, Hanan. *The Locust and the Bird: My Mother's Story*. Translated by Roger Allen, Anchor Books, 2010.

———. *Story of Zahra*. Translated by Peter Ford, Anchor Books, 1986.

———. *Women of Sand and Myrrh*. Translated by Catherine Cobham, Anchor Books, 1992.

Al-Shidyaq, Ahhmad Faris. *Leg over Leg; or, The Turtle in the Tree: Concerning the Fariyaq, What Manner of Creature He Might Be*. Translated by Humphrey T. Davies, vols. 1–4, New York UP, 2013–14.

Al-Tahawy, Miral. *The Tent*. Translated by Anthony Calderbank, American U in Cairo P, 1998.

Al-Tahtawi, Rifaʿah Rafiʿ. *An Imam in Paris: Account of a Stay in France by an Egyptian Cleric, 1826–31.* Translated by Daniel L. Newman, Saqi Books, 2004.

Al-Udhari, Abdullah, editor and translator. *Victims of a Map: A Bilingual Anthology of Arabic Poetry.* Saqi Books, 1984.

Asqalani, Ghareeb. "Hunger." *Anthology of Modern Palestinian Literature,* edited by Salma Khadra Jayyusi, Columbia UP, 1992, pp. 380–88.

Bakr, Salwa. *The Golden Chariot.* Translated by Dinah Manisty, Garnet Publishing, 1995.

———. *"The Wiles of Men" and Other Stories.* Translated by Denys Johnson-Davies, Quartet Books, 1992.

Barakat, Hoda. *The Stone of Laughter.* Translated by Sophie Bennet, Interlink Publishing, 2006.

Ben Bouchta, Zoubeir. *Shakespeare Lane.* Translated by Rajae Khaloufi, edited by George F. Roberson, International Centre for Performance Studies, 2008.

Booth, Marilyn, editor and translator. *My Grandmother's Cactus: Stories by Egyptian Women.* Quartet Books, 1991.

Choukri, Mohamed. *For Bread Alone.* Translated by Paul Bowles, 2nd ed., Telegram Books, 2007.

Chreiteh, Alexandra. *Ali and His Russian Mother.* Translated by Michelle Hartman, Interlink Publishing, 2015.

———. *Always Coca-Cola.* Translated by Michelle Hartman, Interlink Publishing, 2012.

Darwish, Mahmoud. *In the Presence of Absence.* Translated by Sinan Antoon, Archipelago Books, 2011.

———. *Unfortunately It Was Paradise: Selected Poems.* Translated by Fady Joudah, U of California P, 2013.

El Saadawi, Nawal. *The Hidden Face of Eve: Women in the Arab World.* Translated by Sherif Hetata, Zed Books, 2007.

Enani, Mohamed, translator. *Angry Voices: An Anthology of the Off-Beat New Egyptian Poets.* Compiled by Mohamed Metwalli, U of Arkansas P, 2003.

Ghandour, Zeina. *The Honey.* 1999. Interlink Publishing, 2008.

Gibran, Khalil. *Broken Wings.* Translated by Juan Cole, White Cloud Press, 1998.

Habiby, Emile. *The Secret Life of Saeed: The Pessoptimist.* Translated by Salma Khadra Jayyusi and Trevor LeGassick, Interlink Publishing, 2001.

Handal, Nathalie, editor. *The Poetry of Arab Women.* Interlink Publishing, 2001.

Humaydan, Iman. *Other Lives.* Translated by Michelle Hartman, Interlink Publishing, 2014.

Ibrahim, Sonallah. That Smell *and* Notes from Prison. Translated by Robyn Creswell, New Directions, 2013.

———. The Smell of It *and Other Stories*. Translated by Denys Johnson-Davies, Heinemann, 1971.

Idilbi, Ulfat. Sabriya. *Damascus Bitter Sweet*. Translated by Peter Clark, Interlink Publishing, 2003.

Jayyusi, Salma Khadra, editor. *Modern Arabic Poetry: An Anthology*. New York: Columbia UP, 1987.

———, editor. *Short Arabic Plays: An Anthology*. Interlink Publishing, 2003.

Jayyusi, Salma Khadra, and Roger Allen, editors. *Modern Arabic Drama: An Anthology*. Indiana UP, 1995.

Johnson-Davies, Denys, editor and translator. *Egyptian One-Act Plays*. London: Heinemann, 1981.

Kabbani, Nizar. *Arabian Love Poems*. Translated by Bassam Frangieh and Clementina R. Brown, Three Continents Press, 1993.

Kanafani, Ghassan. *Palestine's Children: "Returning to Haifa" and Other Stories*. Translated by Barbara Harlow and Karen E. Riley, Three Continents Press, 2000.

———. *"Men in the Sun" and Other Palestinian Stories*. Translated by Hilary Kilpatrick, Three Continents Press, 1999.

Khaled, Leila. *My People Shall Live*. Edited by George Hajjar, *WordPress*, Oct. 2011, leilakhaled.files.wordpress.com/2011/10/my-people-shall-live-leila-khaled.pdf.

Khalifa, Khaled. *In Praise of Hatred*. Translated by Leri Price, St. Martins Press, 2014.

Mahfouz, Naguib. *Miramar*. Translated by Fatma Moussa-Mahmoud, Doubleday, 1978.

———. *Palace Walk*. Translated by William Jutchins and Olive Kenney, Doubleday, 1989.

Mikhail, Dunya. *The War Works Hard*. Translated by Elizabeth Winslow, New Directions Publishing, 2005.

Munif, Abdelrahman. *Cities of Salt*. Translated by Peter Theroux, Random House, 1987.

Omareen, Zaher. "A Bedtime Story for Eid." Translated by Alice Guthrie, *Words without Borders*, www.wordswithoutborders.org/article/a-bedtime-story-for-eid.

Salih, Tayeb. *Season of Migration to the North*. Translated by Denys Johnson-Davies, Three Continents Press, 1993.

Sha'arawi, Huda. *Harem Years: The Memoirs of an Egyptian Feminist, 1879–1924*. Translated by Margot Badran, Feminist Press, 1987.

Shibli, Adania. *Touch*. Translated by Paula Haydar, Interlink Publishing, 2010.

Taher, Walid. *A Bit of Air*. Translated by Anita Husen, Center for Middle Eastern Studies, U of Texas, 2012.

Tergeman, Siham. *Daughter of Damascus.* Translated by Andrea Rugh, Center for Middle East Studies, U of Texas, 1994.

Wannous, Saʿdallah. *Four Plays from Syria.* Edited by Marvin Carlson and Safi Mahfouz, translated by Carlson, et al., Martin E. Segal Theatre Center Publications, 2014.

Notes on Contributors

Michelle Hartman is professor of Arabic literature at the Institute of Islamic Studies, McGill University. She is the author of *Native Tongue, Stranger Talk: The Arabic and French Literary Landscapes of Lebanon* (2014) and *Jesus, Joseph and Job: Reading Rescriptings of Religious Figures in Lebanese Women's Fiction* (2002). She has translated from Arabic seven novels and a short story collection.

Allen Hibbard is professor of English and director of the Middle East Center at Middle Tennessee State University. He is the author of *Paul Bowles: A Study of the Short Fiction* (1993) and *Paul Bowles, Magic and Morocco* (2004). With Osama Esber, he is completing a translation of Haidar Haidar's *A Banquet for Seaweed* into English.

Rebecca C. Johnson is Crown Junior Chair in Middle East Studies and assistant professor in the Department of English and the Alice Kaplan Institute for the Humanities at Northwestern University. She has published scholarly articles on Arabic literature in *Modern Language Quarterly*, *Eighteenth Century Studies*, and *Novel*. She is the cotranslator (with the author, Sinan Antoon) of *Ijaam: An Iraqi Rhapsody*.

Rula Jurdi is associate professor of Islamic history at the Institute of Islamic Studies, McGill University. She is the author of *Converting Persia: Religion and Power in Safavid Iran* (2004) and the coauthor, with Malek Abisaab, of *The Shi'ites of Lebanon: Modernism, Communism and Hizbullah's Islamists* (2014). She is also a published poet in Arabic and in English translation.

Maya Kesrouany is assistant professor of literature at New York University, Abu Dhabi. She has published scholarly articles on Arabic literature and translation in *Comparative Literature Studies* and other journals.

Anne-Marie McManus is assistant professor of modern Arabic literature and culture at the University of Washington, Saint Louis. Her academic writing has appeared in *Arab Studies Journal*, *Journal of Middle East Women's Studies*, and *International Journal of Middle East Studies*. Her translations from Arabic to English appear in the anthology *Syria Speaks: Art and Culture from the Frontline* (2014).

Philip Metres teaches in the English department at John Carroll University. He is the author of *Behind the Lines: War Resistance Poetry on the American Homefront, since 1941* (2007). His poetry collections include *Pictures at an Exhibition* (2016), *Sand Opera* (2015), *A Concordance of Leaves* (2014), and *abu ghraib arias* (2011), and the last two won the Arab American Book

Award for Poetry. He has translated four collections of poetry from Russian into English.

Mara Naaman, an independent scholar based in New York City, is associate director of programs and ADFL at the MLA. She is the author of *Urban Space in Contemporary Egyptian Literature: Portraits of Cairo* (2011).

M. Lynx Qualey, an independent scholar, is editor of the online magazine *Arabic Literature (in English)*. She reviews and edits for a variety of publications and works with publishing projects, including Kitab Sawti, an Arabic audiobook company, and the Library of Arabic Literature.

Ken Seigneurie is the 2017–18 Edward Said Professor of American Studies at the American University of Beirut and professor of world literature at Simon Fraser University. He is the author of *Standing by the Ruins* (2011). His translation from Arabic of *'Awdat al-almani ila rushdih* ("How the German Came to His Senses"), by Rachid al-Daif, appears in *What Makes a Man? Sex Talk in Beirut and Berlin* (2015).

Caroline Seymour-Jorn is associate professor of comparative literature and Arabic translation at the University of Wisconsin, Milwaukee. She is the author of *Cultural Criticism in Egyptian Women's Writing* (2011) and articles on Egyptian women writers. She has translated into English the Arabic fiction of Etidal Osman and of Ibtihal Salem.

Stephen Sheehi is Sultan Qaboos bin Said Professor of Middle East Studies at the College of William and Mary. He is the author of *Foundations of Modern Arab Identity* (2004), *Islamophobia: The Ideological Campaign against Muslims* (2011), and *The Arab Imago: A Social History of Indigenous Photography, 1860–1910* (2016).

Index of Names

Abbas, Hassan, 204
Abboushi Dallal, Jenine, 56
Abdo, Diya, 82
Abdulhadi, Rabab, 42
Abdul Jabbar, Wisam Khalid, 134
Abdullah, Abdul Majeed, 172
Abisaab, Rula Jurdi. *See* Jurdi, Rula
Aboul-Ela, Hosam, 14
Abu al-Nuwwas, 136–37, 138–39, 233
Abu El-Haj, Nadia, 42
Abu Golayyel, Hamdi, 15, 184, 185,
    191–96, 197
Abu-Khalid, Fawziyya, 155
Abu Lughod, Lila, 81, 82, 87–89
Abu-Lughod, Ibrahim, 100
Abunimah, Ali, 59n1
Adonis. *See* Said, Ali Ahmad
Agamben, Giorgio, 51
Ahdal, Wajdi al-, 170, 178–80
Ahmad, Aijaz, 12–13, 133
Alaidy, Ahmed, 15, 170, 175–76, 184,
    185, 187–91, 197
Albakry, Mohammed, 162–63
Al-Ghadeer, Moneera, 171
Al-Hallaj, 137–38
Ali, Mehmet, 104, 105
Ali, Taha Muhammad, 67
'Alim, Mahmud Amin al-, 56–57
'Ali, Muhammad. *See* Ali, Mehmet
Allan, Michael, 24
Allen, Roger, 3, 8, 26, 27, 85, 121, 128,
    157
Allman, Paula, 42
Alsanea, Rajaa, 56, 82, 86–87, 88, 170,
    171–73
Alsultany, Evelyn, 55
Amine, Khalid, 159–60
Amireh, Amal, 16, 82, 84, 85, 88
Amyuni, Mona, 133
Anis, 'Abd al-'Azim, 56–57
Antoun, Naira, 157
Appiah, Kwame Anthony, 97, 109, 170
Apter, Emily, 51, 111, 113, 120, 121–22,
    129
'Aqqad, Abbas Mahmoud al-, 137

*Arabian Nights. See One Thousand and
    One Nights*
Arafat, Yasser, 62
Aragon, Louis, 25
Arnold, Matthew, 27
Asad, Talal, 135
Ash'ari, Muhammad al-, 56
Ashour, Radwa, 35
Asqalani, Ghareeb, 63, 69, 72, 74
Assad, Bashar al-, 6, 159, 200, 208, 211,
    217
Assad, Hafez al-, 203, 204, 208, 210, 211
Assad, Rifaat al-, 204
Aswany, Alaa al-, 57, 135
'Attar, Hassan al-, 43, 105
'Attiya, A. M., 126

Badawi, M. M., 3, 156
Badr, Taha, 119, 127
Baheyya, 187
Baker, Mona, 7
Bakhtin, Mikhail, 212
Bakr, Salwa, 174, 176, 178–79
Banfield, Grant, 134
Barak, On, 101
Barakat, Hoda, 35
Bassnett, Susan, 7
Batatu, Hanna, 203, 204, 209
Battushig. *See* Myanganbayar
Bauer, Thomas, 24
Bayyati, Abdul Wahab, 28
Beeston, Alfred F. L., 127
Beinin, Joel, 177
ben Bouchta, Zoubeir, 159, 160, 161
Ben-Gurion, David, 47
Benjamin, Walter, 111, 113, 121, 201
Bennett, Jill, 213
Berman, Antoine, 107
Best, Steven, 59n1
Bhabha, Homi, 7, 51
Bin Laden, Osama, 161
Blatherwick, Helen, 23
Bloomfield, Louis, 234
Blumenstyk, Goldie, 226–27
Boccaccio, 118

243